SCRIPTS:

LIBRETTOS FOR OPERAS

AND OTHER MUSICAL WORKS

James Reaney, photographed at his family's farm just east of Stratford, Ontario, by Michel Lambeth, 1962.

SCRIPTS:
LIBRETTOS FOR OPERAS
AND OTHER MUSICAL WORKS

by James Reaney

edited with an introduction by John Beckwith

COACH HOUSE BOOKS

Dedicated to all the Performers   J.R.

first edition

Published with the assistance of the Canada Council for the Arts and the Ontario Arts Council. The publisher also acknowledges the assistance of the Government of Canada through the Book Publishing Industry Development Program and the Government of Ontario through the Ontario Book Publishing Tax Credit Program.

 Canada Council   Conseil des Arts
for the Arts   du Canada

 ONTARIO ARTS COUNCIL
CONSEIL DES ARTS DE L'ONTARIO   Canadä

LIBRARY AND ARCHIVES CANADA CATALOGUING IN PUBLICATION

Reaney, James, 1926-
Scripts : librettos for operas and other musical works / James Reaney ; edited by John Beckwith.

ISBN 1-55245-149-6

1. Operas--Librettos. 2. Librettos.   I. Beckwith, John, 1927- II. Title.

ML49.R288 2004   782.1'0268   C2004-905071-0
Copyright © 2004 by James Reaney

CONTENTS

INTRODUCTION

Dear Jamie,

Your writings for music cover more than fifty years and make up a substantial part of your prolific production. Of the scripts collected here, all but one (*Canada Dash, Canada Dot*) were published in some form or other; but of those published all but one (*Twelve Letters to a Small Town*) are now out of print. It seemed appropriate and timely that this body of your writing be made available. My task as editor has been relatively easy since I composed music for all but one of these ventures, and our collaborations – by mail and by phone mostly – were so close that I know large portions of the scripts by heart. In Toronto in the late 1940s you gave me the typescript of your first publication, *The Red Heart and Other Poems*, and I was bold enough to ask if I could set the six poems of *The Great Lakes Suite*. In the early fifties we somehow developed by correspondence (you were in Winnipeg, I was in Toronto) a joint ambition to write an opera. Nowadays everyone is writing operas, and the standard greeting to a young composer is 'How's your opera coming along?' But back then the works produced were few in number and short and modest in design. *Night-blooming Cereus* fit that pattern; other features included its resolutely Southwestern Ontarian ambience and its rather static plot (all the sex and violence occurred before the curtain went up). Mrs. Brown's fifteen-minute 'domestic song cycle' in Scene 2 was a new (and perhaps very Canadian) form of kitchen-sink music-drama.

How lucky we were at the start to have had CBC Radio. Not only were their producers ready to give network coverage to the chamber setting of *The Great Lakes Suite*; but when someone heard we had put together a short opera, they offered to 'commission' it and give it a live broadcast prior to the first staging. In the sixties Robert Weaver initiated poetry broadcasts and asked me to provide music for your cycle *A Message to Winnipeg*, which became the first of our radio collages. You and I had discussed W. B. Yeats's aversion to simultaneous music-and-poetry performances; Yeats thought the rhythms of spoken poetry and instrumental music could not successfully coexist. The solution appeared to be a give-and-take of different rhythmic foregrounds and backgrounds, for which radio was an excellent medium. I composed *A Message to Winnipeg* to an already complete script, but we developed the subsequent collages collaboratively, eventually incorporating sung as well as spoken verse. The *Toronto Telegram*'s reviewer of the published text of *Twelve Letters to a Small Town* became apoplectic at the 'Gertrude Stein nonsense' of the music-lesson scene, ignoring its musical imagery and its known origins in your own piano studies with a Stratford musical legend, Cora B. Ahrens. As for Ms. Stein, she has hovered over many later passages, right down to the 'cabbages and apples' sequence of *Taptoo!*, Act 1 Scene 5.

Critics? There we've been both lucky and unlucky. Against the sympathetic and detailed reviews of *Night-blooming Cereus* by Milton Wilson and Chester Duncan we had to endure the hostile comments of John Kraglund (a defender in the letters column of the *Globe and Mail* found they 'bordered on malice'). *The Shivaree* was generally well reviewed in the press, but when the CBC went gathering audience comments in the intermission the interviewer found it hard to hide her distaste, even though most of the miked comments were favourable (one exception, a teenage voice, 'absolutely hated' the work). A surprise compliment was that of a veteran opera producer, Nicki Goldschmidt, who came backstage beaming: 'At last – a r-r-real allegro!' When *The Shivaree* was remounted by Toronto's Opera in Concert organization in 2000, Urjo Kareda, who had been one of the main critical champions of your play cycle *The Donnellys* in the mid-seventies, went on a revisionist rampage, calling the opera 'twee' and 'smug' – this in the pages of the *Globe and Mail*, surely Canada's smuggest newspaper. In his vituperative haste he managed to get the hero's name wrong – an amusing detail in view of the plot, which hinges on Quartz's inability to remember names. Fortunately for the performers – possibly the best all-round group of singers we have ever worked with – there were some highly favourable reviews as well. As Patricia Rideout, the original Mrs. Brown, used to advise us, 'Just remember the good ones.'

Jamie, you have been accommodating and patient beyond what any collaborator could expect. By contrast, I have been an incorrigible buttinsky. In your program note for *Serinette*, you describe your happy collaboration with Somers, recalling how pleasant it was in that case to have 'no rewrites.' With me there were always rewrites, and re-rewrites, and throwaways; but the occasions when you have dug in your heels have been mighty few.

When the original draft of the *Night-blooming Cereus* libretto proved too long, you cheerfully rewrote Scenes 2 and 3. I recall my pangs of regret at having to sacrifice that local-colour gem of a couplet from Scene 2, where Mrs. Brown, setting her table for supper, was to sing:

> And somewhere I away have laid
> A jar of Wagstaffe's Marmalade.

When the characters of Miss Beech and Aunt Annie in *The Shivaree* and Ebenezer in *Taptoo!* appeared to me interesting and in need of further development, you readily supplied aria scenes for them – in Annie's case, another operatic innovation, probably the first aria in history on the topic of penis envy. A whole transition sequence in *All the Bees and All the Keys* had to be cut when the score appeared to be getting too long, and you not only agreed but approved my cornball one-line substitute, 'But meanwhile...' I wondered if spectators of *Crazy to Kill* would be puzzled when Agatha Lawson, a mental-home patient, produces a pair of scissors, so you had another character ask her, 'You're allowed sharps?' – which I proceeded to set on a rising semitone.

Some of my other utility suggestions have indeed ended up as lines in the scripts. Among these, I think, is Aunt Annie's 'I can handle him,' in the finale of *The Shivaree*. When we were working on the finale of *Canada Dot*, someone (you, me, our producer Jim Kent?) suggested the period hockey game should be correlated with a contemporary game, and with the help of an avid hockey player and fan, my son Jonathan, then twelve, I inserted phrases for an imaginary Foster Hewitt and some found texts from the sports page of a newspaper.

The scenario which became *Serinette* was one of two you pro-
posed for our Guelph Spring Festival assignment in the late
eighties, the other being Ann Cardwell's mystery novel *Crazy to
Kill*. I leaned more to the latter. I loved the concept of *Serinette*
but personally felt, as I said at the time, 'Sharon-ed out,' having
worked on the Children of Peace material numerous times from
The Line Up and Down through my choral piece *Sharon Fragments* to
the annual concerts of the Music at Sharon festivals throughout
the eighties. When I saw *Serinette* in production I realized I could
never have achieved Somers's beautiful solutions for the Bird
Girl scene or the choral finale in the illuminated temple.

But if Somers was the second composer to consider *Serinette*,
I was the third composer to look at the draft libretto of its
sequel, *Taptoo!* At a point when another opera was not in my
plans, this script looked long and sprawling and in need of a
buttinsky's rewrites; at the same time it struck me as bursting
with invention and with musical clues that were immediately
and originally operatic. You expressed surprise when I told you
I thought it was about the best thing you'd ever written.

Taptoo! illustrates a special characteristic of your libretto
technique. Few librettists look, as you do, for musical incorpora-
tions in their scripts – hints that will tailor a literary work for
musical setting. In this case, you had already researched the his-
torical sources for 'How to play a drum' used in Act 1 Scene 3,
and your typescript already included many quotations from
period songs. This recalled for me your incorporation of hymn
sequences in *Night-blooming Cereus*, of pots-and-pans percussion
scenes in *The Shivaree*, and of thirties balladry in *Crazy to Kill* – not
to forget the psalmody references in *Serinette*. Better than most
writers, I think, you appreciate the difference between play and
opera.

Jamie, for all this, on behalf of your many music fans, a mil-
lion thanks.

Love,
John

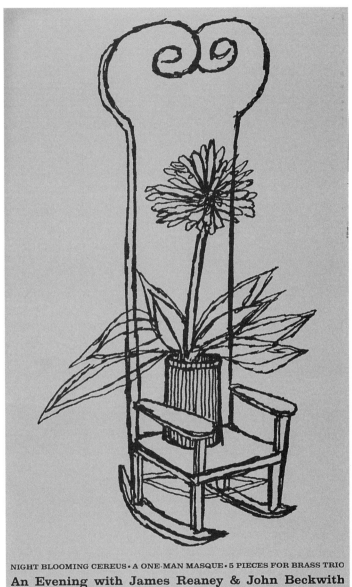

NIGHT BLOOMING CEREUS • A ONE-MAN MASQUE • 5 PIECES FOR BRASS TRIO

An Evening with James Reaney & John Beckwith

HART HOUSE THEATRE   Tues. & Wed. APRIL 5th & 6th   TICKETS $2.00

William Toye's poster design for the 1960 stage premiere of *Night-blooming Cereus* won a prize in a typography exhibition.

The Great Lakes Suite

The Great Lakes Suite
for soprano, baritone, clarinet, cello and piano

First performance; CBC Radio, 15 February 1950
Lois Marshall, *soprano*
Bernard Johnson, *baritone*
Leslie Mann, *clarinet*
Cornelius Ysselstyn, *cello*
John Beckwith, *piano*

First concert performance; Toronto, 10 March 1950
Lois Marshall, *soprano*
Glenn Gardiner, *baritone*
Leslie Mann, *clarinet*
Rowland Pack, *cello*
John Beckwith, *piano*

LAKE SUPERIOR
baritone, instruments

I am Lake Superior
Cold and grey.
I have no superior;
All other lakes
Haven't got what it takes;
All are inferior.
I am Lake Superior
Cold and grey.
I am so cold
That because I chill them
The girls of Fort William
Can't swim in me.
I am so deep
That when people drown in me
Their relatives weep
For they'll never find them.
In me swims the fearsome
Great big sturgeon.
My shores are made of iron
Lined with tough, wizened trees.
No knife of a surgeon
Is sharper than these
Waves of mine
That glitter and shine
In the light of the Moon, my mother
In the light of the Sun, my grandmother.

LAKE MICHIGAN
soprano, baritone, instruments

> For I'm a michigoose
> And he's a michigander.
> > – Old vaudeville song

By the shores of Lake Michigan,
Chicago sits
Filled with jawbreakers
Filled with lawbreakers.

By the shores of Lake Michigan,
Lives the Michigander,
Lives the Michigoose.
Very silly people they
For they had the nerve to say
When they used to visit us
In the days of yore,
'That the Yankees,
The Yankees won the war!'

'Bah!' said we
Patriotically.
'How your wits do wander
You Michigoose, you Michigander!'
Right then and there we had a fight
With our cousins from Michigan
Who shortly after went back there again,
And since we won, we knew we were right.

LAKE HURON
soprano, instruments

Yoohoo Yoohoo
I'm blue, blue
Lake Huron.
By my shores
In fratricidal wars
Indians killed each other.
At Bayfield
The people stop
To see me slop
Against the pier.
At Grand Bend
The people tend
Instead to
Look at each other.
The Au Sable River and the Maitland
Flow into me.
They think I'm a sea.
But haw haw
They're not through yet.
For blue and wet
I flow into Lake St. Clair
And Lake St. Clair into Lake Erie
So very very weary
And Lake Erie into
Lake Ontario
Like a blue grain bag
At which that frowsy hag
Of a city Toronto nibbles.
And then the River St. Lawrence!
Whose waters resemble those
Dark barrelled waves that
Drowned the Duke of Clarence.
So haw haw you Maitland River
And you Au Sable one too.
For when you flow into me
You're not at all through.

LAKE ST. CLAIR
baritone, instruments

I once knew a bear
Who swam in Lake St. Clair
And after the experience
Said, 'Hoity Toit
I don't like the way Detroit
Pollutes the air there.'
Then after a while
He added with a smile,
'And I don't like the way Windsor
Does, either.'

LAKE ERIE
soprano, baritone, instruments

Lake Erie is weary
Of washing the dreary
Crowds of the cities
That line her shores.
Oh, you know
The dirty people of Buffalo
And those in Cleveland
That must leave land
To see what the water's like.
And those that by bike,
Motor car, bus and screeching train
Come from London in the rain
To Port Stanley where they spend
The day in deciding whether Grand Bend
Might not have been a nicer place to go.
Up and down in thousands
They walk upon Lake Erie's sands.
Those in Cleveland say, 'Plainly,'
As they gaze across the waters
Where swim their sons and daughters,
'That distant speck must be Port Stanley.'
Those in Port Stanley yawn, 'Oh,
That lump in the mist
Over there really must
Be populous Cleveland in Ohio.'
But Lake Erie says, 'I know
That people say I'm shallow
But you just watch me when I go
With a thump
And a plump
At the Falls of Niagara into Lake Ontario.
When you see that you'll admit
That I am not just a shallow nitwit
But a lake
That takes the cake
For a grand gigantic thunderous tragic exit.'

LAKE ONTARIO
soprano, instruments

Left! Right! march the waves
Towards the sandy shore
Where I stand and motionless
Stare at their blue roar.
Oh, they would stop and listen
And be my blue audience
If I could leap and glisten
More than they, more than they.
But although within me rush
Waves Death cannot deny
I must upon these coasts
Only listen to their cry.
My voice is soft while theirs is loud.
Loud their wavy boasts
That do drown out all reply.
I am one, they are a crowd.
Yet though I'm still and alone
Upon these thin saltless sands,
Thousands only shall hear the waves
Clap their fresh young hands
In lawless blue applause,
Because I held a megaphone
To their blue green blue noise,
Because I made this seashell,
This poem, for your ear,
My dear Monseer,
Of their blue continual hell.

Night-blooming Cereus

Louis de Niverville's set design for the 1960 stage premiere, Toronto. The curlicued chairbacks dwarfed the singers and had to be cut back.

Night-blooming Cereus

Chamber opera in one act (three scenes)

Libretto, James Reaney
Music, John Beckwith

Cast, in order of appearance:

Alice, *soprano*	Mrs. Wool, *contralto*
First girl, *soprano*	Ben, *baritone*
Second girl, *mezzo-soprano*	Barbara, *soprano*
Mrs. Brown, *mezzo-soprano*	Mr. Orchard, *bass baritone*

Orchestra:
Flute/piccolo, oboe/cor anglais, clarinet/E flat clarinet, bassoon, trumpet, trombone, piano, two violins, two violas, two cellos, contrabass.

First performance; CBC Radio, 4 March 1959
Anne Stephenson, Alice
Patricia Snell, First girl
Jean Marie Scott, Second girl
Patricia Rideout, Mrs. Brown
Irene Byatt, Mrs. Wool
Alexander Gray, Ben
Phyllis Antonini, Barbara
Bernard Johnson, Mr. Orchard
Ettore Mazzoleni, conductor

First stage performance; Hart House Theatre, Toronto, 5 April 1960
Anne Stephenson, Alice
Sheila Piercey, First girl
Ruth Ann Morse, Second girl
Patricia Rideout, Mrs. Brown
Irene Byatt, Mrs. Wool
Alexander Gray, Ben
Patricia Snell, Barbara
Bernard Johnson, Mr. Orchard
Ettore Mazzoleni, conductor
Pamela Terry, director
Louis de Niverville, designer

CHARACTERS

ALICE, *soprano*, is a beautiful young girl whose shoes look like bare white feet and whose hat looks like long fair hair.

MARY looks like the First Girl and looks like a First Girl or a domino or a china cat.

EMMY is the Second Girl and looks like the First Girl, partly like a loaf of bread, taller you see, and like a dress too, but mostly like a china dog or pig.

MRS. BROWN, *mezzo-soprano*, is old but she is not old as the hills, she is quite straight with steel-rimmed glasses and could easily take care of granaries. That is, if you were to offer her the job of fixing and running a threshing machine she could do that and plant and harvest a whole farm full of crops too. Instead of a farm she has a windowsill, each flowerpot a field and no harvest except a heart and mind filled with the delight of watching and waiting.

MRS. WOOL, *contralto*, is the mother of either china dog or china cat and has a voice like a telephone ring produced by a small crank, silver currants tin raspberries metal strawberries wild iron grapes and glass pears spilling out of the tonsil cornucopia down the hundreds of gray telephone poles playing comb and paper with the wind.

BEN SMITH, *baritone*, has two eyes, a nose, a mouth, a good mow of hair and lots of space between all these so that they seem checkers on a board where squares have disappeared into a blank of healthy skin.

BARBARA CROFT, *soprano*, is a professional poor girl who has dead leaves for hair, teazles for eyes, dead Queen Anne's lace for mouth and is a walking walk on a fall day down the road that isn't used much by the forest.

MR. ORCHARD, *bass-baritone*, knows the mysteries of the writing in the hand, the fire in the branch, the dark lake in the head, the Saviour in the thigh, the gold ring the rat has swallowed and the hot summer picnic shady blazing green lawn in the brown seed bed of a snowy day inside the granary.

SCENE ONE

(*Takes place in front of a painted curtain that represents the village of Shakespeare, Ontario. Although it is late March, the fields and roofs and yards are still covered with white snow. The houses grouped about the red-brick tower of the First Presbyterian Church are either red, brown, blue or yellow. They have the look of trees and the large trees feel like houses. Dragging a dark brown bushy long fleece of smoke hair after it, the train that has just brought Alice to Shakespeare may be heard calling out the crossings on its way into the white and blue distance. Late that night, this train with a huge golden eye will return through the village. The sky is an even soft grey all over.*)

ALICE: (*fast*) I want to find Mrs. Brown's house, please.

FIRST GIRL: Which Mrs. Brown, ma'am? There are quite a few in this, even in this small small town.

ALICE: Mrs. Conrad Brown. She must be quite an old old lady by now.

FIRST AND SECOND GIRL: Mrs. Conrad Brown.

SECOND GIRL: There's Miss Coral Brown and Mrs. Tod Brown and Mrs. Sidney Brown. The first one is no relation to the last ones, but the last two are sisters whose husbands run the turnip-waxing factory. But we never heard of a Mrs. Conrad Brown.

ALICE: I want to find Mrs. Brown's house, please. I said Mrs. Conrad Brown's house, didn't I?

FIRST AND SECOND GIRL: She said Mrs. Conrad Brown's house, didn't she?

ALICE: (*aside*) Marching up and down the streets of this little town in soft March weather. Having come a stranger to this very little town in March early in a snowy soft winter spring evening.

FIRST GIRL: Yes, Emmy. Yes, by jingo, Emmy, you're right, there is another Mrs. Brown. It's that – fancy our not knowing her right off when there's only six hundred people to know in this place here and most of them Smiths, Browns or Whites

– names like that, easy to remember if you've got the first names straight. I guess my mother could have told you right off because she's the part-time central telephone operator here – and she can tell all the telephone numbers' owners with what their special ring is right off in her sleep.

Yes, Emmy, there is a Mrs. Conrad Brown. Yes, ma'am, there is a Mrs. Conrad Brown. Only we'd almost forgotten her, because no one goes near her much, us children being always a bit scared of her.

ALICE: Why were you always a bit scared of her?
She must have been
just a poor old woman, all alone.
Who would be scared of Mrs. Brown?
The poorest dweller in this town.
She must be as much all alone
As field surrounded single stone.

SECOND GIRL: (*spoken*) Then you have met her?

ALICE: (*spoken*) No, I have not. I have just heard about her.

SECOND GIRL: Yes, she is old and she is poor
And never stirs beyond her door
Except when in the fall she's found
That there are apples on her ground
Blown down by the wind whose blowing
Is, beside those come with sewing,
Sole visitor to her cottage grey ...
Grey with the beating of an age
Of wind and rain and snow and time.

ALICE: Apples?

FIRST GIRL: Windfalls. Just lying there. She wanted us to come and pick them up, but we wouldn't.

ALICE: How mean, girls, really, how mean.

FIRST AND SECOND GIRL: What do you mean, how mean?

ALICE: Not to steal the old woman's apples when you knew perfectly well she wanted you to – so you'd come close enough for her to talk to you.

FIRST GIRL: But some nights I used to watch her with my elbows on her windowsill. I'd watch Mrs. Brown getting her supper ready. I'd watch her, through all her houseplants sitting on her windowsill – watch her light her old poky kerosene lamp and eat her supper.

SECOND GIRL: We'd both watch her and she'd never let on she saw us. The poor old dear.

FIRST AND SECOND GIRL: (*They mime their spying on Mrs. Brown.*)
Hello, Mrs. Brown.
Guess who's looking at you.
Well, Mrs. Brown,
I wouldn't know,
But you're not alone.

SECOND GIRL: And that kettle looks as if it's boiling over to me.

FIRST GIRL: Well, well, well, Mrs. Brown. Mrs. Brown.

SECOND GIRL: Mrs. Brown.

FIRST GIRL: And do you know what,
Oh it's so sad,
But we always wondered why she set the second place for a person who never came. At first we thought …

SECOND GIRL: Mr. Brown!

FIRST GIRL: Mr. Brown!

SECOND GIRL: But then … My mother told me the whole story. A long time ago Mr. Brown died. But just a bit longer time ago their only child, a girl, ran away from them. Never to come back. They say it broke poor old Mrs. Brown's heart and she's never given up hope her daughter will come back from wherever she went to. Gone to her head, you know … Oh, she was so funny to watch.

FIRST AND SECOND GIRL: Mrs. Brown, oh, if only you'd look out, Mrs. Brown.
Mrs. Brown…
Hello, Mrs. Brown.

Guess who's looking at you.
Well, Mrs. Brown,
I wouldn't know,
But you're not alone.

FIRST GIRL: But the girl did not come back. Never.

ALICE: No. She did not come back. But if she had come back, where could she have gone to? Tell me where Mrs. Brown lives if she still lives. For I've come hundreds of weary miles to see her.

FIRST GIRL: Why, if I might ask? I always like to know why people come.

SECOND GIRL: Mighty few come here, I can tell you. We saw you get off the train ...

FIRST GIRL: And the stationmaster phoned my mother right away to say there'd been someone get off, so everyone knows you're here by now.

SECOND GIRL: Mrs. Brown's daughter run off with a man, you know.

ALICE: Yes, I know.

SECOND GIRL: And the old girl never got one letter.

ALICE: Yes, I see.

FIRST GIRL: So why you'd come? You Mrs. Brown's daughter or something preeprosterous like that?

ALICE: I've come with a message for her.

SECOND GIRL: So, naturally you'd want to know where the old lady lives. Well, she lives at the end of the humblest street. In a humble cottage with two rooms and a woodshed. Just where the street jumps off into Farmer Smith's farm. Go south along this street.

FIRST GIRL: This street's called Draper Street.

SECOND GIRL: Till you come to a jog in the street.

FIRST GIRL: Or otherwise where the blacksmith's is.

FIRST AND SECOND GIRL: Turn left and count three houses,
You can't go wrong again this time
Because if you turn south again
You should be on Walnut Street,
And that's where we think the old woman lives.

ALICE: Thank you very much.

SECOND GIRL: To be exact, ma'am, she lives in a cottage beneath a big maple tree on Walnut Street.

ALICE: Thank you for your kind directions.

FIRST GIRL: Well, Emmy, it's either that, either Mrs. Conrad Brown lives in this town beneath a big maple tree on Walnut Street or a big walnut tree on Maple Street.

ALICE: Thank you …

SECOND GIRL: It could be that …

ALICE: Nice directions. Very much appreciated.

SECOND GIRL: Oh, it could too be that because there are a lot of streets named after trees in this town, but in any case she, Mrs. Conrad Brown, lives in a cottage beneath some sort of a big tree on a street named after another big tree. And we're not even sure it's the right Mrs. Brown for you.

FIRST GIRL: There are so many Smiths and Browns. A Mr. Brown started this place.

SECOND GIRL: But we hope we have helped you.

ALICE: Yes, you have. Oh yes, you have. Thank you very …

(*They stand tableau still as if time had quietly and suddenly stopped while in the grey sky above the village appears a vision of the Nightblooming Cereus opening in slow beach crashing swarming splendour and glory, a blossom larger than airplanes or zeppelins, four times really the size of the village, three times the size of Toronto, twice the size of Bethlehem and once the size of Eden. Then it fades as time comes back.*)

FIRST GIRL: By the way I now remember
Mother said that she was going

To old Mrs. Brown's tonight.
A very rare plant will bloom
On old Mrs. Brown's windowsill
To everyone's great delight.

ALICE: I have heard, yes I have heard
Old Mrs. Brown had such a plant
On her kitchen windowsill.
Only once in a hundred years
Does it bloom, does it ever bloom.
So long, so green and so still.

SECOND GIRL: If we get time we'll go over and look through the
window at it, Mary. I missed the comet.

ALICE: What is the name of this flower?

FIRST AND SECOND GIRL: Unlike other, unlike other
Flowers that bloom in the bright day
This comes out in night's deep dark.
Not like Patience or Geranium
Plant but more like a cactus.
Blossom in the midnight sad hour
Rising in the humble cottage
Night-blooming Cereus Flower

ALICE, FIRST AND SECOND GIRL: Night-blooming Cereus Flower.

FIRST GIRL: Do you think that you'll find your own way?
Night-blooming Cereus Flower.

ALICE: Yes thank you so much and good day.
Night-blooming Cereus Flower.

(*The two girls, Emmy and Mary, disappear. Alice turns and steps into the
village scene. She walks away from us until her figure gets smaller and
smaller until actually it gets larger and larger since in the twilight the
dark tree trunks and the darkening air flow into her figure. The four street
lamps might have been about to come out but, instead, the snow descends.*)

SCENE TWO

(The sky, the trees and the houses of the village and snowy ground float up, disappear, to reveal the interior of Mrs. Brown's house, a very crowded place, but in a two-room cottage everything gets mixed in together – kitchen, parlour and bedroom. The things in Mrs. Brown's house look so familiar and have been where they are so long that they seem to be part of a card game for children. Here is a very worn thick card with a door upon it that has a battered tin doorknob. This next card has a blue granite-ware basin, water pail and dipper on it. This card has an iron stove on it much dampered, lidded, doored and chinked – fire pulsing within. This card has a chair on it and this one a rocking chair and this one a broom. This one has a table set for supper with a lamp. This is a window with house plants instead of a windowsill and with a dark green window-blind at the top and so a fuzzy, furry, smooth, spurgy, portable green blind at the bottom. On this card there is an harmonium which is a sort of stove; that is, if the stove contains a forest of trees jumping back into light and sun, the harmonium contains the forest sighing into the darkness of the demon summer midnight storm, blowing pipe twigs, bugle branches and trumpet boughs. The front door is on this card, it has a white china doorknob and has been locked since the leaves fell off the trees. The game is to put down the cards so that Mrs. Brown has just finished her supper. After taking the last of her tea she looks at the lamp for a few moments, then folds her hands and bows her head for a blessing.)

MRS. BROWN: My Lord I thank for bread and meat
    You give more bread than I can cut,
    More for to drink that I can cup
    More to myself than I can eat.

    These pitchers and these platters hold
    The milk and honey of thy love
    And I am grateful for thy grace
    As starving prophet was of old.

    But in between my praying hands
    And in between my fast shut eyes
    The table of thy manna stands
    From whose delight may I not rise. Amen.

(She gets up and begins to clear up the dishes, shaking out the tablecloth, going to the stove for hot water and dishpan.)

WASHING DISHES

Now I will gather up and wash the dishes,
Plate cup knife fork spoon and jug.
Now will my plate and cup be just like fishes.
There used to be so many more to gather up.

Even I, an old woman, have servants and children,
Plate cup fork knife jug and spoon.
Unlike children away they cannot run,
Safe on the shelves of the cupboard in this room.

I suppose we are his china and cutlery,
Plate cup jug spoon fork and knife.
He washes us when we Him see.
Easier to wash these than wash a life.

But when I, the old woman, am taken from the table,
Cup fork knife spoon jug and plate,
If they are not broken, before I break, will
Faithful remain behind to demonstrate

To others who may own them after,
Plate cup knife spoon jug and fork,
Daily to baptize themselves in the water
Of thinking how they can for Heaven work.

(*The dishes are put away, the cupboard door closed, the dishwater some-how disposed of. She gets the broom from behind the stove.*)

SWEEPING

Look at the faces on the floor
In the wood of the boards they are
Faces of dust I sweep with a broom,
Sweeping the dust in this room.
Sweeping sweeping sweeping sweeping
Has a sound like weeping.
If I kept all the dust I've swept
It would be she I have wept
Whose face appears more often than not
In the dust and the fire and the knot,
And the blowing rain on the window

And the tree branches' shadow
Contain your face there! and again there!
My lost girl in the dust in the air.
But it is best to go on sweeping
Over the faces better than weeping.
Here is the face of an old man peeping.
Here is the face of a young man reaping.
Here is the face of an old woman sweeping.

(A bit tired with so much activity, she sits in the rocking chair.)

ROCKING

Rocking rocking, rocking rocking
Very very slowly.
What I have been doing rocking,
Most of my life lately.

Sewing at a shirt or stocking
As quickly as I can
And what the people to me bring
I sew at while rocking.

Like selling footsteps to all houses
My stitches go through cloth
Of caps and nightgowns and blouses
Dresses, handkerchiefs and vests.

I sew for everyone here,
I the restless stillness,
My thread looks through cloth for tear
And the butcher's apron.

The sewing connects each one
To myself except for her.
She walks about beneath the sun
Without my sewing snow.

As the white snow fills fields and lanes,
Till they cover me all.
Upon my old and long-used bones
Rocking and sewing fall.

(*Mrs. Brown gets up and begins to move the plants away from the windows. She brings them to the table. She carries the Night-blooming Cereus to a special stand of its own in the centre of the room.*)

A PLANT SONG

The night
Comes now with its frost
Unless from windowsill
Their keeper keep them day until.

Patience Plant
Come here now
To this table
And Elephant Ear
The frost to get you won't be able.

Christmas Cactus
Busy Lizzie too
Red geraniums
And the farthest Wandering Jew.

Night-blooming Cereus
Night-blooming Cereus
Now for us
You will come out
After a century
To see my friends and me.

Dark green
Dark green, dark green,
Your leaves, your leaves,
As time without
Her being seen,
The years her mother sadly grieves.

Within
Your blossom may I see,
Within the leaves of grief,
The face of my lost girl,
Or if that is not to be
May somehow lighter be my sheaf.

Poster design by Jeremy Carlson for the 1992 revival by Opera Nova, University of Victoria.

(She sits at the harmonium, finds her place in the hymn book and sings to her own accompaniment.)

A HYMN

Our Lord has prepared for us
Houses in Heaven.
How many rooms have they?
They number seven.
And what will we do
In this Heavenly House?
Watch flowers come out
All the day through.

In his cellar you'll find
Cool milk and sweet wine
And those so inclined
May spend all the day there.
And what will we do
In this Heavenly House?
Whatever you want to
All the day through.

In the woodshed you'll notice
Trees chopped up ready
And fine dry split kindling
For fires all so steady.
And what will we do
In this Heavenly House?
Watch the fire burn
All the day through.

In the pantry you'll find loaves
That ravens have brought,
Loaves everlasting
All fresh and hot.
Our Lord has prepared for us
Houses in Heaven
With tables of wheat bread
Spiritually leavened.

In his parlour the carpets

Refresh tired feet
Like valleys of green grass
All dewy and sweet.
And what will we do
In this Heavenly House?
Always be visiting
All the day through.

And up in the bedroom
Four angels are bedposts
Who each with a gold broom
Sweep care from your eyes.
Oh what will we do
In this Heavenly House?
Dreaming true dreamings
All the day through.

And in the seventh room should be
A pair of folded hands
Praising him who built for thee
A house that ever stands.
All children and cousins
All brothers and sisters
And fathers and mothers
And relatives lost,
Lost loved ones
Dear faces
Will be with you there
If not here, there.

(*a knock at the door*)

SCENE THREE

(*Mrs. Brown waits uncertainly, then answers the door. Alice enters.*)

ALICE: At last I have found whom I have been looking for.
What were you singing before coming to the door?

MRS. BROWN: I was singing a hymn.

ALICE: I knew I would find you at some such holy thing

As up and down the streets here I have been wandering.

MRS. BROWN: You are a ghost I've often seen.

ALICE: I am no ghost. My feet touch the real ground.
Touch me, hear me, if like a ghost I feel or sound.

(They walk around the room, Alice in pursuit. She tries to make Mrs. Brown touch her, but the old lady nimbly evades her.)

MRS. BROWN: I do not want to touch you!
I do not want to hear you!

(Alice, fearful of causing a scene, retires to a shadowy corner.)

Like a snowflake in a stream
You will disappear
As all the other times I've seen
You, my dear.

No, she wouldn't look like you.
She would be older
Now she would be older too,
Than you are, older, older.

Yes, you may smile and smile
My dear
But in a little while
You will disappear.

(Another knock. Enter Mrs. Wool. She is one of those people who reach out and tap you on the shoulder to emphasize what they are saying.)

MRS. WOOL:

THE TELEPHONE'S SONG

Hello, Mrs. Brown!
Don't tell me that it's out yet
(I'm fine, Mrs. Brown)
Or tell me that I've missed it!

(shedding coat and hat)

You know, Mrs. Brown,
I tried to get away as soon

But there was
The longest conversation.

Hello it began and
Goodbye it did end.

Working – telephone
Means – listen – everything.
Hello, Harold, this – Pete,
Your cow's in ring, ring.

Lift her up to the telephone.
No – mustn't stay – supper.
All want to call each other
Because they seem to feel alone.

Hello it began and
Goodbye it did end.

And I as you know, Mrs. Brown,
Have made the connections these many years
The country up and the country down
Between a thousand mouths and ears
Between a thousand mouths and ears.

Who all is coming to see you tonight?

MRS. BROWN: Yourself, Mrs. Wool and Barbara Croft,
And young Ben Smith and Mr. Orchard.

MRS. WOOL: Hello it will begin and
Goodbye it will end.

By the way, Mrs. Brown,
My girl tells me –
I saw a lady get off the train
And look for you all over town.

MRS. BROWN: I do not understand.

MRS. WOOL: Are you going to introduce me
To that lady in the corner?

MRS. BROWN: I cannot, Mrs. Wool. She's not there.

MRS. WOOL: Hello it won't begin then and –

MRS. BROWN: I do not understand.

MRS. WOOL: Goodbye it won't end.

(Enter Ben.)

BEN: Good evening, Mrs. Brown.

(Mrs. Wool walks rather aimlessly around the flower. She also gets a good look at Alice.)

MRS. WOOL: Night-blooming Cereus
When will you bloom for us?

BEN: In my father's store
I've worked all day.

MRS. WOOL: When will you bloom for us?

BEN: So, I'm ready to see this flower.

THE SONG OF THE STOREKEEPERS'S SON

I come
I come
From sweep
Ing out
My faw
Ther's store
My faw
Ther's store.

MRS. WOOL: What's the matter with that?

BEN: It's the life of a dog or a cat.
Have you
Dear flow'r
Ever
Swept out
My faw
Ther's store?
No nev
Er could

You have,
Dear flow'r.

MRS. WOOL: The young people   BEN: Dear flow'r
    Weather vanc steeple!   Dear flow'r
    I'd like to tie you to   Dear flow'r
    three hundred telephones tied to you.   Dear flow'r

BEN: I come
    From sweep
    Ing out
    My faw
    Ther's store
    It is
    The sweeping out of my father's store,
    A dead
    Ly dumb
    And boor
    Ish bore.

(*Enter Barbara. She is pretty but dishevelled and raggedly dressed.*)

MRS. WOOL: What's so dull about that?

BEN: It's the life of a dog or a cat.

BARBARA: What's the matter with their lives?
    Mine is far worse than that of a rat.

MRS. BROWN: Barbara!

BARBARA:

THE ORPHAN'S SONG

    Foundling, foundling, foundling, foundling
    I was found.
    Find a foundling, find a sound one,
    I'm not sound.
    Orphan, orphan, orphan child
    Hear the wind sing!
    Beneath a thorn tree growing wild
    Was a thing.

Mother, father, mother, father,
Hear the wind sing!
Family family family neither
I am nothing.
Where do, where do, where do I stay?
In a loft
Sleeping free on the sweet smelling hay!
My name is Barbara Croft.

And here are some gifts for you:
(*to Mrs. Wool*) Two pebbles for your ears.
(*to Mrs. Brown*) And a meat pie for your tears.
(*to Ben*) And a key to stir your tea.
(*to Alice*) And... and a berry for you there too!

MRS. BROWN: Barbara, you're a wild wild girl
Wild as the night the villagers found you.

A DUET

BARBARA: I can see that you'd like to be
What I am, if you please an orphan.

BEN: Yes, I would but still a man
Because then I would be free!

BARBARA: If I were you you know what?
I'd love my dear old storekeeper father
And I'd really work and swot
To show him that I did.

BEN: I wish that I could change my name.
The surname is so very lame.
I would change my name to George
And work all day at a forge.

MRS. BROWN: Ben, I wonder if you would.

BEN: A blacksmith beating on the anvil!
Bring that black horse in!

BARBARA: Lead me up and down the place till
I find a mother and father.

BEN: Not an orphan girl but it would be nice
  To be a blacksmith's orphan apprentice.

BARBARA: Oh, I'd like to be a storekeeper's son all right
  And have food, father and mother, all day and night.

MRS. WOOL: If you had them, could you love them?

BEN: Never more
  Would I sweep the floor of my father's store.

BARBARA: Never again
  Would I wander through the rain and through the wind.

BEN:	BARBARA:
If I were you	Never again
Never more	Would I wander
Would I sweep	If I were you
The floor of my father's store	Never again through the storm.
If I were you	If I were you
Never more.	Never again.

(They execute a dance during this last part, like 'churning butter,' the children's game – only not quite touching each other's hands.)

MRS. BROWN: The eye looks at, beholds the star.
  The bright star longs to be the eye.
  The eye longs to be the bright star.
  Night-blooming Cereus longs to spy
  The human beings come from far
  And near to see its lonely beauty.
  It will be the Kingdom of Heaven
  When this shy flower blooms.
  It will open like stars in the night –
  Stars that are eyes filled full of sight
  Of Kingdoms of Heaven where lives
  My lost child.

ALL: Where lives –

MRS. BROWN: My lost lost child.

ALL: Where is –

BEN: My wonderful anvil.

ALL: Where my –

BARBARA: Mother lies long hidden.

ALL: Where things –

MRS. WOOL: Are just the same as here.

(The last knock on the door.)

MRS. BROWN: This must be Mr. Orchard.

(Enter Mr. Orchard. He is large and bears a small seedling apple tree, its roots encased in a large earthen ball covered with burlap.)

MR. ORCHARD: Good evening, Mrs. Brown.
There are some of you that do not know me.

MRS. BROWN: Now you are come we can have some tea.

MR. ORCHARD:
(while Mrs. Brown starts handing cups around)
I have brought along this small apple tree.
Feel that trunk now for two
Years old
It will grow up to be I am positive
Very bold.
(to Barbara)
You look as if you lived mostly outside.

BARBARA: I do.

MR. ORCHARD:
(to Ben)
And you look as if you lived mostly inside.

BEN: I do.

MR. ORCHARD: Aha! I've guessed it. You are the
Village orphan,
And I think I know that you are Benedict
The storekeeper's son.

46

BARBARA: I am.

BEN: I am.

MR. ORCHARD: Mrs. Wool, how is that
Convolvulus?

MRS. WOOL: The one that you sold me last spring, Mr. Orchard,
Has climbed right over the house.

MR. ORCHARD: Young man, I need someone turnip rows to scuffle
And juniper trees to trim and dig up.
Young girl, I'm sure you could in the greenhouse ruffle
The sweet-smelling rows of white carnations.

THE GARDERNER'S SONG

You must all come
When the sun
Of summer shines.
You must all come
When the sun
Of summer shines
On the plants of
My plantation
Up at Sunfish Lake.

In my nursery
You will see
Trees and flowers and vegetables.
In my nursery
You will see
Up at Sunfish Lake
Trees and flowers and vegetables
You'd like away to take.

And if you cannot come
In the summer shining sun
Through the cold and wintry air
I've brought with me seeds of these plants there.

(He hands out seed packets.)

MRS. BROWN: Thank you for this blue flower.

BARBARA: Thank you for this green gourd vine.

MRS. WOOL: Thank you for this patience plant.

BEN: Thank you for these golden sparks.

ALL: Thank you. Thank you.

(*They lift the cups of tea to their faces or push them down through the air to the saucers. This is a card with a cupboard on it which has a clock made in Connecticut on top of it that is another sort of stove and harmonium since it burns time with a slow golden winking pendulum fire and at regular intervals impelled by secret cogwheel digestive processes and steel spring blood it takes a hammer and beats a bangly whirring drum as it does now – bangly whronng! bangly whrong! bangly whrong! bangly whrong! bangly whrong! bangly whrong! bangly whrong! bangly whrong! bagly whrong! bangly whrong! bangly whrong! bangly whrong! – twelve o'clock midnight.*

As if summoned by the clock, and it the clock's huge monster angel, there drops down the card of night in the village and the fields – tons of thick flying snow, tons of thick grey cloud, a small yellow roundness accompanied with piercing melancholy hollers from its early whistle and steady lookings from its gold piece eye. This is the card of the night train that has always passed thunderously close to Mrs. Brown's – like a huge front door lock on wheels roaring and crying: Cease your dreams. I am (unless stopped for a train strike) that which is. Your plant with its angel flower can't change me. It is, thinks Mrs. Brown, is. It is is. And there's no use trying to shut it out.

The clock strikes midnight, the train is right upon Mrs. Brown's cottage shaking everything, drowning everything – then not so upon as the passenger cars rattle by – travellers intent on Kitchener or Guelph or Georgetown or Limehouse or Weston or Toronto. Dirty-mouthed trainmen in their dark blue uniforms discussing some girl who was laid by some impossible number of men before she married somebody who hadn't – cuspidors, mere reproductive machines, all the personality of tickets rattling on, slaves of the whirring clock until just a receding red light blurred in snow blurs, black branches. For a moment the houses of the villages that had windows, and Mrs. Brown's was one of them, felt like being trains too – why not? with our square headlights through the snow – but the trees held them back and the houses settled back and some of the windows went out. The clock stopped striking. Beside it stood a huge book, Mrs. Brown's

Bible. It too was a sort of stove, a harmonium, a clock and a thunderous train and in it the whole world burned and did not, spoke and did not. Mr. Orchard puts down his cup.)

MRS. WOOL: Let me play for the hymn, Mrs. Brown.

MRS. BROWN: It is Sunday morning
　　　Nothing grows on a Sunday.
　　　Shall we sing a small hymn
　　　To encourage it to blossom?

MR. ORCHARD: Yes we'll sing it, now the train is out of town.

MRS. BROWN: One hundred and fifty please Mrs. Wool.

ALL:

THE SECOND HYMN

　　　I hear a voice that carries
　　　In the fields of rain.
　　　Through heavens of anxiety
　　　And weeping vales of pain.

　　　Oh sweet bird sing now
　　　Whistle everlasting
　　　Oh sweet bird sing now
　　　Of my soul's new spring.

ALICE:

(She appeals from her long-held place while the others sing a verse without words.)

　　　When will you see me, hear me, touch me?
　　　I have been waiting here all this time.
　　　When will you, when will you, when will you?

ALL: This voice is like the south wind,
　　　My heart is like the snow.
　　　But when I hear its gentle sigh
　　　I feel my winter go.

　　　Oh sweet bird sing now
　　　Whistle everlasting
　　　Oh sweet bird sing now

Of my soul's new spring.

MRS. BROWN: If you are no ghost
    If you are no shadow
    Come to me so I may
    May I touch your hands.

ALICE: At last you've asked me to come.
    I waited and waited for that.

MRS. BROWN: But are you really her?
    Can your looks be still the same?

ALICE: Here is a handkerchief that you gave her
    On her twelfth birthday, do you remember?

MRS. BROWN: But are you not my daughter then?
    I am too old to think what you should look like.

ALICE: I am your daughter's daughter.
    She died a month ago.

MRS. BROWN: My girl –

ALICE: But I'm here –
    And I've come miles to see you
    To bring her love and ask for
    Her forgiveness, my grandmother.

MR. ORCHARD: Mrs. Brown! The flower! The flower!

BARBARA: I will see my mother and father.

BEN: I will see my blacksmith's shop.

MRS. WOOL: I will see Night-blooming Cereus come out.

MR. ORCHARD: I will see why I work in the earth.

ALICE, MRS. BROWN: And we see our happiness and joy
    We hardly need to see.

(The flower's petals gradually open.)

ALL: When I behold
    All this glory
    Then I am bold

To cross Jordan.
    Open, flower.

Then I am bold
To call on God
When I behold
All this glory.
    Open, flower.

I am gold
With his deep love
I am bold
To end my story
When I behold
All this glory.
    Open, flower.

(They all kneel before the flower as they sing.)

Twelve Letters to a Small Town

James Reaney's drawings were prepared for the 1962 publication by Ryerson Press.

Twelve Letters to a Small Town

poetry/music collage for radio

Child's voice (C), Female voice 1 (F1), Female voice 2 (F2), Male voice (M)
Flute, oboe, guitar, harmonium/piano.

Commissioned by CBC Radio.

First broadcast; CBC Radio, 26 July 1961
Rex Hagen, C
Maxine Miller, F1
Beth Lockerbie, F2
Ron Hartmann, M
Anthony Antonacci, flute
Roy Cox, oboe
Al Harris, guitar
John Beckwith, keyboard
James Kent, producer

ALL   Twelve Letters to a Small Town

MUSIC   *Intro*

FIRST LETTER

M   First Letter: *To the Avon River above Stratford, Canada*

MUSIC   *Cue 1: continue under...*

M   What did the Indians call you?
For you do not flow
With English accents.
I hardly know
What I should call you
    Because before
I drank coffee or tea
    I drank you
    With my cupped hands
And you did not taste English to me
    And you do not sound
    Like Avon
    Or swans and bards
But rather like the sad wild fowl
    In prints drawn
    By Audubon
And like dear bad poets
    Who wrote
    Early in Canada
And never were of note.
You are the first river
    I crossed
And like the first whirlwind
    The first rainbow
    First snow, first
    Falling star I saw,
You, for other rivers are my law.
    These other rivers:
    The Red and the Thames
    Are never so sweet

To skate upon, swim in
    Or for baptism of sin.
    Silver and light
The sentence of your voice,
    With a soprano
Continuous cry you shall
    Always flow
    Through my heart.
The rain and the snow of my mind
Shall supply the spring of that river
    Forever.
Though not your name
Your coat of arms I know
    And motto:

MUSIC   *Starts under…*

A shield of reeds and cresses,
    Sedges, crayfishes,
The hermaphroditic leech
Minnows, muskrats and farmers' geese
And printed above this shield
One of my earliest wishes
'To flow like you.'

SECOND LETTER

M,C   Second Letter:
MUSIC   *Up*
M,C   *Instructions: How to Make a Model of the Town*
MUSIC   *Up and out*
M   First take two sticks and two leafy branches.
C   First take two sticks and two leafy branches.
M   Put their ends together so they form spokes.
C   Put their ends together so they form spokes.
M   The spokes of an invisible wheel.
C   Coming together at the centre and fanning out?
M   Coming together at the centre and fanning out –
    These sticks and branches are

The principal through streets of the town.

C   Huron Street and Ontario Street can be leafy branch streets.

M   Downie and Erie can be the bare stick streets.

C   Now, what will we do with these glass bubbles?

M   Put the three blue ones at the end of
The three Great Lakes streets – Erie Street, Ontario Street

M,C   and Huron Street.

M   They eventually reach those lakes but
Hang the green glass ball at the end of Downie Street
Because it fades into farms and fields and townships.

C   I can't think what we're going to make the houses of.

M   We'll make model houses out of berries.
Take some berries. Ripe gooseberries for red houses.
White raspberries for yellow brick houses.

C   White raspberries for yellow brick houses.

M   Sprinkle white and red currants, cherries,
And trees can be represented by their leaves.

C   And trees can be represented by their leaves.
One elm leaf for a whole elm tree,
And streets laid out with rows of berry houses.

M   From the air, you know, a small town
Must look like rows of berries in the grass.
Now take some red apples and some russet apples,
Put these along the main streets for the business places.
Three potatoes for the Court House
St. Joseph's Church (R.C.) and St. James's (C. of E.).

C   Three potatoes for the Court House
St. Joseph's Church (R.C.) and St. James's (C. of E.).

M   Buildings around Market Square – ditto.

56

C	Buildings around Market Square – ditto.
M	With a rather sharpside brick-coloured tomato in the centre of the Market Square – to stand for the three-towered City Hall.
C	What'll we do to represent the people?
MUSIC	*Cue 2 starts under ...*
M	Well we could dress up ladybugs.
C	It's a hot July day and I hear a band. Please, couldn't we finish this later And see the band now?
M	Fall down then! Fall down! Into our model of the town.
C	Hey! Look at all those bugs! Lady and gentleman bugs!
M	Regard the carved potato Court House And observe the firm tomato City Hall.
C	And streets like branches and boughs Hung with the orchards and pears of Houses, houses, people, houses, houses.
M,C	Fall down! Fall down! Into our model of the town!
MUSIC	*continue under (March) ...*

THIRD LETTER

M, F1, F2, C Third Letter: *Orange Lilies*
On the twelfth day of July
King William will ride by
On a white horse
On a white charger,
King William and Queen Mary.

C	He bears an orange lily In his hand
M	(He in front and she behind, On a white horse On a white charger)
F1	And so does she

On a white horse.

F2, M   They're riding to see
And to jump the Boyne
With a white horse
In their groin.

M, F1, F2, C On the twelfth day of July
King William will ride by
With a white horse
King William and Queen Mary.
MUSIC   *Up and out*

FOURTH LETTER

M, F2   Fourth Letter: *Voices and Prepositions*
F2   Up here is the Water Tower, down there's the Sewage
Farm
F1   Down there's the Old Folks' Home, up here's the
Theatre
F2   Up here's a pillared house, down there is Kent Lane
M, F1, F2, C The roof of a small brewery by moonlight

M   Up here's the Hospital and across here is the graveyard
F2   Up the Stone Bridge, along the Dam, into the Churches,
C   Across the Market Square and on the Crimean cannon

M, F1, F2, C   Sunlight on a two-headed eagle

F2, M   Through the market with Amish bonnets and beards,
F2   Eggs and gladiolis, sausages and cooked cheese
F1   An old negro with a lump on the back of his neck
Sitting forever in the silent Saturday summer sun

M, F1, F2, C   In the door of the livery stable

F2   A girl with a branch of lilac in her hand
M   Walking down summer Wellington Street
F2   A white Sunday factory in the waste outskirts
Like a monastery: lonely, empty, austere

M, F1, F2, C A girl with no hair playing by the dam

F2, C   Huge gold paper bells swinging over Northway's store
F2, M   Recorded ding dongs from a loudspeaker
A hundred gold paper Christmas tree angels
M, C   In Kresge's dime store just after the war.

FIFTH LETTER
MUSIC   *Cue 3A*
C   Fifth Letter:
F1, C   *The Cloakroom at the High School*
M   The high school is the palace of Merlin and Cheiron
Where governors and governesses teach
The young Achilles and young Arthurs of the town.

The radiators teach the rule of monotony
Cheep cheep cheeping in the winter classroom
Timid fingers learn to turn a fire on.

A stuffed hummingbird and a stuffed sandhill crane.
In the dusty looking glass of grammar,
Number, the young see the shape of their brain.

But what and where did I learn most from?
High, dark, narrow as its single window
In the old high school there was a cloakroom –

A cloakroom! In winter stuffed with cloaks
Soft with outside things inside,

Burrs, mud, dead leaves on some of the coats.

At four o'clock there are forty-nine bare hooks
    As a hundred hands reach up
And I, lingering, rearranging my books

See sweeping face peer in of janitor
    Alone in the winter twilight
The old janitor! An image to ponder over.

Of course I learnt snow dripping windows
    Corridors of words, cobwebs of character,
The ninety-two elements in a long row,
    But most I learnt
The insoluble mystery of the cloakroom
    And the curious question [MUSIC: *cue 3B under* ...]
        of the janitor
        In some way so centre and core
        January man and cloakroom
From which the moon each month unlocks upon the
        wave
        A white bird.

MUSIC   *Out*

SIXTH LETTER
M, F2   Sixth Letter: *A House on King William Street*
M   Like the life here
        The wallpaper repeats itself.
MUSIC   *Cue 4, under ...*
M   Up and down go the roses
          Similar blows struck out
       By air-banging green fists:
       A bright rose and a blue one
       A pink blow and a blue one

       The years have not changed their likeness
       Except that those behind the sofa
       Have kept their original blaze
       And these opposite the window
          Have turned yellow.

MUSIC   *Cue 4A*
C   Aunt Henny says to Aunt Penny:
F2   'Have you read *She*? Oh, a terrible book,
         An awful book! Yes, it's by
             Haggard Rider Haggard.'

C   Aunt Lurkey says to Aunt Turkey:
F1   'I nearly slipped today, I nearly
             Slipped today.
         We should put a piece of carpet
             On that particular step,
                 We should,'
C   Says Aunt Lurkey taking another should
             Off the would pile.

MUSIC   *Cue 4B*
M   No one remembers when
         The wallpaper was new, except
             The wallpaper itself
         In the green smothered darkness behind
         The sofa and the cupboard.

         And I, I their awkward fool
         Board there while I go to school.
MUSIC   *Out*

SEVENTH LETTER
C, F1   Seventh Letter: *Prose for the Past*
C   What was it like in the past?
M   Find out in the archives of the Public Library.

MUSIC   *Cue 5 under ...*

M   In a small cellar room, there they keep the tea-coloured files of the town's newspapers. A shaky fading paper rope into the darkness of the past some more than a century long. You open the door with a skeleton key – the door, has it a white china doorknob? And there in the dark little room, the summer sunlight smothered by a frayed yellow drawn-down window blind – there is the past.

MUSIC   *Out*

C   Long ago Stratford was a small little embryonic amoeba of a place. Things were paid for in pounds and shillings.

F1   The price of grain and cordwood would go up in the winter and down in the summer, as I remember. Each fall there was a list of the crimes to be tried at the assizes – respectable crimes, too. People – I remember a Swiss traveller – stabbed in a tavern.

C   There were fairs at which young men rode at the ring, bears ran away with little boys and ate them up, Indians stole an ancestor's clothing while he was in swimming,

F2   ... flax was grown in huge quantities and it was laid out to ret on land east of the city which still looks as if it had been used for some peculiarly damp purpose.

C   Two boys, David and Jonathan, drowned in the river.

M   When the Crimean War comes, someone writes a poem that starts Hail Britannia, Hail Terrific Gal. Next week we are informed that he didn't mean Gal, he meant Hail Terrific Gaul. Haha.

   As we read the weekly paper then one can't help noticing how winter affects the little place. Nothing happens except cordwood is consumed in stoves and there are stage coaches and toll gates but still – what is happening is snow. Then in the spring the heart begins to beat more quickly again and there are actually more words in the paper.

F1   The railway attempts to come to town, sinks down in a very powerful slough, causeways itself out and changes things. Gaslight and train whistles and running trees, moons and clouds.

MUSIC   *Cue 5 repeats …*

M   I can hear all the wheels of the past – grinding, singing, creaking, whirling in a fountain of sound at the place where the four branches meet and there have been footsteps and voices without stop now for more than a century. Cutters and sleds dashing and jingling like elegant wooden fish this way and that. Then the flower or is it a seed pod of all the words spoken at the crossroads of the town, the footsteps stopped and the wheels turned, bursts open into figures from the deep past I didn't have to read about for we heard of them from ancestral voices or saw them just the once with one's own eyes.

MUSIC   *Out*

C   There was the Indian woman who worked at pulling flax and drank vinegar.

F1   In the past people showed what they thought of themselves much more openly than they do now. You saw very very happy people striding down the street with their hands clasped behind their backs. You saw very very proud people – a doctor's wife say, of high degree, walking down Wellington Street – with their noses literally in the air and their eyes proudly averted.

C   There was an old blind fiddler who always played at the gate of the fairgrounds and people put pennies in his violin case.

M   There were the old ladies who stopped the church bells from ringing after midnight because it disturbed their slumbers.

F1   An Indian crossing the Market Square in the November twilight with a long feather in his hat.

MUSIC   *Cue 5A under…*

M   There was an old woman called Granny Crack who every child has heard about who wore seven dresses all at once and walked the length and breadth of the country begging for a living, trading and begging. She speaks from the past:

MUSIC   *5B*

F1   I was a leather skinned harridan

I wandered the country's roads
Trading and begging and fighting
With the sun for hat and the road for shoes.

You saw me freckled and spotted
My face like a bird's egg
When, berry picking kids, you ran from me
Frightened, down the lane by the wood.

MUSIC *Out*

M They saw her as an incredible crone
The spirit of neglected fence corners
Of the curious wisdom of brambles
And weeds, of ruts, of stumps and of things despised.

MUSIC *5C*

F1 I was the mother of your sun
I was the aunt of your moon
My veins are your paths and roads
On my head I bear steeples and turrets
I am the darling of your god.

M The old woman of the country, Summer Wanderer,
The old man of the town, Winter Janitor,
  Old Woman, Granny Crack
  Old man, old woman
   Revolving back to back
    Looking down
   Granny, Janitor, Angel
    On my town.

MUSIC *Out*
PAUSE
MUSIC *Cue 6*

EIGHTH LETTER

M Eighth Letter: *The Music Lesson*
In the old fantastic house which one remembers as
having huge green elm trees, red velvet curtains tied
back with pink and gold butterflies (but I add this from
my Great Aunt Mary's front parlour), marble fireplaces
like Roquefort cheese and much-carved chairs, clock

64

under glass bell, a steel engraving of John Knox with
calves on his legs so huge they might be Bibles he was
smuggling past the border in his stockings: so strange –
at my music teacher's house at the back there was a rail-
way track with trains going by. In dreams the engine of
the train always stands still and starts one off on the
scales with a big blast on the steam whistle.

After waiting in the hallway with the Fathers of
Confederation, the History of the Dutch Republic, pic-
tures of Greek Statues interestingly disfigured and De
La Motte Fouqué's *Ondine* gorgeously illustrated by
Edmond Dulac.

MUSIC   *Cue 6A*
M   After that – the Lesson.
F1   Now I'll set the metronome.
   [Metronome starts.]
C   I am very far from home
F1   We have half an hour to play
C   In an auditory way
F1   Play us your scales first in the form of our town's streets.

MUSIC   *Metronome continues; Cue 6B*
C   A Baptist minister walking up Nile Street
F2   An Arabian girl running down Douglas Street
   A French teacher on Wellington Street
   A Sunday School teacher on St. Patrick's Street
C   A truant officer on Romeo Street
F1   An uppity type on Downie Street
   A Welshman on Britannia Street
F2   An Irishman on Caledonia Street.

   [Metronome stops.]

F1   Now play me some grocers and storekeepers.
MUSIC   *Cue 6C*
C   There was a grocer who had a sad little store
   He wore straw cuffs at his wrists.

   There was a seedsman whose name was Seed,
   Fat as a well-fed daffodil bulb.

F2   There were twin grocers, Mr. Esau
And Mr. Jacob, white aproned in dimness,
Selling rare First Editions of Kellogg's Cornflakes.

M   There was my Great-Aunt Mary
Who ran the Britannia Grocery
And was held up for what she had in the till
By an Indian ... five bucks.

F2   There were a brother and sister who ran
A bakery: their name was Bread
Miss Bread and Mr. Bread.

M   There was old Mrs. Mallard-Duck
She kept a second-hand store crammed with
The clocks and chairs and dishes of the past

F2   And five children ... grand ... around the store.

M, F2   Creaking rusty-voiced old Mrs. Mallard-Duck

MUSIC   *Out*

F1   That will do now. Now play me your pieces.
Play me *The Storm*. What shall I set the metronome at?

C   Set at summer and pink *[Metronome starts]* and white and
yellow-brick sunlight with blue sky and white feather
dumpling clouds.

M   *The Storm*

MUSIC   *Cue 6D*

M, F2, C A cloud and a cloud and a cloudy
Came into the blue afternoon room
A cloud and a cloud and a cloud
    And a cloud and a cloud a cloud *[Metronome stops]*
      MacLeod
      A Cloud
And a cloud and a cloudy

F2   Down down down came the cloudy
With a windowpane shudder
And mirrors for your feet

F1   People running into stores

M   Darkness in the library

F2   Umbrellas blossom

F1   Church is nearer through the rain

C   A cloud and a cloud and a cloudy
       Came out of the yellow garage.
       Joseph MacLeod in a many-coloured vest
       Danced to the music dying in the west.
F1   Yes, you've got both hands together very nicely on that.

MUSIC *Cue 6E*
F1   Up the tempo now and do keep practising your Snow
       Scenes and Interiors, your Skylines and City Limits.
       Let's have the next piece.
MUSIC *Out*
C   *Two Part Invention: A Year in the Town*
F1   And how fast can you play it?
C   Not very fast.
F1   Then you'd better play it hands separately. Left hand
       first.

MUSIC *Cue 6F*
M, C   Bud bud budling
       Bud bud budling
       Bud bud budling
       Bud bud budling
           Buddy blossom
           Blossom buddies
           Budding blossoms
F1   The right hand for that:
C, F2 The spring winds up the town
       The spring winds up the town
F1   Left hand now:
M   Leafy leafy leafy leafy
       Leaf Leaf Leaf Leaf
       Leafy leafy leafy leafy
       Leaf Leaf Leaf Leaf
       Leaves Leaves Leaves Leaves
       Leaving leaves leaving leaves
       Leafy leafy leaf leaf
F1   Right hand:
F2   Frogs stop: Put out the glass wind lantern

	Tinkling summer on the porch
F2, C	Frogs stop: Put out the glass wind lantern
	Tinkling summer on the porch.
M, C	Twig and branch, twig and branch
F1	Faster!
M, C	Twig and branch, twig and branch
	Bricks, stones and traffic hum
	Twig and branch, twig and branch
	Bricks, stones and traffic hum
	Twig and branch, twig and branch
	Bricks, stones and highway hum
	Bricks, stones and far away
	Twig and branch, branch and twig.
F1	The right hand for that now:
F2	Crickets cry and the owl flies down
	The Ferris wheel and the fall rains fall
F2, C	Crickets cry and the owl flies down
	The Ferris wheel and the fall rains fall.
F1	And let's hear the left hand for Winter.
M	Blue and white, white and blue
	Orion rules the frosty town
	Blue and white, white and blue
	Orion rules the frosty town
	Blue and white, white and blue
	Orion rules the frosty town
	Blue and white, white and blue
	Orion rules the frosty town.
F2	For three days no train or car got into town.
	The bakers had their yeast dropped from an airplane.
F1	Now! Hands together and not too fast, not too slow.
	Spring!

M Bud bud budling
   Bud bud budling   F2 The spring winds up the
   Bud bud budling   town
   Bud bud budling
   Buddy blossom
   Blossom buddies   The spring winds up the
                              town

Budding blossoms
F1 Summer!
M   Leafy leafy leafy leafy   F2   Frogs stop: Put out the
    Leaf leaf leaf leaf   glass wind lantern
    Leafy leafy leafy leafy   Tinkling summer on the
    Leaf leaf leaf leaf   porch.

    Leaves leaves leaves
        leaves   F2,c Frogs stop: Put out the
    Leafy leafy leafy leafy   glass wind lantern
    Leaving leaves leaving leaves   Tinkling summer on the
    Leafy leafy leaf leaf   porch.

F1 Fall!
M,c Twig and branch, twig and branch
    Bricks stones and traffic   F2   Crickets cry and the owl
    hum   flies down
    Twig and branch, twig and   The Ferris wheel and the
    branch   fall rains fall

    Bricks stones and traffic hum
    Twig and branch, twig   F2,c Crickets cry and the owl
    and branch   flies down

    Bricks stones and highway   The Ferris wheel and the
    hum   fall rains fall

    Bricks stones and far away
    Twig and branch, branch and twig

F1 Winter!
M,c Blue and white, white and blue
    Orion rules the frosty   F2   For three days no train or
    town   car

    Blue and white, white and   got into the town.
    blue
    Orion rules the frosty town
    Blue and white, white and
    blue   The bakers had their
    Orion rules the frosty town   yeast dropped

Blue and white, white and   from an airplane.
blue
Orion rules the frosty town.
F1   Twice as fast next time!
MUSIC   *Cue 6G: Up and out*

    PAUSE

NINTH LETTER
F2   Ninth Letter: *Town House and Country Mouse*
F1   Old maids are the houses in town
            They sit on streets like cement canals
            They are named after aldermen
                    And their wives
            Or battles and dukes.

            At a sky scratched with wires and smoke
            They point their mild and weak gothic bonnets.
            The houses of Albert and Brunswick Streets
            Wait for farmers' barns to wed them
            But the streets are too narrow
                    And they never come.

            Out here barn is wedded to house,
            House is married to barn,
            Grey board and pink brick.
                    The cowyard lies between
            Where in winter on brown thin ice
                    Red-capped children skate.
            There is wallpaper in the house
                    And in the barn
            They are sawing the horns off a bull.
MUSIC   *Cue 7 under ...*
M   Out here the sound of bells on a wet evening
            Floating out clear when the wind is right.
            The factory whistles at noon in summer.
                    Going from here to there

As a child, not to a place with a name
    But first to get there:
The red buggy wheels move so fast
    They stand still,
Whirling against sheaves of blue chicory,
The secret place where wild bees nest,
The million leaning pens of grass with their nibs of
    seed,
The wild rose bush – all
    Suddenly gone.
On gravel now where corduroy logs from the past
    Look dumbly up
Buried in the congregations of gravel,
Getting closer to the highway,

Cars darting back and forth,
    In another world altogether.
Past the stonemason's house with its cement lion
Not something to be very much afraid of
    Since it has legs like a table,
Past the ten huge willows, the four poplars,
Far away in a field the slaughterhouse,
    Two gas stations with windy signs,
The half world of the city outskirts: orchards
Gone wild and drowned farms.
    Suddenly the square:

MUSIC   *Cue 7A under …*

F1   People turning and shining like lighted jewels,

C   Terrifying sights: one's first nun!

F2   The first person with a wooden leg,

F1   A huge chimney writing the sky
           With dark smoke.
C   A parrot.
F1   A clock in the shape of a man with its face
           In his belly
C   The swan
F2   A Dixie cup of ice cream with a wooden spoon.

MUSIC   *Cue 7B under …*
M   And then – backwards, the gas stations,
        The outskirts, orchards, slaughterhouse
        Far back the chimneys still writing
           Four poplars, ten huge willows
           The lion with table legs.
        The bump as we go over old corduroy log
        The gamut of grass and blue flowers
           Until the wheels stop
           And we are not uptown
MUSIC   *Cue 7C under …*
M   We are here
        Where barn is wedded to house …

M, F1 ,F2, C   Into town, out of town.
MUSIC   *Up & out*

TENTH LETTER

M, F2   Tenth Letter: *Voices and Conjunctions*
MUSIC   *Cue 8 starts*
C   Who was the old man with two canes and a white beard
     Who walked along the road out of town
     With a huge sack on his back
F2   *Who was that old man?*

MUSIC   *Cue 8A*
M   Mr. Vermeer, the specialist in trusses and supports,
         Lived in a sorrowful red brick house
     Black ribbons on his pince-nez, black Homburg hat,
         Who had two grave bespectacled kids
F2   *Eighty years old at the age of eight.*

MUSIC   *Cue 8B*
F2   The old bookbinder who lived above the creamery
     Huge butter churns walloped just under our feet
     Had a gold and blue sign: printed wedding invitations
M   *Who had bound books in 1890 in Philadelphia.*

MUSIC   *Cue 8C*
F2   There were remarkable boys on the streets
     One who looked sad because his face was
     Covered with whelks; he delivered papers
     With a wagon –
M   – also an evil red-haired boy
     Delivered groceries, said something I didn't hear
F2   *Which made the girl in the store cry.*

MUSIC   *Cue 8D*
F2   Gospel madman who preached on the streets.
         Every day was like Sunday.
     Far off you could hear him at school
M   *Who was like a big buzzing Bible bee.*
MUSIC   *Cue 8E*
M   Two brick tile kilns at the edge of town,

Two huge mosaic roses,
A rose red brick house where twins lived.
Their father called one 'Pete,' the other 'Twin.'
M, F2   *For 'Hey, Twin!' he would shout.*

C   Down the street came a giant man dressed old
With a clock in his belly: I dreamt that.
Babies of six months in their christening shrouds
Reach out for me by the ding-dong churchyard
F2, C   *Which stands on the hill above the dam.*
MUSIC   *Out*
PAUSE

MUSIC   *Cue 9, under...*

ELEVENTH LETTER
C   Eleventh Letter: *Shakespearean Gardens*
MUSIC   *Up and out.*
C/F1   *The Tempest.* The violet lightning of a March thunder-
storm glaring the patches of ice still stuck to the streets.
F2/M   *Two Gentlemen of Verona.* On Wellington Street an elegant
colonel-looking gentleman with waxed white mousta-
chios that came to tight little points.
F2/F1   *Merry Wives of Windsor.* The Ladies' Auxiliary of the
Orange Lodge marched down the street in white
dresses with orange bows on them.
M/C   *Richard the Third.* At last all the children ran away from
home and were brought up by an old spinster who
lived down the street.
F1/F2   *Henry the Eighth.* Mr. White's second wife was the first
Mrs. Brown and the first Mrs. White was the second
Mrs. Brown.
F2/F1   *Troilus and Cressida.* 'Well, I haven't been to that old
Festival yet but since it began I've had ten different
boyfriends.'
MUSIC   *Cue 9A*
F1/M   *Titus Andronicus.* Young Mr. Wood today lost his right
hand in an accident at the lumber yards.

74

F1,F2/C *Romeo and Juliet.* Romeo and Juliet Streets.

M/F1 *Timon of Athens.* Old Miss Shipman lived alone in a weatherbeaten old cottage and could occasionally be seen out on the front lawn cutting the grass with a small sickle.

F2/M *Julius Caesar.* Antony wore a wristwatch in the Normal School production although he never looked at it during the oration.

MUSIC *Cue 9B*

M/F2 *Macbeth.* Principal Burdoch's often-expressed opinion was that a great many people would kill a great many other people if they knew for certain they could get away with it.

F2,C/F1 *Hamlet.* A girl at the bakery took out a boat on the river, tied candlesticks to her wrists and drowned herself.

M/F2 *King Lear.* Mr. Upas was a silver-haired cranky old individual who complained that the meat was too tough at the boarding house.

M/F1 *Othello.* At the edge of town there stood a lonely white frame building – a deserted Negro church.

F1/F2 *The Merchant of Venice.* When my cousin worked for the Silversteins she had her own private roll of baloney kept aside in the refrigerator for her.

M,C,F2/M *Henry the Fifth.* The local armouries are made of the usual red brick with the usual limestone machicolation.

MUSIC *Cue 9C, up and out.*

PAUSE

MUSIC *Start cue 10*

TWELFTH LETTER

M Twelfth Letter: *The Bicycle*

MUSIC *Cue 10, under...*

M Halfway between childhood and manhood,
More than a hoop but never a car,
The bicycle talks gravel and rain pavement
On the highway where the dead frogs are.

MUSIC *Cue 10A*

Like sharkfish the cars blur by,
Filled with the two-backed beast
One dreams of, yet knows not the word for,
The accumulating sexual yeast.

Past the house where the bees winter,
I climb on the stairs of my pedals
To school murmuring irregular verbs
Past the lion with legs like a table's.

Autumn blows the windfalls down
With a twilight horn of dead leaves.
I pick them up in the fence of November
And burs on my sweater sleeves.

MUSIC   *Cue 10B*

Where a secret robin is wintering
By the lake in the fir grove dark
Through the fresh new snow we stumble
That Winter has whistled sharp.

The March wind blows me ruts over,
Puddles past, under red maple buds,
Over culvert of streamling, under
White clouds and beside bluebirds.

Fireflies tell their blinking player
Piano hesitant tales

MUSIC   *Cue 10C*

Down at the bridge through the swamp
Where the ogre clips his rusty nails.

Between the high school and the farmhouse
In the country and the town
It was a world of love and of feeling
Continually floating down

On a soul whose only knowledge
Was that everything was something,
This was like that, that was like this –

MUSIC   *Cue 10D; continues under…*

In short, everything was
The bicycle of which I sing.

MUSIC   *Up and out.*

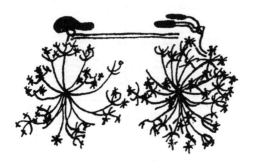

Canada Dash, Canada Dot

78

Dear John, Keep hold of
this letter — I might need it back!

VI, 15, 65

This is a much belated letter on our 3 part Canada project.
I think I can get the first part word done very quickly
now, but first I'd like to get an idea of the whole or-
ganization — & to know how to do this I'll have to
get some ideas from you re music organization.

What I'd like to do is call it tentatively, Canada in
Three Parts, Very Big, Not so Long and Smaller. The
idea is that at the centenary you think about your
country & it's big! (I) & you cross it or go round
it like the St Peck in time & in space. I worked up
all this material for a children's play which is going to
do — so that's all put.

Now Part II — instead of racing all the way across
Canada you examine a smaller slice — say Yonge St —
which you walk up — to Holland Landing. You walk backward
into time of course ending up with Joseph Willson & the
Silver Band at Sharon — which won 1st prize for bands at Philadelphia
Exposition in 1875. John, I just read some more about him
then the chap wrote in Alphabet & he is a charmer.
Just sued on religion in music & vice versa & apparently
wrote hymns — with his own music? This might be worth
looking up — to get a Shaker-like tune à la Copland.

The Third Part is a still — or short, short walk where
you put all the images of the country together & push at random
— the most brilliant ones. Glacier/poetry/ Calico coveralles/
Eskimo names for snow. This will be a contemplative
interesequence which pick out things from the other 2
sequence & makes them into a sort of timeless crown. I realize
that people in the rest of Canada may sort of feather up at
Yonge St — but I know it — & I can mention similar
journeys I know about like by the Red River — & across Nova
Scotia from Windsor to Halifax.
I was thinking in the first part — see editorial for ABC
#9 — you could have a 78 R.P.M. ending where you go thro'

Part of a 1965 letter from Reaney to John Beckwith outlining the rationale
for this 'collage trilogy.'

all you turn Canada maps very, very quickly
Do we have just 20 minutes for each part?

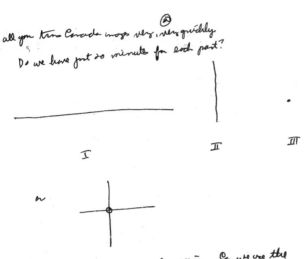

Now, I know there are mode in music. Can we use the
sequence of modes to suggest crossing a country — going
from mosaic to mosaic bit?

It strikes me that the 2nd part should be the musical
system equivalent of the still point feeling — 12 tone? The
first part or the large, large view is the — what kind of music?
19th century. Linear? New archive for 2nd part?

The reason I'm asking all these questions is that if you
can throw me a thematic style arrangement — I'll have some idea
of what comes to make the libretto turn — for the whole.

The idea behind the whole 3 parts that you see the
whole world in a local grain of sand. I wrote a short article on this
in Edge 3. The big legend about Canada is that it was once

'ABC' refers to *Alphabet*, the literary journal of which James Reaney was editor and printer.

Canada Dash, Canada Dot
A Centennial Collage-Trilogy
commissioned by the Canadian Broadcasting Corporation

Part 1: *The Line Across*

Singers: soprano (s), alto (A), baritone (BAR), bass (B)

Speakers: boy (BOY), female voice (F), male voice 1 (M1), male voice 2 (M2)

Instruments: Flute/piccolo, trombone, percussion (one player), violin, contrabass/mandolin, piano/celeste.

First broadcast; CBC Radio, 23 November 1965:

Mary Morrison, s
Patricia Rideout, A
Alexander Gray, BAR
Maurice Brown, B
Reid Needles, BOY
Nancy Kerr, F
Arch McDonnell, M1
Alexander Webster, M2
Robert Aitken, flute
Ted Roderman, trombone

William Wakefield, percussion
Corol McCartney, violin
William Kuinka, contrabass
John Beckwith, piano
James Kent, producer

Canadian Pavillion; Expo 67, Montreal, 23 May 1967

Mary Morrison, s
Patricia Rideout, a
Richard Braun, bar
Walter Verikaitis, b
Jonathan Beckwith, boy
Virginia McLeod, f
Arch McDonnell, m1
Sandy Webster, m2
Robert Aitken, flute
Murray Ginsberg, trombone
Vair Capper, percussion
David Wulkan, violin
William Kuinka, contrabass
John Beckwith, piano

CANADA DASH, CANADA DOT
PART 1: THE LINE ACROSS

SPEAKERS

ALL: Canada Dash, Canada
Dash, and Canada Dot

M1: Canada dashes and Canada
dots

M2: Morse code for our country
on its Hundredth Birthday.

M1: Morse code, or, Two Lines
and a Dot.

F: Now, in real Morse code,
'Da da dit' means – G. But
we've changed that.
Now it means to us –

ALL: First Dash:

SINGERS

ALL: Canada Dash, Canada Dash
and Canada Dot
(*under*) da da dit, da da dit, da da dit, …

(*… out*)

M2: 1965: Draw a line across our country.

ALL: Second Dash:

F: 1966: Draw a line from south to north, up and down Canada.

ALL: Lastly –

M1: 1967: Draw a dot. In a speck of time and now and here where you stand or think or remember – that's where your country is. So, here and here and here and here and here – the first part of this New Morse Code for my country is:

ALL: 'The Line Across.'

MOTTO ONE

M1: From East to West I walk / Across my country …

BOY: (as if learning it) From East to West I walk / Across my country …

M1: Forests and cities are my view / People from the past too / As I walk from sea to sea.

BOY: Forests and cities are my view / People from the past too /

As I walk from sea to sea.

OVERTURE

M1: Overture! (*sotto voce:*) Maritime shanty overtones ... The roar of Atlantic breakers ...   (*Violin: fiddling*)

M2: Spouting whale and a leaping dolphin

F: White sail

M2:   White sail

BOY: Plaice and halibut

F, M1: (*sotto voce:*) Grunt, as if pulling a rope.   ALL: The sea!   BAR, B: (*rhythmic grunts, in - out ...*)

M1: Mackerel Tuna Cod and Shad   S, A: Ocean

F: Alewives Smelt Swordfish   Atlantic

M1: Salmon Pollock and other Flounders   The Strait of Belle-Isle

F: Salmon Pollock and other Flounders

M2: Spouting whale and a leaping dolphin   (*Violin: fiddling*)

BOY: White sail

M2: Smoke smudge

BOY: Lobsters! Ouch!

RIDDLE

M1: A Riddle:

S: My laughter causes terror
I am a wonderful white lady
Travelling over the waves
Two-thirds of me the blue wave hides
My mother is soft and falls from the sky
But I am as hard as a million granite
    grindstones
Who am I?

My laughter causes terror

I am a wonderful white lady

BOY: Her laughter is terrifying.

M1: Icy refrigerator cackles.

ALL: The sea!

S: (*laugh…*)

Travelling over the waves
Two-thirds of me the blue wave hides

My mother is soft ...

    ... and falls from the sky

But I am as hard as a million granite grindstones
Who am I?

Who am I?

Ahhh – la la la la la la –

BOY: A white lady?

F: Two-thirds hidden ...

BOY: Could her mother so soft ...

M2: Falls from the sky?

BOY: Snow – now snow is soft ...

F, M1: and falls from the sky

BOY: Her mother is soft, but she is so very very hard ...

F, M1, M2: Soft snow falls on – Greenland's icy mountains and becomes –

M1, M2: Iceberg!

F: Iceberg!

ALL: You're an iceberg sailing off Newfoundland!

Correct! – and my great greatgreat greatgreatgreatgtgt aunt DESTROYED THE TITANIC!!!

(*Instruments establish Galop ...*)
BAR: Calixa Lavallée

ALL: Lavallée écrivait

BAR: Calixa Lavallée

ALL: écrivait

BAR: Calixa Lavallée

ALL: sa musique

GALOP TO QUEBEC

M1: Galop to Quebec.*

M2: Calixa Lavallée, the composer of our national anthem, was born in Verchères. The long narrow fields and farms and counties of Quebec are like the bars of

Based on Calixa Lavallée's 'War Fever Galop,' for piano, 1861

BOY, F, M1: Calixa Lavallée's music!

M2: This is a galop he wrote long ago. The place names you will hear are the names of counties in Quebec, coming up the St. Lawrence towards Montreal, the last-named county being that in which

BOY, F, M1: Calixa Lavallée was born!

M1: Charlevoix

BOY, F, M2:   Charlevoix

M1: Montmorency

BOY, F, M2:   Montmorency

M1: Québec

BOY, F, M2:   Québec

BAR: Calixa Lavallée

ALL: est né

M1: Portneuf

BOY, F, M2: Portneuf

M1: Champlain

BOY, F, M2: Champlain

M1: St. Maurice

BOY, F, M2: St. Maurice

M1: Maskinongé Berthier

BOY, F, M2: Maskinongé Berthier

M1: Joliette Montcalm

BOY, F, M2: Joliette Montcalm

M1: L'Assomption ...

BOY, F, M2: L'Assomption ...

M1: Verchères!

BAR, B: la la la la la la la

S, A: la la la la la la

BAR, B: Calixa Lavallée

S, A: la la la la la la

ALL:

Ahhh–

BOY, F, M2: Verchères!

ALL: (*cheers, whistles ...*)

BOY, F, M1: On St. Jean Baptiste Day

BOY, F, M1: Eighteen-eighty

M2: ... at the Pavillon des Patineurs in Quebec was first heard that other song by

(*Instruments: phrase from 'O Canada'*)

M2: On January twenty-first, eighteen-ninety-one, after a long exile from the country where he was born ...

(*cheers, whistles...*)

BAR: Et sur la fête de Saint Jean Baptiste

ALL: Mille huit cent quatre-vingts

ALL: Calixa Lavallée

BAR: Calixa Lavallée

ALL: est mort

BOY, F, M1: Calixa Lavallée died

M2: ... in Boston, Massachusetts, U.S.A.

MOTTO TWO

BOY, M1: From East to West I walk / Across my country / Forests and cities do I view / People from the past too / As I walk from sea to sea.

CONVERSATION WITH THE PAST

BOY: People from the past too.

M1: Can you guess with what Ontario persons the following dialogue took place? One person from far back, the grand-father of the second person – who died not so very long ago.

ALL: The grandfather said:

M2: Victoria Guelph, the bloody Queen of England.

ALL: The grandson said:

M1: I would say that a man with as great wealth as Mr. Rockefeller has should use it to improve conditions not only as far as his own employees are concerned, but for the benefit of his fellow men generally.

ALL: The grandfather said:

F: (July 26th, 1837)

M2: Not to this country and continent alone, nor chiefly, is this revolution confined. It reaches the old world. The millions downtrodden for ages by kings, hierarchies, and nobilities, awake ... Aye, and the puffed up, angry little creature, who sits perched upon a mahogany throne in a chamber up here in Toronto, playing the petty tyrant of an hour, might just as well –

ALL: The grandson said:

M1: I did have something to do with the dance at Colorado and for starting him

F: (Rockefeller)

M1: whether for good or ill, a little on that path.

ALL: But the grandfather said:

M2: You give a bounty for wolves' scalps. Why? Because wolves harass you. The bounty you must pay for freedom (blessed word) is to give the strength of your arms to put down tyranny at Toronto. One short hour will deliver our country from the oppressor.

ALL: And the grandson said:

M1: I decided at all events not to publish the article on 'sweating,' till the government had had its chance.

BOY: Who was the grandfather?

F: Who are these Ontario men?

BOY: The grandfather was –

ALL: William Lyon Mackenzie!

M1: The grandson was –

ALL: Mackenzie King!

WATER, RIVERS AND LAKES

M1: Water, Rivers and Lakes

of water

BOY: From Lake Ontario!

BOY: Niagara River, Niagara Falls!

B: Where has this cup of water come from?

A: It has come from – I will tell you where this cup has come from.

which flows out of

which flow out of

BOY: Lake Erie, and up the Detroit River

which flows out of

BOY: Lake St. Clair, and up the St. Clair River

which flows out of

BOY: Lake Huron and up the Sault –

which flo-o-ows out of

BOY: Lake Superior!

Ahhh, ahhh–, Aa–rrgkh!!

M1: There, at Cape Thunder, lies the Sleeping Giant,

O-o-o ...
Nanabozho ...!

M1: ... Nanabozho, the god of the Ojibway Indians.

BOY: Why are you sleeping up here on top of Cape Thunder, Nanabozho?

M2: I had no more work to do. I had killed off all the monsters. I had made the land again after the great flood. I had caused the black marks on the white birches. I whipped them for being evil to me. But to those who know and love their country I awake once more. Cape Thunder where I lie is in the very centre of the land. What season is this that you make your journey up the rivers and lakes?

BOY: It's St. Jean Baptiste Day. A day in June, the day Calixa Lavallée's song was first sung at the Pavillon des Patineurs.

M2: A day in – June? You have changed the names of the months. Before I fall asleep again I will teach you the names of the Indian months.

INDIAN MONTHS

M2: Their May is our

M1: Our June is their

M2: Their July is our

BAR: Frog moon

A: The moon of trees

B: Moon of the deer

S: When the young birds fly

BAR: The deer cast their horns

B: The deer are running

S: Hoar-frost moon

A: Stay-at-home moon

S: Whirlwind moon

BAR: Big moon

B: Eagle moon

A: Wild-goose moon

M1: Our August is their

M2: Their September

M1: Our October

M2: Their November

M1: Our December

M1, M2: January

M1, M2: February

M1, M2: March (*getting tired ...*)

M1, M2: Ap - ril –

M1, M2: (*exhale ...*)

ALL: (*exhale ...*)

PULP FACTORY

F: (*hand clap*) This will never do. We'll never get a line
across the country this way. Get a move on! There's
work to be done. Here! Here's a pulp factory. Standing
idle. Turns our forest products into – all sorts of things.

BOY: What's a forest product, mother?

F: Wood! ... and I'll show you how to turn it into almost
anything.

B: Listen to the forest by the lonely lake ...

A: Cedar Hemlock Spruce Pine

A, BAR: Tamarack Larch Aspen White birch

B: Dark spruce

A, BAR: White birch White birch

B: Dark spruce

A, BAR: White birch White birch

98

M1: Chop them down!

M2: Chop chop chop chop

M1, M2: chop chop chop chop

ALL: chopchopchopchopchopchopchop (*continuing under ...*)

ALL: Hydraulic barkers!

S: Listen to the forest by the lonely lake...

A, BAR: White birch ...

BAR: Down the river the forest stumbles and lurches and swims.

S: Cedar Hemlock Spruce Pine

S, B: Tamarack Larch Aspen White birch

BAR: Dark spruce

S, B: White birch White birch

A: Down the river the forest comes to –

B: R-r-rip the bark off!

BAR: OUCH!!

M1: The chipper takes it over –

ALL: Soak Soak Soak –

F: Stir the digester and –

M2: Cook it in the chemicals

ALL: Pulp ... pulp ... pulp ...

BOY: Blow upon it, blow upon it

F: Bleach it and whiten it

ALL: Press it down! Press it down!

M2: thinner

M1: ... and flatter

F: A piece of paper!

A: Chip chip chip chip chip

S: Screen screen screen screen

A: Steam steam steam

S: Hiss-ss-ss –

   Hiss-ss-ss –

B: Pulp ... pulp ... pulp ...

BAR: Blow ... blow ... blow ...

B: White ... white ... white ...

S, A: Thinner and thinner ...

BAR, B: Flatter and flatter ...

M2: 'Forever Amber'

BOY: 'Dick, Jane and Puff'

ALL: Twelve acres of Canada's forest: one *New York Sunday Times!*

M1: Cut the tree down!

ALL: Bark that tree!

M1: chip

ALL: soak

F: digest

M2: cook

ALL: pulp ... pulp ... pulp ...

BOY: blow

F: bleach

ALL: A piece of paper!

ALL: The *New York Sunday Times!!!*

B: Crack!

BAR: TIM-BER!!!

B: R-r-rip!

BAR: Ouch!

A: chip chip chip

S: screen

A: steam

S: Hiss-ss-ss—

B: Pulp Pulp

BAR: Blo-o-ow

B: Bleach

M2: acetic acid!

M1: solvent!

M2: spin spin spin

BOY: spin spin spin spin

ALL: spin spin spin spinspinspinspin …

TRAIN

M1: Last summer I took a railway journey from London, Ontario, to Vancouver. Previously we had – more than five summers ago – taken a train from Halifax to the centre of Canada. In the East – and in Southern Ontario – the

S, A: Ouch ouch ouch

BAR, B: Acetate acetate acetate

S: Ladies' lingerie!

A: A red dress!

BAR, B: A plate of hamburgers!!

ALL: The *New York Sunday Times*!!!

fields are small, trees and thickets and fence-bottoms close up – cows, ducks, herons. Then – Metro Toronto – buzzing with machinery and cars. And then – Northern Ontario. Do you know it takes a whole day and night to cross the huge district of Northern Ontario? – a day and a night across, whitebirched and mysteriously rocked. Mishepeshoo the Ojibway water-demon foams down towards us just when you hear the train wheels give a hollow sound – as they cross over a small stream, a large stream, on a bridge or culvert. Now the forest stays behind us. Rocks and stones disappear. There are huge fields now. And three kinds of prairie ahead of us. The first kind of prairie is

M2:
Eagle River Gunne
Pine Hawk Lake
Keewatin White-
mouth
Sioux Lookout
Redditt
Ottermere White
Elma
WINNIPEG

BAR, B:
Vermilion Bay
Edison
Scovil Kenora
Hudson McIntosh
Farlane Minaki
Winnitoba Hector
Anola

Elie
Molson
Lydiatt Oakbank
North Transcona

Portage la Prairie
Deer
Cloverleaf
Hazelridge
WINNIPEG

Shilo

Harte

North Brandon

Brandon

Rosser Meadows

Marquette Poplar Point

High Bluff

Portage la Prairie

Burnside Bagot

McGregor Austin

like this: (MUSIC...) – and your eyes
regard not just the distance with the
grass lands and great fields swinging
away into as huge a sky – your eyes
look not at *the* distance, but distance
itself.

M1:   Geology says that the low green
hills of Southern Manitoba originally
came as gravel and erosion in glacial

rushing rivers that flowed from the
Rocky Mountains.

Between the Red River Lowlands and
the Rocky Mountains lie these
names of railway stops you hear.

Between the lowlands of the present,
our present time, our present selves,
and the giant mountains of the
ancestral past lie lists of names, stops
on the railway of the mind.

F: Jacques Cartier
Samuel de Champlain
Louis Hébert

M2: Louis the Fourteenth
Sieur de Maisonneuve
BOY: Sir John A. Macdonald
F: George the Second
George the Third
George the Fourth
BOY: Alexander Mackenzie
F: VICTORIA!
M2: Viscount Monck
BOY: Sir John Joseph
Abbott
Sir John Sparrow

BAR, B: Carberry Hughes
Douglas Chater BRANDON
Kemnay Alexander

A: Second kind of prairie...
BAR, B: Griswold Oak Lake
Routledge Virden Hargrave
Elkhorn Kirhella Manitoba
Fleming Saskatchewan
Moosamin Red Jacket
Wapella Burrows
Summerberry Wolseley
Sintaluta Indian Head
Qu'Appelle McLean
Balgonie Pilot Butte
REGINA Grand Coulee
Pense Belle Plaine Pasqua

The names of the kings and queens who have ruled over Canada. Governor generals – governors general – and lieutenant governors. Passengers lists on boats that flew across the Atlantic with white wings.

Lists of names in graveyards. On war memorials. Lists of names in old directories.

Sir Robert Laird Borden

Thompson
F: Baron Lisgar
Earl of Dufferin
M2: Marquess of Lorne
Marquess of Lansdowne
BOY: Sir Mackenzie Bowell
M2: Baron Stanley of Preston
F: Earl of Aberdeen
M2: Earl Minto
BOY: Sir Charles Tupper
M2: Earl Gray Duke of Connaught
Duke of Devonshire

F: Baron Byng Viscount Willington
BOY: Sir Wilfrid Laurier
M2: Earl of Bessborough
F: Baron Tweedsmuir
Earl of Athlone Viscount
Alexander

BOY: Sir Robert Laird Borden

MOOSE JAW Boharm
Caron
Morse
Rush Lake
Waldeck
SWIFT CURRENT
Beverley
s: Whitesail, whitesail
wings... Ahhh...
BAR, B: Gull Lake Tompkins
Piapot, Walsh Irvine Pashley
MEDICINE HAT
Crowfoot Strangmuir
Indus Shepard
Ogden CALGARY
Bearspaw Glenbow
Cochrane Radnor
Morley
– puff –
Ozada

Arthur Meighen	Arthur Meighen	
Mackenzie King	Mackenzie King	– puff –
		Seebe
Mackenzie King	Mackenzie King	
	BOY, F, M2:	– puff –
Mackenzie King	Mackenzie King	Kananaskis
Mackenzie King	Mackenzie King	
		– puff –
Mackenzie King	Mackenzie King	Exshaw
Mackenzie King	Mackenzie King	– puff –
– puff –		Canmore
Mackenzie King!	– puff –	– puff –
	Mackenzie King!	BANFF!!

BOY: Is the reason you're puffing so much – ?

F: It's so hard getting up these mountains.

BOY: The Rocky Mountains?

F: The Rocky Mountains. Now, if we can just find the source of the Fraser River we can finish drawing our line across Canada.

BOY: Look back. There's the Sleeping Giant at Fort William.

F: These mountains are the home of his father – West Wind.

(M1, M2 – *voices off*)

BOY: Who are these people climbing up towards us? They're walking towards the east.

F: Travellers across –

M2: We've done it. We've drawn a line across Canada from east to west and now we're drawing it back.

BOY: How can we do that same thing?

M1: Just as we did, you'll come to the source of the Fraser and you'll slide down it.

M2: Past all its tributary creeks and bars – all the way to Vancouver and the Sea!

(MUSIC: *Finale starts under …*)

M1, M2: A whirlwind dancing by itself.

BOY: The chinook?

F: You saw it on the Alberta prairies.

M1, M2: Wheels, wheels, wheels ...

F: ... from a train.

M1, M2: A mountain with four horns.

BOY: You saw two deer in the mountains?

M2: Yes. And high up in the mountains we sang this:

FINALE

M1: Finale!
(*sotto voce:*) Suggestions of a voyageur song

   ... or maybe a square dance

S, A: (*rhythmic clapping*)
B: From Fort George down ...!
   Road River
     Naver Creek
   Stone Creek
     Big Bar Creek
BAR: Envoyons! Down ...!
   Grande Rapide Fort à gauche
 B: Rapide Couverte
     Woodpecker River

Soda Creek Risk Creek
          Dry Creek French Bar
BAR: Chimney Creek Alkali Creek
  B: Yulahan River Texas Creek
          Thompson River – !
BAR: Gaspard Creek Watson Bar
          Lilloet Stein River – !

B: Boston Bar

BAR, B: Hell's Gate!!!

ALL: Spuzzum!!!
BAR, B: Mills Bar
S, A: Emory's Bar
BAR, B: Chillukweyuk River
S, A: Chilliwak
BAR, B: Vancouver –

S, A: The sea!

M1:
     Music suggests turbulence of Hell's Gate …

ALL: … Spuzzum!!!

ALL: The sea!

     The sea!

BAR, B: The sea!
(*cheers, whistles …*)

MOTTO THREE

ALL: From East to West we walk / Across our country / … Forest and cities do we view / People from the past too / … As we walk from sea to sea.

ALL: (*cheers, whistles …*)

Canada Dash, Canada Dot
Part 2: *The Line Up and Down*

Singers: hymn singer (alto, H), pop singer (bass-baritone, P)

Speakers: female voice (F), male voice (M)

Instruments: clarinet/bass clarinet, trumpet, viola, contrabass, percussion (one player), piano/organ/harmonium

First broadcast, CBC Radio, 27 December 1966.

Patricia Rideout, H
Jack Van Evera, P
Nonny Griffin, F
Arch McDonnell, M
Bernard Temoin, clarinet
Joseph Umbrico, trumpet
Eugene Hudson, viola
William Kuinka, contrabass
Hugh Barclay, percussion
John Beckwith, piano
James Kent, producer

CANADA DASH, CANADA DOT

PART 2: THE LINE UP AND DOWN

(*Instruments: hymn tune*)

M: From East to West we've walked / Across our country
Forests and cities did we view, people from the past too / As we walked from sea to sea.
Now we sing, now walk forth / From South to North.

F: Is this the beginning of Yonge Street?

M: Right in Lake Ontario.

F: So we start walking north?

M: As we walk north through the city of Toronto, put down anything that strikes your fancy. What you...

F: ...see!

M: What I...

F: ...hear!

M: What you...

F: ...touch, taste, smell, feel, imagine – TRAFFIC!

M: What did you say? I can hardly hear you.

F: Traffic. All that flashing glass and metal and chrome on the cars.

P: Honk! Beep-beep! A-hooh-ah!

M: F:

M:	F:
Red	
Orange	
Green	
Red	Stop
	Go
Orange	Walk
	Don't Walk
Green	
	Stop
Red	Go
	Walk

Orange — Don't Walk

Green — Stop / Go / Walk

Red — Don't Walk / Stop / Go

Orange — Walk / Don't Walk

Green — Stop / Go / Walk

Red — Don't Walk

Orange — Stop / Go / Walk

Green — Don't Walk

Red — Stop

Orange   Go
                Walk
                Don't Walk

Green   Stop!

H: Neee-ow!

P: (raspberry sound)

M: Chrysler '65

F: $3995!

H, P: Chevrolet Buick Oldsmobile Dodge Meteor

M: Chrysler '64

F: $2538!

P: Scree-eech!

H: Ee-eek!

M: Chrysler '63

F: $1987!

M: Chrysler '62

F: $1467!

M: Chrysler '61

F: $795!

H: Chugchugchugchugchug chugchug

P: Whoo-oo-oosh!

M: F:

                                              Orange
                                              Red
                                              Green
                                              Orange

         Go   Red
                                              Green
         Stop   Orange
                                              Red

Walk

Green
Orange
Red
Green

Run!

Orange
Red
Green

Don't Walk

Orange
Red

Go

Green
Orange
Red

Stop

Green
Orange
Red

Walk

Green
Orange
Red
Green

Run!

Don't Walk

Go

Orange

Red

Green

Orange

Stop!

F, M: (*gasp, then exhale with laughter, as if they have just escaped across the intersection in time*)

F: Haven't you always wondered what you'd do if when you're in the middle of the street it flashes to 'Don't Walk' if you just stayed absolutely still and did what it said, 'Don't Walk' – ?

M: There's a loophole there. Of course you'd get killed.

F: They expect you to figure that out for yourself, don't they?

M: Look at that plough carved up there over the window of that old bank.

F: Sleep, baby, sleep / Father robs the bank

M: Look at the street.

F: The cement of this street has pebbles in it and slivers of stone. Like grey candy which the shoes eat up.

M: 'No turns at any time!' ... Look at that shop window.

F: BAN for sale!

M: Perfume for sale!

F: The different colours of the cars. The different faces of the people – coming towards us. The faces are each letters in a sentence that the city keeps trying to say to you... but... down Yonge Street, what does it say?

M: People like being downtown.

F: ...that the city keeps trying to say to you but – down Yonge Street – what does it say?

M: Wholesale clothing!

F: A peachstone on the street.

M: A pigeon feather.

F: A German family. Very chic and tall are the parents. Like ads in magazines.

H: Mercedes-Benz...

P: VolkswagenVolkswagenVolkswagenVolkswagen...

M: Simpson's and Eaton's exude a dignity –

F: Look at the windows.

M: Simpson's and Eaton's exude a dignity –

F: Over and over and over again the papier-mâché cobra comes out of the basket for the papier-mâché boy with the pipe – an Easter window!

M: Simpson's and Eaton's exude a dignity that disappears until you reach –

F, M: Simpson's and Eaton's exude a dignity that as you go farther up Yonge Street disappears until (*majestic music*) Eaton's College Street again!

F: Come inside to get the granny look.

M: Sam the Record Man!

F: Coles Books! Coles Notes!

M: Seven seconds delayed when flashing.

M, F: Raw truth nailed to the screen!

M: Off in the distance on another north-and-south street I see a brand-new skyscraper made all of black marble – looking like a fourteen-storey radio.

F: Moloch's temple, you mean. All the new buildings – save the City Hall – look like Moloch temples smeared with napalm.... Three young men in black.

M: Various sorts of nuns. They all have their own special way of facing one's look.

F: That man in green shoes is looking at some suede shoes in the window.

M: A faded mother in slacks and curlers with fresh-coloured children.

F: ...Out of one of the side-street rat holes.

M: South Yonge Street.

P: Traveller, r you travellin' far?
  Walkin' up and down, back in town.
  Yessir, I am travellin' far,
  For I travel on a star,
  As I walk up and down, back in town.
  Floatin' up and down,
  Yessir, I am travellin' far.

M: CHUM, CKEY...

F: The high-school kids are out.

P: For y' sorta get the yen, in Kingston Pen,
  T' move in a line fr as far as you can.

M: A whole succession of youths with pipes.

F: College – come for their pre-supper downtown stroll.

P: Traveller, r you travellin' far?
  Yessir, I travel on a star.
  And it takes me, as you can see,
  Back, back, back t' town,
  Floatin' up and down –
  Walkin' up and down –
        Back in town.

F: All these people with dark glasses: are they blind?

M: No, they're not blind…. People with small babies.

F: Have you seen a tree yet?

M: No, but should there be trees? All this property's too valuable for – just a tree.

F: A recurring type is the pasty-faced woman in black slacks, cigarette in mouth, dyed red hair – often with a baby in her arms.

M: Step with me into this tavern.

H, P: (whistling, laughter, smooch sounds, snapping fingers…)

M: Now that your eyes are accustomed to the darkness and the brightness, what do you see there hung from the ceiling in a cage?

F: A dancing girl. À gogo!

(*Organ, drums: dance music*)

M: South Yonge Street.

Existence waked me here on this cement tapeworm
   Called Yonge Street
Take a step, take a breath, take a step, take a breath
   This day and every day
   Called Yonge Street
I can remember the tokens that made it all go
   Eliza Regina Imperatrix
It was a sort of weather in your pocket.
I can remember a fishhead at Savarin's Grill
The crowds of other-me's walked above the rush
Beneath them lakeward of their own sewerage

G: By the way, where is the golden branch I gave you?

M: A cunning Melinda Street boss ate it like a candy stick
   He wore a grey suit and had bellies under his eyes.

G: And where is the silver cup and grail we gave you?

M: A paper King Street woman with installments for eyes and typewriters for feet – she pawned it.

But I have here instead this long grey vertebrae
The backbone of a city; my backbone as a matter of fact.
Now that I'm dead
Will it do instead
Of the golden branch and the silver cup
I was given when
First I journeyed to the world of men?

… But outside the auto-accessory store – a rack of real sponges. Smell this sponge. What does it smell of?

F: The sea! … Coming down Yonge Street later on, in the early dark, round about Charles Street, there's a rhythm of fruit stores. Softening at you.

P: Yes, I travel on a star…
        Doo-da-doo-doo…

F: Sometimes when there's a crowd of people all going the same way – say, in the subway station – and their voices get caught in a shallow space – a wall pitched just the right way with an overhang – the wall makes all their conversation and chatter into… (*loud music interrupting*) the wall catches the echo-murmur of all their talk at once – and you hear a giant voice. Sad and wonderful. A giant voice, saying – (*music again interrupts*)

M: We never quite catch what the giant voice says.

F: Oh yes we do. Don't you know that we have two voices – the one we hear and the one voice that's overheard, under-heard: the undertone? (*music softening*) The tone of voice says, often, something quite different from what the words of the voice are saying.

H: Lord, where the willows clothe the stream,
    And the deep waters gently run,
    The spirit of thy Son is seen,
    And there the feet of Israel come.

M: Is this what the modern crowds on modern Yonge Street are really saying and longing for?

F: I don't know. But long ago – in 1802 – another traveller up Yonge Street, David Willson, thought like this. As we go up north we go not into present subdivisions but into the past – the deep past of Sharon, where David Willson once built his Temple and preached to the Children of Peace and taught them to play and sing together.

(*Instruments: hymn tune*)

M: In 1878, owners of farms along Yonge Street were:

F, M: Alex Brown, Jonathan Strathy, Mrs. Weir, Montgomery's Tavern, Sir Henry Pellatt's Tomb

M:

We are drifting back in time...

F, M: T. Hamilton Mercer, The Golden Lion, Dempsey's Store, St. John's Church

M:

Is this her copy of David Willson's *Hymns and Prayers for the Children of Sharon* that we hold in our hands?

M: In 1802 David Willson came to this section in East Gwillimbury, some thirty-five miles northeast of York, and obtained a grant of land under the hand and seal of King George.

F: Settlers coming into Canada from the south brought ox-goads with them, made out of poplar saplings.

M: After settling in Sharon, David Willson and his wife joined the Quakers, but the ways of worship did not suit the newcomer.

F: He liked music and they did not.

F: Jonathan Stibbard, J. R. Strathy, Jonathan Lawrence, Peter Lawrence, The Honourable William McDougall, Thomas Nightingale,

F: Mrs. Van Nostrand

Joseph Duff, Joshua Shepard Senior, Joshua Shepard Junior, The Green Birch Tavern... *(fading...)*

M: In 1812 Mr. Willson seceded from the Quakers, half a dozen joined him, and the Children of Peace were organized.

H: Now we sing the songs of Sharon,
   Hopeful, and oh, peaceful land.
   The Church doth bear that once was barren;
   Children in our father's lands.

M: In 1825 the Temple was begun.

F: Let's build it again.

M: It took seven years to build.

F: Faith has seven garments.

M: Build Willson's Temple again? But it's still standing.

F: The new one will be different from the old – although the pattern will be the same:

M: Stone   F:

   Tree   Three

   Vine   Four

Seven
Twelve
Three
Four
Seven
Twelve
Three
Four
Seven
Twelve

Three
Four

Seven
Twelve

Twelve
Seven
Four
Three

Milk

Vine

Tree

Stone

Tree

Vine

Milk

Bread

Twelve
Seven
Four
Three

Heart
Jordan

Shepherd

Bread

Milk

Vine

Shepherd

Jordan

Heart

Twelve
Seven
Four
Three

Twelve
Seven
Four
Three

Three
Four
Seven
Twelve

Tree
Stone

Three
Four
Seven
Twelve
Three
Four
Seven

Tree
Vine
Milk

Twelve
Three
Four
Seven
Twelve

Vine
Tree
Stone

M: Although I hungered for communion, I could not comply, without transgressing my inward law. My natural food left me in despair.

H: O hollow, empty, lonesome space,
Without a friend, or God, or grace.
Where Death and Hell triumphant reigns,
And life doth feel their binding chains.

M: Sixty feet square! Seventy-five feet high!

F: He liked music and they did not.

M: I became a stranger to myself, and there was none to comfort me, but God alone.

H: I see the sun to set and rise,
I hear loud thunders in the skies,
I see the restless ocean roll;
All these are emblems of my soul.

M: Twenty-four windows on the first floor.

F: Where's the pulpit?

M: No pulpit. ... Mr. Willson knew as early as 1814 that he was disliked by the Family Compact, and that some even planned to have him sent from Canada.

H: The heart of man's a bounded space,
Reduced by sin, enlarged by grace.
The bounds thereof do go and come,
As God doth visit by his Son.

M: Twelve pillars with the apostles' names.

F: Four central pillars.

M: Faith, Hope, Love, Charity.

F: An ark, like a small pagoda, containing...

M: a Bible. ... I saw a stream of pure water descending from the east. Its progress was rapid, and its course towards the west. I saw an infant travelling therein against the current, towards the east.

F: It was the size of a newborn babe, and

F, M: the word of God said unto me, 'Dress the child and keep it warm.'

H: I'll haste to Jordan's stream,
Where wisdom doth chastise,

I'll bow my neck and wash me clean,

And watch with wakeful eyes.

F: A curved beam for Noah's Rainbow.

M: Three storeys for the Trinity.

F: Four doors for four directions.

M: Yet in 1837 he and his two sons were arrested and taken from their homes. The father was soon after released, but the two sons, Hugh and John, were confined each five months in Toronto Jail, and the former was taken to Kingston, where a further incarceration of seven months was endured.

H: Down the pale cheek the tears did flow,
       At home the little orphans cried:
       Our rulers filled our hearts with woe,
       That Justice to our Land denied.

F: More windows in the second storey.

M: Twenty-seven feet square.

F: Three thousand panes of glass.

M: The third storey is nine feet square.

F: Both reached from below by a Jacob's Ladder.

P: *(lining out)*

    Clothed with the shadow of the vine,
    We eat our bread and drink alone;
    Lord! We confess these crumbs are thine:
    This day thy love we freely own.

(Instruments play hymn tune; H sings descant; then, reprise.)

H: Clothed with the shadow of the vine,
    We eat our bread and drink alone;
    Lord! We confess these crumbs are thine:
    This day thy love we freely own.

M: At their feast of illumination in September...

F: One hundred and sixteen candles placed in the windows.

M: Of course he died –

F: January, 1866

M: – and the Children of Peace faded away. He died – but not before saying:

F: – Life taketh her servants by the hand, she leadeth them through the chambers of death to the windows of everlasting light – and they shall stand in the presence of God forever.

(*music: quiet bell sounds…*)

M: (*very quiet*) Held by chains from the lanterns of the tower hangs a golden globe…

F: …a golden globe inscribed with one word: PEACE.

M: Settlers coming into Canada from the south brought ox-goads with them made out of poplar saplings.

F: They planted these ox-goads, and they became trees, two trees growing on either side of the gate to their farms.

(*music becomes more animated, leading into final hymn*)

H, P: Lord, where the willows clothe the stream,
    And the deep waters gently run,
    The spirit of thy Son is seen,
    And there the feet of Israel come.

THE CANADIAN BROADCASTING CORPORATION
in co-operation with
BMI Canada Limited
presents

Canada dash, Canada dot'

The words mostly by James Reaney
The music mostly by John Beckwith
Commissioned entirely by the CBC

Thursday, November 23, 1967
Concert Hall, Edward Johnson Building,
University of Toronto

NOTE: This program is being recorded for broadcast on the CBC radio network's CBC Tuesday Night, (Toronto CBL, 740) November 28th, 8:10 p.m. EST.

Program cover, concert premiere, Toronto, 1967.

Canada Dash, Canada Dot

Part 3: *Canada Dot*

Singers: soprano (s), alto (A), baritone (BAR), bass (B)

Speakers: boy (BOY), female voice 1 (F1), female voice 2 (F2), male voice 1 (M1), male voice 2 (M2), male voice 3 (= folksinger) (M3)

Instruments: flute/piccolo, clarinet/bass clarinet, trumpet/Fluegelhorn, trombone, percussion (one player), violin, viola, contrabass/mandolin, piano/celeste/harmonium/organ (two players)

First broadcast; CBC Radio, 28 November 1967 (complete trilogy)

Mary Morrison, s
Patricia Rideout, A
Richard Braun, BAR
Walter Verikaitis, B
Jonathan Beckwith, B
Nonny Griffin, F1
Virginia McLeod, F2
Arch McDonnell, M1
Sandy Webster, M2
Jack Van Evera, M3

Robert Aitken, flute
Bernard Temoin, clarinet
Fred Stone, trumpet
Ted Roderman, trombone
Vair Capper, percussion
Corol McCartney, violin
Eugene Hudson, viola
William Kuinka, contrabass
John Beckwith, keyboard 1
Gordon Kushner, keyboard 2
James Kent, producer

CANADA DASH, CANADA DOT
PART 3: CANADA DOT

PRELUDE

SPEAKERS:

F1: Draw a line across Canada, east to west.
     From here to here to here... to there,
     here.
     The Line Across.

     Draw a line up and down crossing the first
     line.
     This second line is of time.
     We drew it north, north into the past.
     Now and now and now and now from now to
     now to now to now to then, then, then,
     then now, now now.
     The Line Up and Down.

M1: Now: Where the two lines cross is a dot

SINGERS:

     Walking,
        moving,
           going...

     Time past...

           Time

                    past...

     Past time past...

that is neither here nor now, neither there nor then – but is timeless, spaceless. Listener, these are dots – objects of love – things that are always present in my mind. Things my country gave me the chance to love.

ALL: Dots. Such as:

BOY: A Bon Ami Can

F2: A Can of Bon Ami Household Cleaning Powder.

F1: An Arrowhead

M1: Found in a walk through the fields.

M2: Municipal Coats of Arms

M1: In this case – those for the town of Oshawa.

F2: A China Doll – three inches?

F1: Two inches high dug up in a garden.

BOY: Phrases from a Weed Book

Dot
dot
dot
dot dot...

(*Continuing, with instruments...*)

M2: A Government book devoted to describing the weeds of this country.

M1: From a pamphlet describing the Folk Names of Birds – French, English, Gaelic.

BOY: A Tintype

F1: Of Ancestors: Newlywed.

F2: Lines from the poet Isabella Valancy Crawford

M1: Nineteenth Century, lived on King Street, Toronto.

M2: A Lesson in Skating

BOY: And a description of a Hockey Game by a World's Champion.

BON AMI

ALL: Dot One!

BOY: Bon Ami, Bon Ami
Makes porcelain gleam –
(Directions!)
Nettoie les fenêtres –
Polie tout en nettoyant –

S,A: Polishes as it cleans
Ne rougit pas les mains
Mode d'emploi:
No red hands
N'a pas encore engratigné:
(hasn't scratched yet.)

Bon Ami

M1: I guess it's odd that a can of household cleaning powder should be so magic. A very early thing. Red and yellow. The chicken. Also (it's made in Montreal) the first indication that the country was bilingual. Where do you first live? In the kitchen where your mother can keep an eye on you. Humble, simple objects in a kitchen can be deeply loved and remembered.

BOY: Polishes as it cleans.
Ne rougit pas les mains.
Mode d'emploi:
No red hands!
N'a pas encore engratigné: hasn't scratched yet.
Bon Ami, Bon Ami (*fading…*)

S,A: Bon Ami, Bon Ami
Makes porcelain gleam
Directions:
Nettoie les fenêtres
Polie tout en nettoyant
Bon Ami (*fading…*)

ARROWHEAD

F1: Dot Two!

BAR: Arrowhead

Stone bird

B: Your wings
    Were a hunter's shoulder-pull

BAR: Arm-push, arm-pull

B: Lost by whom, how long lost arrow?
   A whole pond of tree-rings ago

B: Arrowhead
   Stone bird

BAR: Your wings
     Were a hunter's shoulder-pull

B: Arm-push, arm-pull

M1: For thirty years I searched for arrowheads
    in the fields. One morning I purposely walked
    a different way – refusing a car-ride. And
    there it was. Half-hidden by the new barley
    blades. I feel that the arrowhead – the
    patiently chipped centre of a wild forest world
    – the arrowhead found me.

BAR: Lost by whom, how long lost arrow?
A whole pond of tree-rings ago

BAR, B: (A whole pond,
A whole pond of tree-rings ago...)

THE OLD AND THE NEW ARMS OF OSHAWA

M2: Dot Three!
The new and the old arms of Oshawa, a town east of Toronto.

ALL: Oshawa, Ontario
Oshawa means: Where the road crosses the stream.

M2: Azure on a bend argent a gear wheel

BOY: between an upright piano and a sedan automobile

M1: with in base of bend an angle iron and a staple

BOY: between in chief semy of trees a road palewise enarched

M1: between two factories and a warehouse

M2: and in base semy of trees a river bendwise nebuly

BOY: surmounted by a road bendwise

M1: and the dexter bend line surmounted by a culvert with opening at base.

BOY: Crest: a beaver.

M2: Motto: 'Nulli secundus.'

ALL: Oshawa, Ontario
Oshawa means: Where the road crosses the stream.

F1, F2: The old arms were

F1: quarterly (1) gules a tram-car;

F2: (2) argent a lake steamer;

F1: (3) argent a beehive beset with bees volant;

F2: and (4) azure Minerva's head couped.

CHINA DOLL

ALL: Dot Four!

F1: A nineteenth-century two-inch China Doll

s: *(vocalize)*

found in the garden.

Nnn... ah oo mm...

White China Baby Doll
Found while hoeing
Almost Armless, Partly Legless
Plump, quite fat and glazed

Noo... ah...(gk!)

White China Baby Doll
With your Battenberg face
Rhubarb cradle, Burdock bed
Poppy seed rattle, fell asleep

Mm... Heh hah oo ah-hah...

Grandmother Earthworm spun for you
Star-nosed Mole lit your way
Centipede, Millipede danced for you
Until my hoe woke you today

Baa.. oh eh...
oh eh...
Da... oo hah mm... ee..hoo...
Ah..ee... nnn...

(White China Baby Doll...)

FROM A WEED BOOK

BOY: Dot Five: From a Weed Book

F1, F2, M1, M2:
Where does Shepherd's Purse grow?

S, A, BAR, B:
pastures, old meadows, roadsides, waste places

And where does this weed grow?

Rocky pastures, riverbanks, roadsides, fencerows

And where this weed?

railway embankments, old fields, meadows, riverbanks, ditches, waste places, waste places

M1: Come to your doorstep – or into your yard or down a street where pavement is cracked and shaded and not much used and I'll show you...

pastures, old meadows, roadsides, waste places, waste places

WHITE-THROATED SPARROW

M2: Dot Six:
    White-Throated Sparrow
    Now – the White-Throated Sparrow is
    sometimes called the Canada Bird because
    some say it sings...

A: sweet sweet Canada Canada Canada

But some say it sings...

S: hard times Canada Canada Canada
   Canada

BAR, B: poor poor Kennedy, Kennedy

B: old Sam Peabody, Peabody, Peabody

While others say it sings...

S: p'tit, p'tit Fréderic, Fréderic, Fréderic

BAR: *(gargle in falsetto range...)*

B: *(whistling...)*

BOY: Tu-wee, tu-wee...

M1: Brr-rt, brr-rt, brr-rt...
M2: White-Throated Sparrow; Canada Bird

A PICTURE OF ANCESTORS NEWLYWED

BOY, F1, F2: Dot Seven:
A Picture of Ancestors Newlywed*

BAR:

Dearest, sweetest, fondest, best,
Lean your head upon my breast.
Loving arms shall thee entwine,
Loving hands be placed in mine.
Grief and care shall flee away,
Darkest night shall turn to day,
Winter snows to summer showers,
Autumn leaves to fresh Spring flowers:
Oh....
Mmm....

Picture of a living love,
True as angel notes above.

BOY: Great-grandfather sits, great-
grandmother stands, in the parlour of a
photographer.

*based on 'A Souvenir of Love' – words by John Imrie, music by Edwin Gledhill – Toronto, 1886

150

A hundred or more persons are in existence so far because these two came together – in love, in 1851, and – *in camera.*

(In love, in 1851... and... *in camera.*)

LINES FROM ISABELLA VALANCY CRAWFORD

M1, M2: Dot Eight!

F2: Lines from Isabella Valancy Crawford:

For love, once set within a lover's breast,
Has its own sun, its own peculiar sky,
All one great daffodil, on which do lie
The sun, the moon, the stars, all seen at once
And never setting, but all shining straight
Into the faces of the trinity –
The one beloved, the lover and sweet love.

M1: Who was Isabella Crawford?

Constant as the Polar Star,
Shining in the heavens afar...
La la la...

She was a poet who lived and died on King Street in Toronto during the late nineteenth century. At Peterborough – her father was a doctor come out from Dublin – she could read Dante at the age of twelve. She is one of the very first poets to speak – like this:

F2: ...The sun, the moon, the stars, all seen at once,
And never setting...

M1: She died in 1887, aged thirty-seven – but this still lives:

F2: (whispered) ...its own peculiar sky, all one great daffodil...

LESSONS IN SKATING

BOY: Dot Nine!...

F1: Dot Nine!...

F2:   Dot Nine!...

M1:   Dot Nine!...

M2:   Dot Nine!...

BOY, F1, F2, M1: Dot Nine!
Lessons in Skating!

ALL: Dot... Nine!...

B: (free vocalize...)

M2: 'Lessons in Skating, by George A. Meagher, Champion Figure-Skater of the World since 1891, with suggestions respecting Hockey, its laws, etcetera...'

M2: The Names of Skating Figures:

F1: Figure Eights

F2: Loops

M1: Rail Fence

BOY: On to Richmond Forward!

F2: Pig's Ears

M1: Grapevines

F1: Crosscuts or Anvils

BOY: On to Richmond Forward!

F2: Pig's Ears

M1: Grapevines

(Clarinet: skaters' waltz motifs)

A: (free vocalize)

F1: Crosscuts or Anvils

M2: The Fundamental Movements of Skating:

BOY: Jumping on Skates
Locomotive Steps

M1: Locomotive Steps: These are certainly very odd, and very attractive steps, and when properly executed give much pleasure to the performer. This may be done noisily (resembling the clatter of a locomotive) or may be skated quite noiselessly. We have six distinct changes in this movement, namely:

BOY, F1, F2, M1: Single Forward; Single Backward; Double Forward; Double Backward; Single Sideways; Double Sideways!

F2: Combined Skating:

(Flute: skaters' waltz motives)

BAR: (free vocalize)

154

(*Celeste: skaters' waltz motives*)

F1: Combined Grapevine!
BOY: Combined Rail Fence!
M1: Combined Sea Breeze!

BOY, F1, F2, M1: The Sea Gull!

M2: The Sea Gull: Two persons join and cross hands in front...

F2: (lady and gentleman, for instance)...

M2: Both begin on the right foot forward outside edge...

F2: On the right foot forward outside edge...
until a complete revolution has been made, at
the same time the gentleman raising the lady's
hands, passing first the right, then the left,
gently over her head... This figure certainly is
a 'beautiful ideal' of 'hand in hand' skating.

S: (*free vocalize...*)   S, A, F2, M1, B: BAR:

M3: (*announcer*)
Cournoyer
Pilote
Jacques Lapierre

M2: From marbles to football I have played
them all, and it has been my experience that in
hockey the player's mental and physical

Narration	Announcer	Sounds	Vendors
powers are given wider scope than in any other game. Where, may I ask, can be found a more enthusiastic audience than at a championship hockey match?	Tremblay / Talbot	Cheering, crowd	peanuts / eskimo pies / peanuts / eskimo pies
	Richard / No 9, Belliveau / Boivin	noises	programs!
The very roof-timbers seem to creak with excitement; yells and shrieks that would silence a band of Sioux warriors are heard from every nook and corner of the building.	Face-off		
	Blue Line	Roaring / cheers…	
BOY: Johnny Bower wanted a shutout to celebrate his forty-fourth birthday but he got a present he will likely cherish even more – an assist.	Armstrong		
	Hull		
F1: Although November is the 'worst month for tension,' Mrs. Pappin says, like most players her husband is also jumpy during playoff time.	Harris / Wharram		
BOY: Ellis and Oliver messed up a passing play	No 9, Gordie Howe		

with only one defenceman back.

F1: Home should be restful and relaxing, Mrs. Keon believes.

BOY: Erickson jammed the puck in from a scramble to the side of the net.

F1: Mrs. Brian Conacher, left, exhibits tension hockey wives experience at a game.

BOY: Less than a minute later, Leafs took a three-nothing lead when Pappin hit the far corner from twenty-five feet.

F1: Mrs. Horton, like other hockey wives and mothers, is likely to suffer from some tension herself Saturday afternoons. That's when everybody has to be quiet so Father can get the sleep he needs to make the 'Three Star Selection.'

BOY: Accepting the cake, Bower thanked president Barry van Gerbig: 'I counted the candles on the cake and there's only forty-two.' A bottle of champagne was stuck in the

Gamble

McDonald

Bob Pulford

Two minutes

High sticking

top of the cake.

M2: The clashing of sticks, the stamping of
feet, the ya-yahs of the admirers when a long
and well-aimed shot for goal is fired, or
perhaps when one player more cunning for the
time than the rest, by his superior judgment,
and surprising ability, darts with the puck,
gently coaxing it from one side to the other
while travelling at lightning speed through an
entire line of adversaries until finally, like a
pistol shot, it cracks through the goals, when
a thousand, yes, five thousand throats shout
and scream until the pandemonium reminds
one of a dynamite factory cutting loose!

Amongst the countless numbers of crack
Canadian Hockey Clubs there have been some
hard fought and well-earned battles, but never

Sawchuk
Vasco
Eddie Shack

del Vecchio
No 27, Mahovlich
Stan Mikita

Ullman
14, Keon

13 seconds
12
11

crescendo
of
whistles
cheering
catcalls
&c...!

loud burst!

eskimo pies
programs!

peanuts
eskimo pies
programs!

did the enthusiasm rise to such a pitch as it did
when the 'Shamrocks' of Montreal, won the
World's Championship at the 'Arena' Rink,
March 1st, 1899.

9   PROGRAMS!

8 seconds left   cheers

     loud roar

5...   (loudest...)

4...

POSTLUDE

ALL:
    Bon Ami
      Arrowhead
        Coat of Arms
    China Doll...

    Valancy...

'Shamrocks' of Montreal...

ALL: roadsides...

A: Canada Canada Canada...
BAR: Picture of a living love...

All the Bees and All the Keys

All the Bees and All the Keys
for narrator and symphony orchestra

Commissioned by the Junior Women's Committee of the Toronto Symphony Orchestra through a grant from the Canada Council

First performance; Massey Hall, Toronto, 7 April 1973
Toronto Symphony Orchestra
Victor Feldbrill, conductor; Max Ferguson, narrator

Revised version for narrator and ten instruments
First performance, Young People's Theatre, 11 May 1987
Louis Applebaum, conductor; Jerry Franken, narrator

NOTE Margin numbers in the narrator's script correspond to rehearsal numbers in the musical score. 'GP' means 'general pause,' i.e., no music from the orchestra. An arrow (→) indicates the narrator should wait for a cue from the conductor. A slanted stroke (/) indicates the narrator should take a natural pause and proceed. The sign ℤℤ indicates an electric buzzer to be operated by the narrator.

Cartoons by Ross MacDonald ('Rudy McToots') for the 1975 children's book by Press Porcépic. The publication included a piano reduction of the musical score.

1   Introduction

1A

1B   ➤ 'Hey, what are you putting them in the bottle for?'
Benjamin asked Kenneth. / It was the spring of nineteen
hundred and five and the lilacs were in bloom; bumblebees
were buzzing about them and Kenneth was trapping them
into an empty bottle. 'See, I've got twenty-three so far.
Bottle's almost cram full of bumblebees, Benjamin.' / 'What
are you going to do with them, Kenneth?' asked Benjamin.
Kenneth only smiled. He caught another bumblebee and
then quickly put the cap back on the bottle so that all twen-
ty four bees had no chance whatsoever to escape. /

1C   'Kenneth! Kenneth!' You let those bees out of that bottle.'
'Nothing doing,' said Kenneth. / 'Scram!' / Now, Benjamin
hated seeing anything suffer, particularly bees because his
father was a beekeeper and had taught him to love their
buzzing and humming. He put his hands over his ears and
ran away. Actually, this was a clever thing to do, because
Kenneth now lost interest in his bottle of twenty-four bees.
/ No one was watching him. /

GP   Leaving the bottle of buzzing prisoners in a hot, sunny
place, he went over to the woodshed where he had left the
new trumpet his mother had given him for his birthday.
Tomorrow a music master was coming in on the train from
Toronto to give Kenneth his first trumpet lesson. Kenneth
picked up the trumpet, put it to his mouth and began to try
it out. /

2   Benjamin sneaked back along behind the lilacs. / He
grabbed the bottle of bees and ran off with it. ➤ 'Who stole
my bee bottle? Who stole my bottle of bees? Did you,
Benjamin? Benjamin, if you did... I'll never let you try my
new trumpet now. Never. Benjamin!'
      ➤ But far away, where Kenneth could never find him,

Benjamin took the cap off the bottle.

2A ➤ One by one, the great bees flew up / ... and out / and off / ... away.

2B ➤ What was the matter with the twenty-fourth bumblebee? Had the heat and the crowding been too much for it? Benjamin spilled it out in his hand and petted its furry back with an outstretched finger. / The Queen Bee! Yes, she was still alive. / She woke up. She flew away, away, until Benjamin could no longer see nor hear her.

GP You must now imagine that some years go by and both Benjamin and Kenneth have grown up. Benjamin inherited his father's bee yard, got married and made his money out of honey. He now has a boy six years old called Benjamin Junior. Kenneth has grown up, yes, and makes his money out of – his mother's money, which she left him in great amounts. Having learned to play the trumpet wonderfully well, Kenneth has founded a very famous Silver

3 Band. Here it comes now down the main street of the village. ➤ Kenneth kept shouting directions. 'Louder! /

3A Keep up! / Follow the beat! / Now... a third higher! /

3B ... a *fourth* higher! / one key *lower!* / Softly, softly... / Pianissimo... / We've come to Benjamin the Beekeeper's yard and we don't want to frighten his bees, do we? They might swarm and fly away,

3C which wouldn't be good for someone who makes all their money out of honey.'

GP Of course a great many people wanted to join the Silver Band, but Kenneth turned most of them away.

4 The tryouts were held in June. 'Now,' said Bandmaster

Kenneth, 'who is next?' A young cornetist from New Hamburg began to play. ➤ *ZZ* Stop, stop!

4A Not pure enough. Next?' A young bassoon player from Kitchener stepped forth. ➤ 'Not bad. But,' said Bandmaster Kenneth, 'can you play that tune in other keys? For instance, F sharp? / And how about E flat? /

4B Hmhm. Well. Now one more key. Anybody who is going to play in my Silver Band has to be able to play in all the keys. D flat! / *ZZ* Bah! Out! Not quick enough! Not good enough for my Silver Band. OK. Nobody left to audition? So, no new members this year, eh? You're too small. Why, it's the bee-keeper's son, Benjamin Junior! What instrument was your poverty-stricken beekeeping father able to...

4C ➤ A dandelion horn?' ➤*ZZ* / Well, Benjamin Junior didn't give up. The next year he auditioned on an empty bottle.

4D ➤ *ZZ* Bandmaster Kenneth didn't let him in, nor did he let him in the following ten years when Benjamin Junior kept trying on other homemade, toy and broken second-hand instruments: / Tin whistle,

4E ➤ *ZZ* Toy trumpet,
   ➤ *ZZ* Ukelele,

4F ➤ *ZZZ* Butter-box drum,
   ➤ *ZZZZh* Sweet potato,

4G ➤ *ZZZ* Until the summer when Benjamin Junior was seventeen. There were a great many flowers that year, the bees collected a lot of honey, and there was just enough money left over to buy him a new trumpet.

4H Not enough for proper lessons, but...
   ➤ 'Not bad,' said Bandmaster Kenneth. /

4I 'Here's a piece of sight music now, Benjamin Junior. Play it a tone higher than it's written. / What? You can't read music? You can't transpose? You only play by ear? / *ZZZZZ* / I'm sorry, Benjamin Junior, but I can't let you into the band. Next?'

GP Benjamin Junior wanted so much to belong to that band. 'Why not start your own band?' said his father. 'There are lots of boys in this town who can't get into the Silver Band. Call it the Tin Band. I'll set up two more beehives to pay the

rent on a rehearsal hall.' So a new band called the Tin Band
became a rival to the Silver Band.

5 ➤ They competed in music festivals.

5A ➤ 'And in second place … the Tin Band, conducted by
Benjamin Junior!'

5B

GP ➤ For some time there was no trouble, until the following
poster appeared in all the nearby villages and towns: /

6 Moonlight Excursion Tonight! On the Steamship Georgina!
Music by… the Tin Band!

➤ 'That settles it!' shouted Kenneth to the Silver Band.
'They're beginning to take big jobs away from us. It's those
bees. They made enough honey to get him enough money
to start a Tin Band. Do you know what's happening? Do you
know where it will end? No Silver Band! All Tin Band.
Where's the piccolo tonight? Run away to play with them,
and there's not room enough in this village for two bands.

Attention! We are going to march down the street past the
Beekeeper's yard.

6A ➤ Louder! / Follow the beat! / A third higher! / A fourth
higher!

6B ➤ Louder! / Fortissimo! / We don't want to frighten his
bees, do we? / For they might swarm and fly away, which
wouldn't be good for someone who makes all their money
out of honey.'

6C

6D ➤ 'Benjamin Junior,' said his father, 'all our bees have flown
off. Whatever will we do now? And I have orders for honey
to fill by the end of this month.' 'Never mind, Father,' said
Benjamin Junior, 'I'll get your bees back for you.' And he
walked away across the big meadow at the edge of the vil-
lage until his father could no longer hear him humming –
for the lost bees – or even see him looking for them. /

GP Have you ever tried to look for a swarm of bees? It isn't an easy thing to do. Benjamin Junior searched for his father's bees one whole sunny hot day in June. He fell asleep at the edge of a pasture just as the stars were coming out.

7 As he fell asleep he wondered if the stars might not be his

father's golden bees flown very far away indeed.

7A 'No,' said a tall figure in a dream he had that night. 'The stars you can see behind me are not your father's bees.' The tall figure wore a golden crown, she had silver wings and was dressed in robes of gold and black. 'The stars are my bees and we will come to help you

7B because once your father when he was a boy helped twenty four friends of ours. / When you wake in the morning, Benjamin Junior, return to your father's house. Tell him to set up twenty-four of his biggest hives. Suddenly it will seem as if ALL THE BEES in the world have come to those beehives so they must be the biggest hives he can find. Big enough for

7C ALL THE BEES. They will make your father a great deal of delicious honey, but even more important they will teach you and your fellows in the Tin Band how to play better, how to play in ALL THE KEYS.' / 'Who are you?' asked Benjamin Junior. 'Who were your friends that my father helped?' 'I am someone who loves both stars and bees,' replied the tall lady in Benjamin's dream. 'When your father was a small boy, I watched him save twenty-four bumblebees from certain death. I made a vow then that one day I would help him in twenty-four ways. Wake up, Benjamin. It is dawn. Go back to your father's bee yard and see how I have returned him his bees.'

GP Several days later it all came true as the crowned figure in the dream had said it would. ALL THE BEES in the world seemed to fill the twenty-four hives that Benjamin set out for them. Since each hive hummed in a different key, this

meant that not only wcre ALL THE BEES

8   in Benjamin's bee yard, but also ALL THE KEYS. ALL THE
BEES *and* ALL THE KEYS.

➤ The bees taught Benjamin and all the members of his Tin
Band how to play in tune. / Any mistakes and you got stung.

8A   How to read music from sight. More complicated this, but
the bees used fence wire for music staves and themselves
for the notes. You had to read music from sight quickly. Or
you got

8B   stung! / Transpose up and down the scale. Major keys,
minor keys, B flat... D flat... F sharp minor... / Arpeggios of
augmented fifths, diminished sevenths... / Any mistakes
and you got stung! /

8C   Precision, clarity, feeling, / balance, nuance... / ➤ Or you
got... / ➤ So, with the help of ALL THE BEES, the Tin Band
rapidly improved. But meanwhile:

GP   'Silver Band! Attention!' yelled Kenneth. 'The Governor
General and his lady are going to make a short visit to this
village. Do you know why? Chiefly because they want to
hear my famous Silver Band! They have only ten minutes.
We'll play for them, and then their special train will rush
them to a very important engagement elsewhere.

9   So – Silver Band. We'll practice on the way down to the sta-
tion. / Louder! Keep up! / There's the Tin Band all ready
waiting

9A   to see if we will ask them to join us. Well, their playing has
improved a lot lately but... No!

9B   March right by them! / What's the difficulty back there,
drummer? You missed a beat.' 'Bandmaster Kenneth,' said
the bass drummer, 'there's ALL THE BEES in the world fol-
lowing us.' 'Keep playing,' shouted Kenneth. 'Benjamin,

9C   call those bees off. Benjamin!' / 'Can we join the Silver Band
then?' 'No, Benjamin,

9D never!' 'We can play in all the keys, Kenneth.' 'No.' 'Besides, ALL THE BEES say that you should let us.' 'Never! Scram!'

9E ➤ 'Then,' said Benjamin Junior, 'Bandmaster Kenneth, your fate is on your own head.'

9F

9G ➤ Kenneth told his Silver Band to keep on playing no matter what happened. And, you know, they did. Even when the bees had chased them a good mile or two outside the village. / Despite the bees, you could hear them trying to keep together all over the place farther and farther away.

9H

GP ➤ 'Your excellencies,' said Benjamin Junior, bowing low with his trumpet under his arm, 'the Silver Band has had an accident. They are just now straggling into town. In the limited ten minutes that you have, might your excellencies – like to hear – the second-best band in town, the... Tin Band?' The Governor-General looked at his watch, then – nodded.

10 ➤ The Governor General said that if this was the Second Best Band in town what must the First Prize one be like?

10A Bandmaster Kenneth stepped forward. Dishevelled and red in the face, he said: 'Your excellencies, they are the Silver Band now. Whoever has been teaching them? My band never played as well as that.' 'Perhaps,' said the Governor General's lady, 'your two bands might like to play something together.' 'Well,' said Benjamin Junior, 'who will conduct?'

➤ Bandmaster Kenneth nodded to Benjamin Junior. The despised leader of the once-scorned Tin Band could now lead his Silver Band.

10B ➤ 'Kenneth,' whispered Benjamin Junior. 'The bees wish to play with us.' / 'Never!' shouted Kenneth. 'I draw the line at playing with insects. /

10C Yes, yes. Let them join in. Please, why did I say that? A good idea, Benjamin Junior.' ➤ So they played – the Silver Band, the Tin Band, *and* the Bees.

10D

10E

10F

10G ➤ They were still playing as the Governor General's train had reluctantly to leave.

10H ➤ 'Why, it sounded like a whole symphony orchestra,' said the Governor General. 'Wherever were they hiding the strings?' His wife was going to remark that she rather thought the violinists and cellists could have been hidden behind some beehives she had noticed across the street, / but instead she said, 'Sh!' / She was listening

10I to what you are listening to.

10J ➤ Far away, farther away, came the music from the two bands and the twenty-four beehives – the music that came about because a naughty boy called Kenneth collected twenty-four bumblebees in a bottle and would not let them go and another boy called Benjamin let them go until they grew to be ALL THE BEES AND ALL THE KEYS.

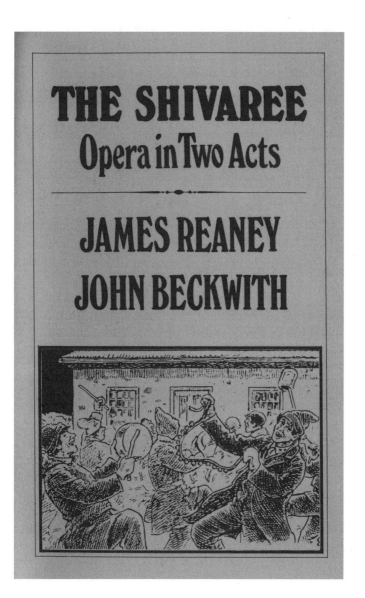

THE SHIVAREE
Opera in Two Acts

JAMES REANEY

JOHN BECKWITH

Edmond-Joseph Massicotte's drawing 'Le Charivari' (*L'Almanach du peuple*, Montreal, 1928) shows an imaginary shivaree in early Quebec. It was reproduced on the cover of the original libretto publication, 1982.

The Shivaree

Comic opera in a prologue and two acts

Libretto, James Reaney   Music, John Beckwith

Cast, in order of appearance:
Ned, the hired man *tenor*
Bo *baritone*
Henrietta Quartz *contralto*
William Quartz *baritone*
Daisy *soprano*
Miss Beech, the schoolteacher *high soprano*
Jonathan *tenor*
The Shivareers:
Jo *bass*
Sam *baritone*
Elmer *tenor*
Russell high *baritone*
Aunt Annie, the tomboy *mezzo-soprano*

Orchestra:
flute/piccolo, oboe, 2 clarinets (second doubles bass clarinet), bassoon, horn, trumpet, trombone, 2 percussion, piano, guitar, 3 violins, 2 violas, 2 cellos, contrabass

First performance; Town Hall, St. Lawrence Centre, Toronto, 3 April 1982.

Henry Ingram, *Ned*
Peter Barcza, *Bo*
Patricia Rideout, *Henrietta Quartz*
Avo Kittask, *William Quartz*
Caralyn Tomlin, *Daisy*
Katherine Terrell, *Miss Beech*
James McLean, *Jonathan*
Thomas Goertz, *Jo*

Paul Massell, *Sam*
John Keene, *Elmer*
Gregory Cross, *Russell*
Susan Gudgeon, *Aunt Annie*
Howard Cable, *conductor*
Paula Sperdakos, *director*
Geoffrey Dinwiddie, *designer*

THE SHIVAREE

Once there was a girl named Persephone whom Zeus secretly promised to his brother Hades, the god of the dead. Stooping to pick a daffodil, Persephone was grabbed by Hades, who bore her away underground in a chariot pulled by six black horses. This story concerns a girl who in stooping to pick up a flower was saved from the Hades of her district.

PROLOGUE

(Light narrows to just Ned, pail in hand, in which he is carrying some cutter bells and a file.)

NED: You see,
   Everyone's been asking what's been going on here
   The smorning.
   Ned, they say,
   With your hair like mouldy hay
   And your wits gone quite astray,
   Can you clear your mind sufficiently –
   No, no, I can't,
   I'm not intelligent
   By daylight.

   Come on, Ned, clear your mind sufficiently
   To tell us
   Why the dogs went barking here, barking there,
   Who the dark-faced people were chased away in fear
   And where,
   Where's the old man, Ned? Where's your boss?
   Not in the store the smorning, where's he gone to – Gosh!
   I say
   Is this some sort of examination I've got to pass?
   I just don't know the answers with the sun up in the sky,
   But when the moon comes out at night – why,
   Then everything will crystal clearly – clar–i–fy.

(Bo enters with a wheelbarrow which contains some chains, an iron pipe and a long bolt.)

BO: Hey, Ned, what's been going on here?

NED: Oh no – examination time again.

BO: Dogs barking, dark people in wagons clattering by?

NED: No, no, I can't.
I'm not intelligent
By daylight

BO: Come now, clear your mind sufficiently.
Explain, explain –
Your boss, he's not in the store,
Is he away? Why is it closed?
Ned?

NED: Hey, Bo, that's one question I can answer.
He's off getting married again.

BO: Getting married again? *(Ned nods.)*
We young men of the crossroads,
We bachelors under thirty of this neighbourhood
Forbid him.

NED: What's forbid without forestall, Bo?

BO: You think the same way I do, Ned?

NED: No. But if he comes back married again
I think I think that I think *(clang)* And you?

BO: Oh I think *(clang)* and even *(clang, clang)*.

(They laugh and play a brief jam session until –)

HENRIETTA: *(From the house)* Stop that dreadful noise!
Ned – stop loafing out there, come back here and help me
lock the cellar doors. Tell your wheelbarrow friend no loiter-
ing in front of the store when it's closed. Or I'll sic the dogs
on him.

(Disappears.)

NED: So she says. But when the moon comes out tonight, why–

BO: Yes –

NED AND BO: Marry again? How dare he? This (*clang*) we do not allow. (*Exit Bo.*)

NED: I'll bet they're coming out of the church right now.

(*Blackout.*)

ACT ONE

OVERTURE

(*The bells of a small country church – a wedding is just over. The bride and bridegroom step up into the bridegroom's buggy drawn by a great black horse and they wheel out of the green churchyard dotted with white gravestones onto the white gravel roads of summer. The buggy – we hear the bridegroom crack his whip – hurtles down into valleys where the swamp forest blots out the sun. It is cool and dark green here. Then up, up to the top of the hill – the ditch of green grass, the white road, the white cloud, the blue sky – past farmhouses where dogs bark, geese fly up out of puddles. The shade of a great solitary tree by the road occasionally catches at them but relinquishes them to a road that goes down through fields of fat green crops, meadows dotted with plump cattle – a jog in the road, a crossroad, and under an ancient elm stands Mr. Quartz's store. It is a large brick house with small paned windows, a little round window in the gable, a white balcony over its front porch. Beside the house is an old orchard and then a large grey barn. The store is closed. Just before the curtain rises the hired boy, Ned, comes out to unharness the horse, and he is just taking it away as we see the bride and bridegroom sitting in the buggy. He is an older man in a rather battered top hat and dress suit: he could be sinister, he could be a buffoon. He has great dignity and force, or he has none at all – it is hard to tell. She is a pretty young desperate girl who is wondering why on earth she is here and also who she is. She wears a white wedding dress.*)

QUARTZ: (*slowly getting out of buggy*)
Hey, Ned! I got a new mare in the buggy!
                              (*laughs*) Well –
My dear. Come down, my dear. Descend, my dear, and
Come with me, my dear, into our house as
My newly wedded wife, my dear.

174

DAISY: I don't
Wish to, Mr. Quartz, thank you very much.
Not at the present, Mr. Quartz, thank you.
I should like to sit here and think a while, Mr. -

QUARTZ: *(interrupting)*
Please call me by my Christian name. William.

DAISY: William!

QUARTZ: Yes, my dear?

DAISY: Nothing, William.
But shouldn't you call me by my first name too?

QUARTZ: *(shyly)* Rachel.

DAISY: Rachel?

DUET
DAISY: That's not my name.

QUARTZ: Good God!
Have I forgot her name already? Is it –
Is it – is it – is it – Elizabeth?

DAISY: No, no, no.

QUARTZ: Oh we married in such a hurry, you see.
Martha?

DAISY: It's not Martha nor Mary.

QUARTZ: Susan, Letitia?

DAISY: Neither of those.

QUARTZ: Is it Helena or Jessica?

DAISY: No, no, no.

QUARTZ: Is it Peterina?

DAISY: No.

QUARTZ: Something from the Bible like Ruth?
Or Rebecca or Adah or Zillah?

DAISY: No – my name's not in the Bible.

It's so odd you don't remember.

QUARTZ: Well, is it the name of a month
Such as June, May or November?

DAISY: My name isn't seen on calendars.

QUARTZ: Is it a flower?

DAISY: You're close!

QUATZ: Well, let me see then. Rose?

DAISY: No!

QUARTZ: Pansy?

DAISY: No!

QUARTZ: Daffodil?

DAISY: No!

QUARTZ: Violet?

DAISY: No, no, no!

QUARTZ: Oh – !
I shall just run into the house
To ask my sister what your name is.

(He goes into house.)

DAISY: *(taking out hand mirror)*
Well, who is that silly girl? She
Is, don't you know, Mrs. William Quartz!
Mrs. William Quartz, Mrs. William Quartz!
She is, she is, she is –

QUARTZ: *(rushing out of house)*
Daisy! I married a Daisy!

DAISY: Yes, Daisy is my name.
Not Faith nor Hope nor Charity.
Daisy is my name, Daisy is my name.

QUARTZ: Daisy is her name.
She's a Daisy, a Daisy is her –

DAISY: – But I'm still not coming down, sir!

QUARTZ: *(He loses his temper and stamps his foot.)*
   You had better come down and come
   Into my house or else!

DAISY: I will not!
   Now I never will!

QUARTZ: *(placating)* That would be foolish
   To live in a buggy for the rest of time.
   No bed in it! No stove! No dishes!

DAISY: William, a person needs so very little.
   If one has love, one has everything!

QUARTZ: Of course I cannot give you love, my dear.
   But I can give you everything. I'm rich.
   William Quartz owns a lot, dear Rachel.

DAISY: Daisy! My name is Daisy!

QUARTZ: Judas Iscariot!
   I keep thinking you're my first wife. Rachel
   Was her name, you see, Martha my dear.

DAISY: My name's not Martha. *(teasing him)* Ebenezer – Ezra –

QUARTZ: My name's not Ebenezer nor Ezra.

DAISY: (No, no, no!)

QUARTZ: Martha was my second wife's name, you know.
   My God! What is my own name? Is it –
   Is it – is it –

DAISY: Ask your sister!

QUARTZ: It surely isn't Ebenezer or Ezra.

DAISY: Run in and ask your sister!

(Quartz does run into the house again.)

   I am falling down a deep deep well.
   That mourning dove is singing: 'Poor silly girl,
   Poor silly girl!'

QUARTZ: *(shooting out of the house again)*
    William! That's my name and yours is Daisy!

DAISY: Yes, William is your name. I'm a Daisy, but William is
    your name.

QUARTZ: I married a Daisy.
    Daisy is her name and mine is William.
    As I was saying – where was I at? –

DAISY: *(mimicking)*   'I'm rich.
    William Quartz owns a lot, dear Rachel.'

QUARTZ: Yes. I own this farm and of course this store:

ARIA I've got mortgages on ten other farms
    Run by widows with infants in arms
    Quite unable to keep up the payment, so –
    Foreclose! Foreclose! Foreclose!
    I've got money in the bank and profitable shares,
    Mahogany tables and rosewood chairs,
    A very profitable stallion, fifty brood mares,
    Grain in my granaries and hay in my mows!
    Fifty black steers and fifty white cows!
    All this is yours, Daisy, all this is yours
    If you – not love me – but give me some heirs.
    Children, babies, infants, younkers,
    Issue, twins, descendants, sons, daughters!
        All this is yours, Daisy,
        All this is yours.
        Give me some heirs, Daisy,
        Give me some heirs.
        All this is yours!

DAISY: Yes. You have everything. And love is
    Everything, but I cannot ever think that
    Everything is love. *(opening her white bride's Bible)*
    You are a rich man,
    But it says in my Bible that rich men
    Have a hard time getting to Heaven.

QUARTZ: *(producing a black Bible from his pocket)*

from the 1982 stage premiere by Comus Music Theatre, Toronto:
Caralyn Tomlin, Avo Kittask

> But in my Bible near the front it says
> David died and went to Abraham's bosom.
> Abram's bosom was Heaven in those days *(leafing pages)*
> And here it says: Abraham was a very *(wetting his thumb)*
> Exceedingly rich rich man. So – Daisy,
> Who says a rich man cannot enter Heaven?
> Why, it says here his bosom *is* Heaven.

DAISY: I wonder if you could be Heaven, William?

QUARTZ: Why naturally. It says so right here!

DAISY: *(putting down the white Bible)*
> Why did I marry you? Why did I marry you?
> Why –

QUARTZ: Come to my bosom, dear, and find out!

(Henrietta Quartz emerges from the dark house. She blinks in the sunlight. She carries a suitcase and is dressed for a journey. She is tall and sharp – a formidable bird of a woman. One is aware of how many years she has spent in the store and the house toting up accounts, entering things in cashbooks and watching her collection of objects.)

HENRIETTA: So, this is the girl you have married, Will.

QUARTZ: Oh, this is my sister Henrietta.
Come down and meet her. Come down and meet her.

HENRIETTA: Do you think she'll be a good wife? Stand up!

QUARTZ: Come down, I say!

HENRIETTA: Stand up, girl, till we see what you look like!

(*Daisy does stand up.*)

Good for you, Will. She looks a good worker.
Pretty face! Attract people to the store –
Maybe! Independent! Has her own will.
Still – she married you for your money
So that'll keep her in tow – maybe.

DAISY: I did not marry Mr. Quartz for his money!

HENRIETTA: Maybe. Why on earth did you marry him?

DAISY: That's what I'm asking myself as I sit
Here in this buggy and as soon as I
See why – why I'll come down – but not before.

(*She sits again.*)

HENRIETTA: Maybe. But more than likely you married William
for his money. The others did.

(*Enter Ned, the hired boy. He is impish, short and redhaired. He is rather a Til Eulenspiegel type.*)

NED: Hey, William!

QUARTZ: Mr. Quartz to you, boy!

NED: Sir: The black cow has disappeared again!

QUARTZ: Great Judas Iscariot! Not again!
That black cow doesn't like me. Where? When?

NED: Right after the gypsies came through at noon.

QUARTZ: Gypsies! Have they been through here again?

HENRIETTA: They were going to camp here, Will, but I

Set the dogs on them.

QUARTZ: Get my spyglass, Ned,
And my gun! I'll find their camp and my cow!

HENRIETTA: Maybe. Get his overalls too, boy.
You mustn't ruin that suit, Will. Daisy dear,
Won't you come down from that buggy and stay?
What's the matter with her, Will?

QUARTZ: I wish I knew!

HENRIETTA: You should order her to come down, William.
If you don't show her who's boss now
You never will.

NED: *(entering with overalls)* Your overalls –

QUARTZ: The gun – and hurry! *(exit Ned)*

HENRIETTA: Are you going to be
A good wife, Daisy?

DAISY: What do you two mean
By a good wife, I wonder?

HENRIETTA AND QUARTZ: A good wife? A good wife? *(laugh)*

DUETTINO *(during which Quartz dons overalls)*
She's up at four to bake the bread,
She can lay out the corpse of the
     Ancestral dead!
She's up at five to churn the butter
And in a pinch she can drive
     The cutter!
She's up at six to rock the cradle
And all day long she will lift
     The ladle!
She switches the flies from her husband's plate
And in every way she's a thrifty
     Mate!

(Re–enter Ned, with gun and a drinking glass.)

QUARTZ: *(to Ned)* Don't point that gun at me, you fool!

DAISY: *(to Henrietta)* Were his other wives like that?

HENRIETTA: Oh, yes, yes, yes.

QUARTZ: What's that glass for, Ned?

NED: *(looking through it)*
It's your spyglass, I think, sir. I – I think.

QUARTZ: Spyglass! You idiot – I meant – telescope!
Go and get it or I'll send you back to
You know where and you know who, boy!

NED: *(exit, still holding gun)*   No! No!

DAISY: Am I like those before?

HENRIETTA: Much prettier.

QUARTZ: *(opening Henrietta's valise for inspection)*
Sister – where are you taking my cashbox?

HENRIETTA: I'm taking both our cashboxes, William.
I'm going to spend a week at Aunt Mattie's
In Toronto. They'll be safe from the gypsies,
And from the confusion of the shivaree.

(During this sequence, Ned is seen lurking by the barn, overhearing.)

QUARTZ: The shivaree!

HENRIETTA: You'll have one, William.

(Ned runs stick along picket fence.)

It may go on every night for a week.
That's why I'm clearing out – account of the noise!
The neighbourhood's young men envy you, Will.

(Ned hits anvil.)

QUARTZ: I'll fix them! I don't mind a bit of noise.

(opening cashboxes)

But it's a good idea to have these safe
And sound somewhere else.

Look, Daisy! Look at the yellow gold, my dear.

HENRIETTA: He's right, my dear.

QUARTZ: This is life, Daisy. This is everything.

HENRIETTA: Come down and touch it, dear.

QUARTET

QUARTZ: Why do the poor starve, Henrietta?

HENRIETTA: Because they lack gold, William.
    Why can the young man not marry?

QUARTZ: Because he lacks gold.

HENRIETTA: Why is the harbour barren of ships?

QUARTZ: And the mill silent by the river?

HENRIETTA AND QUARTZ: There is no gold, no gold,
    But we have gold, and when we wish
    We fill the gaping mouth with bread
    'Tis we unlock the bridal bed.

(*They put the cashboxes on their heads and dance temptingly in front of Daisy. She looks over their heads to the house which she must enter. It is a Mammon's Cave out of which few survivors come.*)

Rich man, poor, beggar man, thief,
    Tinker, tailor, soldier, sailor,
    Minister, butcher, Indian Chief,

(*Ned returns with telescope and gun.*)

We hold you all on our heads.
    Daisy! Come down and dance with us!

(*Ned, who has been watching, lets off the gun at this point and the cashboxes come tumbling down. They scramble about picking up the gold. Ned seizes the opportunity to get up into the buggy with Daisy, just for a second.*)

DAISY: Jonathan!   HENRIETTA: Drat that boy!

NED: Who's this Jonathan?   QUARTZ: My gold! My gold!

DAISY: Someone I loved once. HENRIETTA AND QUARTZ:
    Jonathan! Jonathan!   1, 2, 3, 4, 5
                                  6, 7, 8, 9, 10

NED: I'll bet he couldn't   11, 12, 13, 14, 15, 16!
    count like that!   17, 18, 19, 20, 21
                                  22, 23, 24, 25, 26

DAISY: Do they treat you well? 27, 28, 29, 30, 31, 32!

NED: Oh, I don't mind them.

DAISY: Oh, Jonathan!

NED: (*getting down and eyeing a
    gold coin to steal*)   33 – 34 –
    I'll bet they won't
    miss this coin!

DAISY: Ah! –

NED: Surely they won't find
    out I've got this one.
    By golly, I didn't know there   35 –
    were so many numbers.

(*Ned trips while making off with gold coin; they grab him.*)

QUARTZ: Come here, Ned!

HENRIETTA: You rascal! Oh you rascal!

(*They both turn him upside down until the gold coin he has stolen drops
to the ground.*)

HENRIETTA AND QUARTZ: Thirty-six one-hundred-dollar gold
    pieces:
    Mother's brooch, Father's cufflinks, grandmother's silver
    chain
    And grandfather's diamond stick pin!

NED: (*reminding Quartz*) Gypsies!

QUARTZ: Off we go, lad, and, Daisy, if
    By the time I come back you are not in
    My house, Ned and I will take those wheels off
    And carry you up to my room. Ha ha ha!

184

(He takes gun and telescope from Ned as they go off.)

HENRIETTA: *(producing a red flag from its stand on the porch)*
    I must go too, my dear. The train is due
    At our crossing and I must flag it down.
    Daisy – could you lend me a quarter?
    I haven't just the right change for my ticket.
(Daisy gives her some money.)
    Thank you. I'll be back in a week. Don't let
    The strawberries go unpreserved.

(Exit.)

DAISY: Oh Jonathan, why have you forsaken me?
    Is there still time – to take me away?

ARIA Jonathan, you were a strange young man.
    You never could decide if I was yours,
    So, Jonathan, I tried to make you decide
    By letting Mr. Quartz keep company with me.
    But if flowers and leaves keep company with winter,
    They soon find they're stabbed with a cold icy splinter.
    My heart's like the lane and the fields in fall,
    Rusting and stiffening with cold until all
    Lies buried in colourless snow,
        Jonathan!
    Walk above the snow
    Where the garden was –
    Walk above the snow
    That covers me up,
        Jonathan!
    That covers me o'er.

(Enter Miss Beech on her bicycle. Originally, Persephone's mother, Ceres, rescued her daughter from the clutches of Hell by refusing to let any vegetation grow. In 1900 in Canada Ceres has become a very spirited but gentle old schoolteacher – Miss Beech – who goes about botanizing down the country roads on her bicycle. Her carrier s stuffed with plant specimens.)

BEECH: Well, my girl, you seem to be Mrs. William Quartz.

DAISY: Did you hear my thoughts just now?

BEECH: I'm your teacher:
I know all your thoughts, but why did you do this?

DAISY: It was to make Jonathan decide for
Or against me. I guess he decided
Against. He didn't stop Mr. Quartz
In his courtship at the Strawberry Social.
Mr. Quartz asked me if I would marry him.
He asked with such a look and gesture
For some reason I said – Yes, Mr. Quartz.
Thinking – now Jonathan will be sorry.
And today I made my wedding vows – so
I can't change my mind – I am caught!

BEECH: My dear girl, you must run away this minute.
You've made an error in marrying Quartz.

DAISY: Is he wicked or cruel or what?

BEECH: Not exactly.

DAISY: He's most unlovable and I fear him
Somewhat. I don't love him but I do love
Honesty – so I must stay with him. I vowed,
Miss Beech, I've vowed to and signed my name.

ARIA
BEECH: Run away! Run away! Get on my
Bicycle – before it is too late.
Why should he ruin your pretty innocence?
Why should his sister blight your life with hers?

DAISY: Why did his other two wives die?

BEECH: They caught a sickness called 'being Mrs. Quartz.'

DAISY: Then I'll get it too. What does it matter?
Jonathan doesn't care.

BEECH: Run away! Run away! Look at this
Place; it is – a house of pinching cash.
Can flowers grow from bags of gold?

Do meadowlarks love ravens and owls?

DAISY: Did he ill-treat them, Miss Beech?

BEECH: If he had done so, it would have been better.

DAISY: Be it better or worse – what does it matter?
Jonathan doesn't care.

BEECH: Oh my child! I warn you – if you go
In that house – all the flowers I love,
All fields of grain and gardens vegetable,
The morning dew itself – all shall seem to die.

DAISY: What does it matter? Jonathan doesn't care.

BEECH: But Jonathan does care!
Since you've got married he at last knows
That he should have married you long ago.

DAISY: What use is it to know when it's too late?

BEECH: Poor Jonathan! He only knows anything
He says, when it is just one second too late.
Poor Jonathan!
Poor Jonathan!
Talk to him, Daisy!

DAISY: Is he close by?

BEECH: He's ridden down to the oak tree in the lane.
If you want him to see you I'm to ring
My bicycle bell three times.

DAISY: Do it, Miss Beech!

BEECH: *(rings the bell)*
Now – goodbye. We can't see much of each other.
Mr. Quartz doesn't like me:
I want too many things for the school.
It will be a pretty sunset, I believe.

(She goes off.)

(Jonathan enters: a college boy, rather longish hair.)

DAISY: So you've come at last.

JONATHAN: Do you love me, Daisy?

DAISY: Of course I do.

JONATHAN: Then why have you married this man?

DAISY: Because
    I loved you, silly.

JONATHAN: It has made me know myself.
    I thought it would always be spring or summer.

DAISY: My summer's gone.

JONATHAN: Oh my darling: You shall not
    Go into that dark house of fall filled with
    Dark rooms filled with clouds and rain and dead leaves
    And snow.

DAISY: Now that you cannot have me
    You are so sure you love me.

JONATHAN: Run away!
    Come away with me!

DAISY: Get me a red dress, then!

JONATHAN: I shall never leave this road!
    I shall watch for you day and night!
    I have not lost you!

DAISY: Yes you have, Jonathan.
    If you love me now, do what I tell you.
    Watch the sunset with me and then leave me.
    If you love me – never say you do again.

DUET

DAISY AND JONATHAN: Let's say that this is ours.

DAISY: What do you hear, Jonathan?

JONATHAN: The distant sounds
    So fresh and close.
    The valley's like a bell

Where a dog barks far away.

DAISY: This is ours – the close of this day.

JONATHAN: What do you see, Daisy,
　　　What do you see?

DAISY: The lone heron flying
　　　To his nest by the river
　　　And the clouds like great angels
　　　Twisting the sky.

JONATHAN: This is ours – to watch the day die.

DAISY AND JONATHAN: This is ours – to watch the day die.

DAISY: I'll give you a scarlet thread, Jonathan,
　　　I give you a lengthening shadow.
　　　I give you the swallows turning
　　　In the golden high air.
　　　I give you the darkening earth
　　　Caught in the sun's
　　　Absalom hair.
　　　When a sunset you see
　　　Pray remember me.

JONATHAN: I'll give you the moonrise
　　　Soon through the orchard.
　　　Regard, my love, my moon tonight.
　　　Regard its tears, the silver dew
　　　That chills each flower and
　　　Blade of grass
　　　With my love.
　　　When a sunset you see
　　　Pray remember me.

(*She descends from the buggy; they embrace, kiss and slowly draw apart.*)

DAISY & JONATHAN: When a sunset you see

　　　Pray remember me.

(*Quartz and Ned enter; Quartz has a gypsy's torn dress in his hand.*)

QUARTZ: My bride Daisy!

At last you've come down
From your perch!

DAISY: I am yours, Mr. Quartz!

QUARTZ: I showed those gypsies a thing or two!
This one said you'd never have me
So I tore off her dress! Ned – go in and
Bring me out Father's great Bible.
(*Ned starts to go, then lingers.*)

DAISY: Did you
Tear off a gypsy woman's dress, William?

QUARTZ: I was only bluffing. I meant to give her
A cuffing and she tore away from me.
She called me a nasty name. Ned, (*prodding him*)
Get the Bible... pen and ink. (*Exit Ned.*)
Who's that young man in the shadows?

DAISY: William Quartz – if you should ever strike me
Or offer to strike me or give me a cuffing
I should leave you, ten times vowed though I am.
I won't be struck!

QUARTZ: Judas Iscariot!
What have I done? You've no idea, my dear,
How troublesome gypsies are. I got you
A pretty, pretty dress. Here – Rachel – take it.

(*The old miser offers her the gypsy's dress. She spurns him. Jonathan steps forward.*)

JONATHAN: Mr. Quartz – I beg of you – let this girl go.
She's made a mistake. She was afraid to –
Once it got going she couldn't stop it –

QUARTZ: She didn't have to say yes.

JONATHAN: I know. But –

QUARTZ: I know full well she could never love me.

JONATHAN: (Courage, Daisy!)

QUARTZ: I will not give her up! I want women too!
   My bed is cold and I am childless.

(*Ned brings out the Bible and pen and ink.*)

JONATHAN: You old magpie. You've collected a young girl
   The way you collect gold. You can spend gold
   But I understand you cannot spend her!

QUARTZ: Oh ho! Is that so! At fifty-eight I am
   As capable of wantonness as an eighteen-year-old!
   We shall see. It was you, young capon,
   With your sighs and your hesitations
   That could not bring matters to a head!
   Booh! (*laughing*) Go away, little boy! My dear,
   Let us sign our names in the front of the Bible –
   And, Daisy, swear on the Bible
   That you will not leave me. (That gypsy
   has frightened me.)

(*He signs, hands her the pen.*)

DAISY: I'll sign my name (*She signs.*)
   But I gave my vows this afternoon,
   And I shall not swear them again.

(*starts for the door*)

QUARTZ: Swear!

DAISY: (*entering house*)   No!

QUARTZ: (*closing door after her*)
   Oh you shall never come out of that door
   Again! Ned, throw down hay for the stallion.
   My black beauty, Cerberus! And if I
   See you at the shivaree tonight I fire you!

JONATHAN: (*musing*) A shivaree – a shivaree –

(*Quartz strides about setting things in order; Jonatan lurks in the shadows; the light is fading. At length Quartz sits on the porch, removes overalls, and straightens suit. Daisy reappears on the balcony above for a last look at the sunset. The swallows fly on the highest golden air, where it is still, up that high, only late afternoon. Bats begin to come out of Mr. Quartz's chimney. There is a deer's skull fastened over Mr. Quartz's front door.)*

QUINTET

DAISY: I give you the swallows turning
In the golden high air.
I give you the darkening earth
Caught in the sun's Absalom hair.

QUARTZ: No! *(to Daisy)*

JONATHAN: Let my love go! let my love go!

QUARTZ: No! *(to Jonathan)*

JONATHAN: Give her back! Give her back!

QUARTZ: Ask her! She has promised!

(He goes into house.)

NED: *(busy with pail; to Beech)*
Here I must pump some water
While others mourn their fate.
I'm lucky I am who I am,
Drudging early and late.

Perhaps it's not too late!

BEECH: *(wheeling bicycle; to Ned)*
What ever shall I do now?
I cannot leave her to her fate!
I shall ride to the county capital
To examine the certificate!
Perhaps it's not too late!

(Quartz comes out on balcony behind Daisy.)

BEECH: (Not too late.)
NED: (Not too late.)

JONATHAN: Return this girl to spring and to light.

QUARTZ: No! *(to Jonathan)*

DAISY: What can you give me, love?

BEECH: (I cannot leave her to her fate)

You have only to do with winter and night. Regard, my love,

QUARTZ: Nothing! (to Daisy, answering for Jonathan)

NED: (I'm lucky I am who I am)

my moon tonight. When a sunset

DAISY: Give me stars for my dark

BEECH & NED: Perhaps it's not too late!

you see Pray remember me.

Enough, my love.

QUARTZ: She is legally mine!

(Exeunt Ned, Miss Beech; exit Jonathan.)

QUARTZ: *(mimicking Jonathan)*
Regard, my wife, your husband tonight!

(He places a black gloved hand on Daisy's shoulder.)

CURTAIN

The poster design for the 1982 stage premiere featured a drawing by Miro Malish.

ACT TWO

(The moon is rising. It is a perfect summer evening filled with millions of different shadows multiplied by a south wind. The stars are few and large, the frogs in the pond are singing, an owl cries in the orchard. It is the night of all the year's collection of nights that could be called a wedding night. As they journey to the farmhouse at the crossroads, the young serenaders think of the moonlight.)

SERENADERS: *(behind closed curtain)*
    Silver silver silver white
    Silver silver silver black
    Is the light and shadow of
    This midsummer night.

    The silver dew and the silver pond
    The silver river and the silver moth
       Luna luna luna
    Why do the fields love the moonlight so?
    Why do the roads love the moonlight so?
       Luna luna luna

    Silver silver silver white, etc.

(The Serenaders one by one make for a rendezvous in front of a roller by Quartz's store. They cannot be seen from the balcony. A lantern is lit. The moon is shining now literally as bright as day and we see the serenaders very well by its light. They are not as ethereal as their thoughts about the moonlight: Elmer, a short fat young man; Sam, tall with buck teeth; Bo, the village dandy with electric blue armbands and a bowtie and slicked hair; Jo, an old obscene hired man, always just too smart for his own good, in overalls, a fuzzy grey unshaven face, full head of ashy grey hair (he is quite capable of lurking about long after the shivaree is over); Russell, a plain dumb young man with glasses, very thick ones; Aunt Annie, the tomboy, a rather oldish one, dressed up in men's clothes with her hair under a cap.)

THE SERENADERS' CONVERSATION

(Enter Bo, Jo, Sam.)

BO: Ned, where are you?

JO: *(whistles)*   Hey, Ned

Won't the old man letcha come out?

(*Enter Elmer, Russell.*)

SAM: Elmer!

ELMER AND RUSSELL: Sam!

RUSSELL: Bo! Jo!

SAM: Russell!

BO AND JO: Hey, Russ!

(*Enter Aunt Annie.*)

RUSSELL: (*to Aunt Annie*) Hey, who are you?

ELMER: D'ya think they've
  Got into bed yet?

BO: No.

SAM AND RUSSELL: Sh!

BO: Not yet.
  There's still a light downstairs.

(*Aunt Annie takes Russell's glasses.*)

RUSSELL: Help!
  Somebody took my glasses.

JO: Hey! Elmer!
  Elmer, where's Sam?

(*Light in house goes out.*)

RUSSELL: Bo, you scared me!

ELMER: Look at the moon!

SAM: The light's gone off!
  Not a light on in the house.

JO: Are they there?

RUSSELL: (*to Aunt Annie*) Who are you, anyhow?

BO: All right, what have we?
  What you got, Elmer?

ELMER: I got a bell! Cowbells and trainbells!

BO: What you got, Sam?

SAM: I got a tin horn, Bo. And a policeman's whistle.

BO: What you got – Hey, Ned! You got out.

NED: (*entering*) I don't care if he does fire me.
I heard you singin' down the road
And I climbed out of the window
Onto the kitchen roof. I got a
Tin cakebox filled with nuts and bolts.

RUSSELL: If I could just find my glasses
I could find out where you are.

ELMER: Here they are, Russ!

RUSSELL: Gee, thanks. I got two old rusty lids
Off of molasses buckets to bang together.

BO: Jo?

JO: I thought I'd just yell, Bo.

BO: What'd you bring, over there?

ANNIE: What'd you bring yourself?

BO: I brought my baby brother's drum
And this noisemaker I won at the fall fair.
Hey! Where do you come from?

SAM: You don't live near here.

ANNIE: It's true I'm a stranger in this neighbourhood
But there's no better way we boys know
To get acquainted than to go to a
Shivaree together.

(*They tear off her cap.*)

ALL: She's a girl! She can't come to the shivaree.

(*She is given a hug by Jo.*)

JO: She sure hugs like a girl!

BO: Get your dirty paws off of my aunt.
   Aunt Annie – why'd you come along?

ANNIE: Because I'm – tired of staying at home
   Because I – wanted to see what a shivaree was like.

BO: But you can't have a part in this!
   This is a man's custom!

NED: We can't get drunk
   With a woman around afterwards.

ALL: Go home.

ANNIE: I won't go home! *(She takes Bo's drum.)*

BO: You give me that drum.

(He takes it back from her.)

ANNIE: If little Tom knew you had his drum
   He'd take a fit.

ARIA   I want to be a man.
   I want to swear! I want to drink and chew
   Tobacco! I'm tired of being a girl!

(Puts her hair under her cap as before.)

SAM AND JO: You'd like a beard and moustache then,
   Cut off your hair, would you?

ANNIE: I don't know.
   I'm tired of pushing a broom

ELMER AND RUSSELL: She'd rather push a plough
   If she were able.

ANNIE: Around a dusty room.

NED AND BO: Look, Annie, would you rather – now –
   Clean out a stable?

ANNIE: No. Yes. Yes. No. Yes.

ALL: No. Yes. No. Yes. No, yes, no yes, noyes
         Noyesnoyes. Wear a dress, wear a pants,
         She doesn't know what she wants.

ANNIE: I don't know.
         I don't know if that's what I want.
         Oh, you've got me so mixed up I don't know what I want!
         All I know is – I'm tired of being a girl.
         So, what else is there you can be?
         Nothing. Nothing else evi-dently.
         But there's no harm in fantasy. (*thinks*)
         That I could be a werewolf
         And roam the fields till dawn. (*howls*)
         Or shave the hair right off my head
         And dress like a ghostly nun. (*makes spook sounds*)
         I'll get up at four to bake the bread
         And switch the flies from off my husband's head
         Maybe. (*waves the red flag that Henrietta waved earlier*)
         Or I could ride a bicycle
         And teach the golden rule.
         (*bike bell sounds; mimes bike-riding*)
         Oh, I could be a reluctant bride,
         A potato that's never been fried!
         (*thinks and resolves on something – lets down her hair*)
         Or I could join the gypsies
         Who wander up and down.
         Or next time join the circus
         And be a famous female clown. (*mimes acrobatics*)
         But – there must be something else than what I now
             am that I can be.
         And – obvious solutions – like becoming just one more
             old maid – do not appeal to me.
         So – I swear that this night – mark my words – I shall
         be free
         For –
         Is this or is it not a shivaree!
                     Shivaree   shivaree   shivaree
         shivaree   shivaree

SERENADERS: Shivaree   shivaree   shivaree

(She runs off as they all laugh at her but she really doesn't leave and she may be seen later at one edge of the yard beating a kettle.)

JO: Be a man! Holy Moses!

BO: She means she'd like to *get* a man.

RUSSELL: So let's get back to business.

NED: Yeh, fellows,
If we don't hurry it'll be too late.

SAM AND JO: Sh!
They've just gone up into the bedroom now.
(Light goes on above.)

ELMER: There! The window's lighted up!

BO: All right!
Now how much do we ask for?

(They huddle together.)

ALL: *(sotto voce)* Two dollars to buy us a keg of beer
Or give us a barrel of cider and one dollar.

(Sam gives a hoot on his tin horn.)

BO: Not yet! Let there be an awful and grand silence.

JO: Wait till he's got his pants off!

ELMER, NED, RUSSELL AND SAM: Sh!

(They walk in a group to a position directly facing the balcony. Their instruments are poised and ready.)

SHIVAREE MUSIC 1

ALL: Mister and Mistress Quartz, we serenade you dear.
We won't let you go to bed until you give us some beer!
Shivaree!
Mister and Mistress Quartz, we hope your honeymoon
Will be all the sweeter for the quiet rollicking tune
of Shivaree!

If you don't give us some beer, we'll stay –
Twelve o'clock. One o'clock. Two three four – break of day!
  Shivaree.
If you give us some beer, we don't ask anything more.
William Quartz. You old bugger. Does he wake or does
  he snore?
  Shivaree.

(The noisemakers make their noise. There is a short silence. Then the balcony window flies open and Mr. Quartz emerges with a shotgun.)

QUARTZ: *(from the open window)*
I'll give you lousy bums to the count of ten
To get off my property or I'll shoot.
One two

ELMER: This isn't your property, Quartz.

SAM: It's the king's highway. *(They're standing on the road.)*

RUSSELL: And you give us beer.

BO AND JO: Beer!

QUARTZ: Three four five six

ELMER, NED, RUSSELL AND SAM: Beer!

BO: Don't
  Listen to him, boys.

JO: Give him another blast!

QUARTZ: Seven eight nine ten!

(They have just played a few notes – rather dimly and timidly – when a blast from Quartz's shotgun sends them all flying.)

DAISY: *(at window, still in her wedding dress)*
William. You shouldn't shoot at them.
They're just poor boys who want a drink.

QUARTZ: They want you! They'll get you away!
They think I'm too old for you! The clowns!
Get back in the room and don't come out again.
(She recedes out of sight.)

Who's playing that guitar? Who is it?

JONATHAN: *(unseen as yet)*
    When the bear goes to sleep
    In the winter, my love,
    And the snow falls deep,
    Come to thy window, my love.
    Come south to thy window, my love.

QUARTZ: Stop playing that guitar; do you hear?
    Or I'll shoot! I can't sleep with all this noise.
    (oath as he shuts window)

NED: *(heading back serenaders)*
    Come on, fellows – I just remembered. I put
    All blanks in his cartridge box.

SAM AND JO: Why didn't you tell us that?

ELMER: *(to Bo)* So, what do we do this time?

NED: *(counting them as they return)*
    Bo, Elmer, Jo, Sam, Russell –

ELMER AND BO: *(consulting together)* Three
    Dollars or two barrels of cider and
    A silver dollar.

RUSSELL: Who's playing the guitar?

JONATHAN: *(elegant Orpheus)* Good evening, gentlemen.

BO: Jonathan. What do you do here this night?
    I never thought you'd like this sort of thing.

JONATHAN: Gentlemen, the girl I intend to marry
    Is up in that room with that old bear.

JO: It's too late now, brother!

SERENADERS: It's too late now, to marry her.

JONATHAN: But now's the first time I know that I love her.

JO: Holy Moses – if I fall in love I sure know I have,
    Long before this happens to my girl.

JONATHAN: Well, that's what education does for you.
But it's not too late. Can you get him
Excited again and out of his house
So I can talk to Daisy? (*guitar flourish*)

SERENADERS: Sh!

QUARTZ: (*looking out window*)
At last – all is quiet – even that guitar.
It's all over, my dear girl. Time for bed.
If they should come again – pay no attention.

(*There instantly comes the most deafening roar. The shivaree band skips about the yard shouting, singing and clapping hands.*)

SHIVAREE MUSIC 2

BO: Quartzie – give us quartz of beer!

SAM: Hey, Quartz! Pay for the serenade!

ALL: Quartzie – give us quartz of beer!
Hey, Quartz! Pay for the serenade!

NED: William! Up off that bed!

ELMER: Or we'll come and pull you off.

ALL: Quartzie, etc.

JO: Hey, Will – what did you do with the other two?

RUSSELL: Quartz – no bed till you pay the fiddler.

ALL: Quartzie, etc.

(*Quartz strides out onto balcony, shooting as he comes. They answer each shot with a blast from the shivaree band.*)

QUARTZ: Well, what is it now?

(*Realizing his bullets are blanks, he discards gun*)

ALL: Three dollars to buy us some beer
Or two barrels of cider and one silver dollar.

QUARTZ: I have no money in the house
And my cider barrels are bone dry.

(*Ned hands cake tin to Jo and moves off, after a word to Bo.*)

JONATHAN, ELMER, SAM, RUSSELL AND JO: That's a lie!
Give us or else!

QUARTZ: (*derisive*) Ha, ha, ha.

BO: William – is that a gypsy bell I hear?

QUARTZ: Gypsies?

ALL: Gypsies! Gypsies gypsies gypsies!

SAM AND ELMER: They're leading a great black horse from the
barn.

QUARTZ: Great Judas Iscariot! They've stolen my horse!
Where are they? Show me the way!

(*He swings down from the balcony on a grapevine like a huge spider. All
go out with Quartz except Jonathan.*)

DUET

JONATHAN: Come out and come down my love.
Come onto your balcony,
Come out and come down,
Come out and come down –
And I will show you the moon
Like a bunch of white violets
Held by the negro night.
Come out and come down,
Come out and come down.

DAISY: No, you have lost me,
Past my vow I'll not go.
But the moon will be ours
And the sun and the river.
Only snow will be his.
I cannot come to you,
I cannot come to you
To see the moon.

JONATHAN: Do you not love me enough to run away from him?

DAISY: I love you so much that I stay with him.

JONATHAN: Come out and come down, my love –

DAISY: I cannot come to you, my love –

(Jonathan into the shadows, Daisy into house. Quartz sees her out of the corner of his eye as he returns, chasing what appears to be a gypsy woman rattling some sleigh bells. It is Ned in the gypsy dress.)

QUARTZ: *(seizing a stick)* So it's you, you impudent young swine.
    Tangle my nerves with gypsies, gypsies – eh?
    Well here's a big stick to beat you with
    And home you go to your stepfather tomorrow.
    Who'll be sorry then, eh? Gypsies indeed!

NED: Ow!

(Quartz finishes beating Ned as the serenaders return, then nimbly climbs up on the balcony from the outside.)

QUARTZ: Did I see you out here, Daisy? Were you?
    You are to stay inside the room – or else!
    And this time – my dear little serenaders –
    You will never get me out again – never.
    Not if you play your bells, drums, rattles
    Until your arms and legs drop off. *(shuts window)*

JONATHAN: Get him out again!

NED: *(has removed dress and put aside sleighbells; rubbing his shoulder and bottom)* Oww! He's won. He won't.

BO: Come on, fellows. Another try with the shivaree band!

(They give a desperate blast.)

    He's not coming, Ned. You're right.

JONATHAN: I have five dollars! *(produces bill)*
    I won it in a competition.
    This five dollars is yours *(to all the serenaders)*
        if you, Ned, will go
    And start a bonfire over there in the field, and you –
    The rest of you – serenade him again.

BO: You're too late. The light's gone off.

JONATHAN: Not too late. This time – let's have a slow build up.
We'll slowly affect his nerves.
He hears us getting louder and louder and louder and
By that time the bonfire's burning – louder,
Louder and then we shout – Fire!

(Serenaders' reactions: 'Wow!', soft whistles, etc. Exit Ned.)

If that
Doesn't put the light on again and bring him out –

SHIVAREE MUSIC 3

Ring that bell, Elmer!
It should be my wedding bell!

SERENADERS: Ding dong diggi dong ding dong dong

JONATHAN: Blow that whistle, Sam, and blow the horn,
That's for a baby that's going to be.

SERENADERS: Whistle, whistle like the wind.
Blow for the bride and her lost bridegroom.
Whistle whistle blow blow
Ding dong diggi dong ding dong dong

JONATHAN: Shake that rattle *(to Jo)* for the seeds in our garden,
Our garden that is going to be.

SERENADERS: Shake the rattle for a seed that will grow.
Rattle rattle
Whistle whistle blow blow
Ding dong diggi dong ding dong dong

JONATHAN: Crash those cymbals *(to Russell)* to scare away the fiend!
Opening the gate of our garden to be.

SERENADERS: Stay away devils and spirits of the dead!
Crash crash crash
Rattle rattle
Whistle whistle blow blow
Ding dong diggi dong ding dong dong

JONATHAN: Beat that drum for my heart that's beating
  Fearfully joyously fearfully.

SERENADERS: Beat that drum – Ratatatat Wham!
  Crash crash crash
  Rattle rattle
  Whistle whistle blow blow
  Ding dong diggi dong ding dong dong
    FIRE!
  Fire, Mr. Quartz!

(The light goes on and Quartz appears on the balcony.)

QUARTZ: Get some water – water!
  Get some water in some pails, you fools!
  It looks like my barn! *(He clambers down again.)*
  Get some water – some water! Ohh! –

(All go out save Jonathan.)

JONATHAN: Daisy, my love, will you listen?

DAISY: *(from within)* I cannot come out to see you.

JONATHAN: I will throw up this rose
  To the balcony there.
  If you come and pick it up
  That will mean
  We'll never meet again –
  But keep my rose, my love.
  But if you stay, but if you stay
  And do not pick up my flower
  I shall know that you want me
    To save you.
  These fellows will help me. *(He throws up the rose.)*

DAISY: *(coming out)* Jonathan. I say farewell.
  I shall pick up this flower *(doing so)*
  And never see you again. *(Quartz appears.)*

QUARTZ: Put that down, do you hear? Put it down!
  I told you to stay in your room, didn't I?

(He climbs up and cuffs her. She drops the flower and runs back into the bedroom.)

> There! That's what bad little girls get!
> *(turns to face returning serenaders)*
> So – you fools – you thought a bonfire
> Would keep me away long enough until
> My fool of a wife could make up her mind
> To go off with her guitar-playing friend
> Well –

(Ned flashes in, waving a sickle. He pretends insanity.)

NED: La la la la la

QUARTZ: Great Judas Iscariot! What's the matter with him?

NED: *(racing about)* You can't send me home to my stepfather –
He's even worse than you are.

BO: He's gone mad, sir. He swears he'll kill your cows,
Geld your black stallion, disturb your brood mares –
Scare your chickens, roust up your pigs and –

QUARTZ: Oh God! No!

NED: La la la

ELMER AND SAM: Come down and help us catch him, Mr. Quartz!

ALL: We can do nothing with him. Come down, Mr. Quartz!

DUET

NED: I'll drown all your poultry, Quartz.

QUARTZ: Daisy! Stay there! Remember your sacred vows.

You wouldn't even let
   me call you by your
   first name
This afternoon – I'll
drown every animal
   you own –
Into the horse trough
with the Black
Minorca clucks,
The Golden Necked Sussex
   Layers and the
   Plymouth Rocks.
And then – I'll drown
your Tamworth Sow!

Now don't go away! Oh
God! My pigs and cows.
Stay in the bedroom
sweetheart, till I
Catch this mad scamp of
mine!
I shall have to
Get a rope and tie him in
the cellar!
(*He gets rope.*)

Remember your sacred
vows!
Oh God! My pigs and
cows!

(*Ned goes out during this, and re-enters with a large pig. Quartz comes thundering down and pursues him. Rattling and beating, the serenaders follow. The stage is empty – even of Jonathan.*)

DAISY: (*slowly coming out*)
   Jonathan! Come and take me away from him!

JONATHAN: (*walking towards balcony*) Daisy! At last you will come
   to me.
   My darling bird fly down to me.
   (*She jumps from the balcony into his arms.*)

DAISY: (*They kiss.*) How can we escape him, Jonathan?

JONATHAN: Why, I've some wonderful horses!

(*He puts her in the buggy, then climbs up beside her.*)

DAISY: Have you? I don't see them, Jonathan.

JONATHAN: Here they are!

(*The Shivaree Band – including Annie, but minus Ned – emerges laughing and begins to pull and push the buggy. Annie, Sam, Bo and Jo take positions to pull buggy as 'horses,' while Elmer and Russell act as 'coachmen' pushing it from behind.*)

MARCH

SERENADERS: Here we are. We'll be your horses,
    Gallop a trot!
    We'll trot you to freedom
    We'll trot you to freedom
    And gallop to liberty!
    We'll be your horses,
    Gallop a trot!

DAISY: Here is a swallow turning

JONATHAN: Turning in golden air

DAISY: He sees the morning

JONATHAN: Darkness hides here

DAISY: Darkness hides here

JONATHAN: A morning

DAISY: Where

JONATHAN: See a swallow turning

SERENADERS: We'll be your horses
    Gallop a trot! etc. (*Exeunt.*)

QUARTZ: (*enters, holding Ned by the ear*)
    So! Another clever trick! Just pretending mad, eh?
    Great Jezebel! Where's my buggy? Where's my –

(*He rushes into house – emerges slowly onto the balcony. The serenaders return to face him.*)

    Four barrels of beer if you tell me where she's gone.
    My black stallion can out-gallop his white horse.

SERENADERS: No!

QUARTZ: Five.

SERENADERS: No!

QUARTZ: Six! Which road will they take?

SERENADERS: No!

SAM: Mr. Quartz, we won't tell you.

QUARTZ: *(trying a new tack)*
    Sam, I'll get you fired from the kiln, so fast.
    Russ, I'll call in your father's note. Jo, it's
    the asylum
    For you.

SERENADERS: *(Their responses are weakening.)* No, no, no.

QUARTZ: Will you tell where he's taking her or do you
    Want to be beggars? Will you tell? Will you
    Tell? Do you want to be beggars –
    Even more so than now? Tell – tell –
    You were just about to get married, Bo, weren't you?

(They waver. Dawn is coming. Miss Beech wheels in, her headlight turned on.)

from the 1982 stage premiere by Comus Music Theatre, Toronto:
Katherine Terrell

BEECH: Stop everything! Get them up out of bed!
I've just found out the most amazing thing!

QUARTZ: Judas Iscariot, even schoolteachers
Shivaree poor older married men.

BEECH: Ah! There you are, Mr. Quartz!
What is the first name of your bride?

QUARTZ: *(makes three imperfect gestures and sounds)*
Ah... Mm...
Oh, don't ask me such a silly question.
I can't remember her name just like that.
I get her mixed up with my other wives.

BEECH: What is the first name of your bride?

QUARTZ: Sometimes I forget even my own name.
Her name is – *(laughs)* Wife Number Three. *(extended laugh)*

ALL: Mr. Quartz, what is your wife's first name?

QUARTZ: I can't remember.

BEECH: I thought so.
Well – I've just been to see the County Clerk.
I've just had a look at your marriage
Certificate. Yes, your marriage certificate!
You made a mistake, a mistake in the application
For the licence. You have your bride's name down
As Rachel! Rachel instead of Daisy.

QUARTZ: That was my first wife's name! Rachel!

BEECH: So you are not married to Daisy legally.
She has a chance to change her mind
If it's not too late. Where is Daisy?

ALL: She's gone –

BEECH: Oh, it can't be too late. I've
Bicycled here fifteen mad hilly miles!

SAM: We helped her elope with Jonathan.

BEECH: She eloped with Jonathan. Wonderful!

QUARTZ: Yes, she's gone! Flown the coop. Changed her mind!

ALL: Yes she's gone!

NED: Changed her mind!

ALL: Gone!

BEECH: Then I'm not too late! Hurrah!

JUBILATION SONG

(Miss Beech conducts the Shivaree Band with a stick she has picked up somewhere.)

ALL: Hurray!

BEECH: What do we say when things turn out right?

SERENADERS: What do we say why we say we say

BEECH: Love Triumphant! Oh, Victory of Light!

SERENADERS: We say, we sing of Love's Victory –
    Jonathan fell in love finally.

BEECH: Hurrah hurrah!

SERENADERS: Hurray hurray hurray!

QUARTZ: *(remaining on balcony)*
    Will no one marry me? You – Miss Beech – marry me?
    I'm a very rich man. I'll buy for your school
    A new water pail and an abacus.

BEECH: Heavenly days, no!
    I've saved Daisy from your clutches
    And I'll certainly not get into them.

QUARTZ: Is there no girl will marry me?
    Old foolish ridiculous miser that I am?

BO: We'll find something for you, surely.

ELMER: Will nobody – nobody – marry Mr. Quartz?

ALL: Will nobody marry Mr. Quartz?

ANNIE: I'll have him! I'll have you, Mr. Quartz!

212

QUARTZ: But you're a young man, aren't you?

ANNIE: Not a bit of it. I've tucked my dress in
These overalls which I'll just climb out of.

RUSSELL: Earlier on, you wanted to be a man.

SAM: Swear, chew tobacco...

JO: ... go to shivarees.

ANNIE: But that was before Mr. Quartz courted me.
Lift me up to him! I'll have him!
(I can handle him.) He's mine!

(They lift her up to him. He looks at her.)

All right, Mr. Quartz?

QUARTZ: (pause) Ned! Run for the minister right away!

BO: Holy Moses, boys! We can start the new shivaree
Right now!

(The serenaders perform and dance before Quartz and Annie, who bow to
them. Miss Beech whizzes back and forth on her bicycle.)

ALL: What do we say when things turn out right?

QUARTZ AND ANNIE: What do we say why we say we say

ALL: Love Triumphant! Oh Victory of Light!
We say, we sing of Love's Victory
Mr. Quartz found a wife finally –
Quartz found a wife after all!

CURTAIN

Crazy to Kill

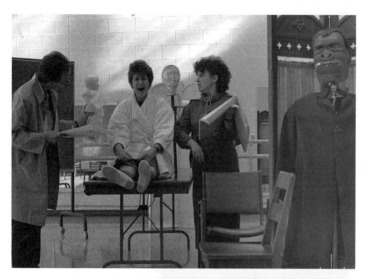

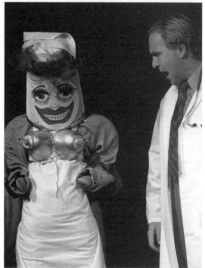

Still photos from the 1988 workshop at the Banff Centre. Students from the art program invented various substitutes for Reaney's 'doll puppets.'

Crazy to Kill
A Detective Opera

Libretto, James Reaney   Music, John Beckwith

Based on the mystery novel *Crazy to Kill* by Ann Cardwell
(New York, 1941).

Commissioned by the Edward Johnson Music Foundation with
a grant from the Ontario Arts Council.

First performance; Ground Round Studio Theatre, Banff Centre,
22 October 1988.
Tom Goertz *baritone*
Michelle Milenkovic *mezzo-soprano*
Peggy Evans *soprano*
Jan Stirling and Dean Dawson *speakers*
David Boothroyd *music director & pianist*
Riccardo Gallardo *percussion*
Michael Ashman *director*

professional premiere, Guelph Spring Festival, Ross Hall,
Guelph, 11 May 1989.
Paul Massel *baritone*
Jean Stilwell *mezzo-soprano*
Sharon Crowther *soprano*
Cheryl Swarts and Jay Bowen *speakers*
Mark Widner *music director & pianist*
Mark Duggan *percussion*
Elyakim Tausig *sound tape*
Jerry Franken *director*
Sue LePage *designer*
Anna Wagner-Ott *puppet designer*

Time: the late 1930s
Scene: Elmhurst, a rest home

Cast, in order of appearance:
Agatha Lawson, a patient at Elmhurst
Tape Operator
Percussionist
Pianist

Detective Fry
John Lennox, age ten
Dr. Lennox, his father, supervisor of Elmhurst
Mrs. Parsons ⎫
Mr. Keene   ⎬ patients
Mr. Small   ⎭
Tim O'Connor, an orderly
Dr. Greer
Madame Dupont, a patient
Miss Jones, a nurse
Dr. Holman, an intern
Miss Scarth, head nurse
Miss Zimmerman, a nurse
Lieutenant Hogan
Amy Johnston, a patient
Dr. Lang, former supervisor
Miss Currie, a policewoman, disguised as a nurse
Miss Maclean, a nurse
Sergeant Coombe
Miss Krug, a nurse
Another nurse

NOTE: Some characters are portrayed 'live,' others as doll-puppets, some as both. The following suggests the distribution of roles among five performers (*doll-puppet).

Baritone Fry, Fry*, Hogan, Hogan*, Coombe*, Currie*, Holman*
Soprano Dupont, Maclean*, Krug*, Parsons*
Mezzo-soprano Agatha, Agatha*, Scarth, Scarth*
Speaker 1, female Jones*, Johnston, Keene*, Zimmerman*, John Lennox*, Nurse in finale*
Speaker 2, male Tim*, Greer*, Lennox, Small*, Lang*

CRAZY TO KILL

(Pre-curtain activity (houselights on): Scene, the vestibule of Elmhurst, a private asylum. A doll show is being prepared. A very correct, harmless older woman – Agatha Lawson – is going back and forth with shopping bags full of dolls she has made out of scraps and pieces, human hair from barbershop floors, hairdressing salons and so on. She attaches them to a carousel of strings hanging down from the loft. She has a doll version of herself. She makes costume decisions about it – finally putting on a dress and hat, dead look-alikes for what she is wearing. Houselights fade as Percussionist enters.

(Tape: amplified sounds of Agatha's sewing-machine.)

Agatha fades out of view. Later we will find out that she is making a doll out of men's suitings cast-offs that is a dead look-alike of Detective Fry. A few non-pitch percussion events, live (tape fades); then –
    A knock.
Fry enters from the auditorium. He treats the whole audience chamber as the private asylum, sings to the audience directly (accompaniment – vibraphone with assorted non-pitch percussion):

FRY: Hey!
    What's been going on here?
    Don't you hide on me!
    Am I in love with someone
    I'm never to see?
    What's been going on here?
    I'm really upset.
    You know that I love you
    Tho' we've never met.
    Come out, come out, my darling
    Wherever you're at,
    Or I'll tip this funny rest home
    This way and that.

(Pianist enters. A few scattered, dissonant piano licks interrupt the flow of the song as Fry continues.)

FRY: That way and this way
    Ev'ry night and day
    Nothing can ever subdue

My love that's strong for you.

(He reaches the stage area and begins to search for clues. Continues his song; adds the occasional dance step – Donald O'Connor or Astaire? Gives the dolls a strong whirl; they gradually slow down.)

FRY: Hiding in this kewpie doll?
       Sunlight slides across the floor.
       All right, I don't care at all –
       I'll hunt for you no more.
       And hide on you: *you* see
       If *you* can find *me*.
       Only I can give you peace of mind,
       Only I your tangle can unwind.

(Piano assumes a fuller and more formal accompaniment to the song; scattershot commentary is now in the percussion part.)

FRY: What's been going on here?
       I'm really upset.
       You know that I love you,
       (spoken) For God's sake,
       Don't play so hard to get.
       Come to me, my darling, come to me.
       Don't you dare hide on me.
       Nothing can ever subdue
       My love so strong for you. *(He laughs – Richard Widmark.)*

(Fuller light now reveals a collection of working doors, a vertical bed, a curtained table whose lamp shines through the curtain, a large stepladder, other curtained alcoves. The set is like Bluebeard's closet – filled with many unpleasant surprises. Above, there hangs a screen for back projection of images in the murderer's soul. Elmhurst has many doors with ground glass where an image, a shadow, boils up as it were from the kettle of space on the other side of the locked door.)

FRY: *(consulting his notebook)*
       Patient: Agatha Lawson. Dementia, general enfeeblement.
       Age: fifty-one. Admitted: April 16, 1930. Imbecility, not congenital but acquired – following severe melancholia.

(*During this, Agatha appears on stage right as if called. She is dressed for travel, with a suitcase and a shopping bag of portrait dolls – which she and the detective will use throughout to help tell her story.*)

FRY: (*to Agatha*)
First question: *You* make all these dolls, love? By yourself?

AGATHA: (*cheerful, businesslike*)
Yes, Mister Fry. Over the years here, I've made a portrait doll for every one of the patients, nurses, doctors, at Elmhurst. (*sinister*) When someone dies, they let me have a swatch of their hair.

FRY: You're allowed sharps?

Costume design by Sue le Page for the 1989 première: Agatha Lawson

AGATHA: O.T. has always let me have scissors. (*cheerful again*) Now, I'm making a doll of you, sir, and – (*with scissors, smoothly taking off Fry's hat*) and – I think he could stand a trim at the back here. Ha! De-li-lah!

(*tape: exaggerated scissors-clipping*)

(*She goes behind him and – crunch! – off with a swatch. He shuts his eyes at the sound of the scissors.*)

AGATHA: I can stay until eleven o'clock, sir, with your questions. Then they've said I am free to leave this place – forever.

FRY: Wouldn't you like to hang around and see if I can produce the person who tried to choke you last night?

AGATHA: No. At eleven o'clock, I leave. (*a tense pause*)

FRY: It all began – how?

AGATHA: (*picking out a boy doll – John Lennox – with red hair, short pants, a small pail in his hands*) Dr. Lennox's son, he started the whole thing. You see, I was allowed to walk about the grounds. Why, I was about to be released in a day or two. And I saw the young Lennox boy furtively running over the fourth fairway. He disappeared into the dusk. I followed him a few yards… then I turned back.

(*During this, we hear the light drumming of his footsteps, we see him look to see if he is observed – cocky little smile. For a moment both he and Agatha disappear into the dusk. With a twang, an emerald Aztec snake writhes in the air above hissing, fading.*)

(*tape: footsteps; twang; prolonged loud hiss, fading*)

FRY: (*from notebook*)
It says here the boy's father came into the breakfast room next morning and said:

LENNOX: (*spoken*)
Did any of you see my son, John, after dinner last night? (*pause*) D'you know that I found him, barely alive, at the bottom of the gravel pit this morning?

AGATHA: I saw John last night, Dr. Lennox. Yes. I was walking on the golf links after dinner – before we started our game of bridge. Mr. Small was smoking a cigarette on the front porch. (*polite smile, obliging*) It was around seven-thirty.

(*During this, John Lennox reappears and bits of the foregoing action are repeated.*)

(*tape: footsteps; hiss up and then fading*)

LENNOX: Thank you, Miss Lawson. You see, my son is quite sure that someone pushed him over the edge.

(*Music becomes wilder and more violent.*)

AGATHA: (*narrating*)
Soon, Dr. Lennox had the whole place in a turmoil with his questions. (*pause; music subsides*) I must say, though, when he made his morning rounds he paid a lot more attention to us, and a lot less to that huzzy Nurse Zimmerman.

(*Exit Lennox. Fry sits; Agatha remains standing. What are they thinking of? We know what they hear: tape and percussion suggest hospital sounds – clink of cutlery and glassware at meals, feet scurrying, a falling dish.*)

(*tape: clinking sounds*)

FRY: (*Observing her, he hums fragments of his opening ballad-tune; occasional flashes of more sinister words from the depths of his shallow mind.*)
…dusty windowpane
…a desperate windowsill
do do da da do
…wire mesh controls your will

(*tape: more clinking and pattering-feet sounds; a muffled scream*)

DUPONT: (*offstage*)
Tiens, ma fourchette… Décrasse-toi le crâne.

FRY: (*uneasily, to Agatha*)
Please continue.

AGATHA: (*controlled*)
On the Friday night, neither Mr. Keene nor Mrs. Parsons felt like bridge. Mr. Small suggested a walk, and I agreed. We

four were the only patients allowed to walk in the grounds alone.

(*Accompanied by Parsons, Keene and Small, she approaches an open door through which sunset light streams invitingly. Tim – hulking, ignorant-looking – blocks the doorway.*)

AGATHA: One of the male nurses, Tim, stood solidly in our path. He refused to move.

TIM: (*spoken, loud*)
Dr. Lennox's orders. There's nothin' I can do about it. He says yous – none of yous – is allowed out tonight.

(*He shuts the door on them. Exit Tim. The others retreat, but Small remains in view.*)

AGATHA: (*continuing her narration*)
So, I prepared myself for bed, went down the hall to clean my teeth, got a glass of water: always like to make myself as little nuisance as possible. I returned to my room.

(*During this, she pulls on a bell rope. Dr. Greer – a dishevelled, spectacled specimen – appears.*)

GREER: You ring the bell, Miss Lawson?

AGATHA: (*now slightly more agitated*)
Dr. Greer, when Tim told us we couldn't take our evening walk – I didn't like the look in Mister Small's eyes. We who have been here any length of time get to know the symptoms, Doctor. I don't like the look of him at all.

GREER: Small?

AGATHA: When he first came here, one of his symptoms was – his face twitched. It usually means he's going to do something quite desperate.

GREER: Gosh, I don't think you need worry about him, Miss Lawson, but thanks very much. We'll keep an eye on him. (*Small retreats.*) Everyone is going to bed just a little earlier tonight.

(*Exit Greer. A twilight sequence: the desk lamp glows in the curtained booth that represents Miss Jones's nursing station.)*

(tape: soft footsteps; the swish of a starched dress)

AGATHA: The usual noises of a hospital at night. Nurse Jones's uniform whispers as she walks down the hallway and returns to her alcove with her little desk lamp.

FRY: *(making notes)*

Nurse Jones...

hallway...

her alcove...
desk lamp...

AGATHA: *(to Fry)* Missus Dupont can't speak a word of French when she's in her right mind. Ten years I've known her, and she's spent six months of every year in Elmhurst here – speaking French.

DUPONT: *(hysterical vocalise)* Nous partirons pour l'Europe nous partirons pour l'Europe nous partirons partirons partirons pour l'Europe...

(Dupont points a finger at Agatha and screams. Miss Jones emerges from alcove.)

AGATHA: Stop that noise, my good woman.

JONES: What is the trouble, Madame?

DUPONT: C'est effrayant... effrayant... *(Exit, with Jones.)*

AGATHA: I left Miss Jones to cope with the poor soul. Why should she scream at me? I'm not so bad looking I frighten people on the street. At last I could lie down on my bed – my little trundle cot – without interruption.

(Laughs, yawns drowsily. Lies down on a vertical bed of the sort she can

Mme. Dupont

stick her head through. Musing –)

Perhaps that sort of person has a sight we more
normal people lack … as if Madame Dupont knew what was
going to happen that night.

*(But the music knows and hints at what now happens. Night lights.
Shadows.)*

*(tape: footsteps; rustling of paper; faint clock ticking, then tolling ten
times)*

AGATHA: Soft pad pad of   FRY: *(again making notes)*
    rubber-soled   pad pad
    shoes …

GREER: *(offstage)*
    Good night, Miss Jones.

JONES: *(in alcove)*
    Good night, Dr. Greer.

AGATHA: ... faint-rustling –
our charts, in the
night nurse's
hands. Closing
and locking of the
big door that
leads to the main
hall. Oh, silence.
A silence more
fearful than the
loudest noise.

FRY: pad pad pad...
patients' charts

big door...

(The music now skittles like a mouse. From it, and from screen images, we sense an unknown figure choking Miss Jones, abstracting her keys, scampering upstairs, unlocking Nurse Zimmerman's door. A flash of vile red-orange on the screen, and Zimmerman is stabbed with scissors. Then, scampering down: many little pauses to indicate that the unknown has had to elude the presence of hulking Tim at his watch.)

(tape: choking; clatter and louder clash of metal; laughing)

DUPONT: *(offstage)*
Nous partirons
pour l'Europe,
nous partirons
pour l'Europe,
nous partirons,
partirons,
partirons... aha,
aha, aha...
(laughing)

AGATHA: Miss Jones, Miss
Jones! Miss Jones,
should stop her or I
am going to
scream, and if I
scream they'll say
I'm not ready to
leave here yet, oh –
only two more
days, if ... if... if...

(Agatha gets out of bed. Narrating:)

AGATHA: I walked quietly down the hall. Paused at the lavatory door. Mrs. Parsons heard me and came out of her room.

PARSONS: What's ever the matter, Agatha? Agatha?

(Agatha twitches at the alcove curtain, drawing it slowly back. A life-size doll of Miss Jones topples from her chair.)

AGATHA: Miss Jones!

PARSONS: Agatha? Agatha?

AGATHA: Please go back to
      bed, Mrs.
      Parsons. I'll ring   PARSONS: I don't understand
      the bell and get   it ... Agatha?
      the intern.   Agatha?

(*Exit Parsons; but later she sneaks back to observe. Agatha walks to bell rope and pulls it carefully.*)

(*tape: bell*)

HOLMAN: (*entering*) Miss Lawson?

AGATHA: Dr. Holman. (*She motions to the body of Jones.*)

HOLMAN: My God, what has happened to Nurse Jones?

AGATHA: I was about to go to the lavatory when I found her like this. Madame Dupont's cries disturbed me. I wondered why on earth Miss Jones didn't go to her.

HOLMAN: My God...

AGATHA: So, I rang.

HOLMAN: My God, it's a good thing you did, Miss Lawson. She's barely alive. Turn the light on in Number Eight and then ... get Nurse Zimmerman. Here... take the keys. Lock the door after you. And – hurry!

(*During this, he gently lifts the Jones doll and takes it to Room Eight. After preparing it for him, Agatha holds up the keys and sings:*)

(*tape: Jangle of keys*)

AGATHA: Shall I run out and away?
      Freedom is a heady thing if you've been closely confined.
      Here I stand with all the keys to this whole place... Shall I
      run out and away?

      Down the avenue of trees,
      Waving poplars in the breeze,
      Clouds race by just overhead

I could touch them if I tried.
>Unlock that gate!
>I
Defy
>My
Fate!

Sun now casts my shadow
Not on floor, nor through a window
But on the green and springy ground
On which my footsteps sound
>Unlock those doors!
>Left
Foot
>Right
Foot
Left...

TIM: (*barring her way*)
>Hey, where do you think you're goin'?

AGATHA: Miss Jones has... met with an accident. She may be dying. Dr. Holman has given me his keys. I'm to fetch Nurse Zimmerman.

TIM: Who did her in? Yous?

AGATHA: How dare you?!

TIM: How do I know you dint do Holman in, too?

AGATHA: My good man: come with me to arouse Nurse Zimmerman... she of the famous red hair; then you shall know I am in earnest.

TIM: Well... okay, Agatha...

(*They walk to the nurses' wing. Agatha knocks on Zimmerman's door.*)

(*tape: knocking; echoes*)

TIM: Knock again. I should be back at my desk. Hey – here's the head nurse.

SCARTH: *(entering in d'eshabille)* What's the meaning of this, Tim?

TIM: Jones had an accident...

HOLMAN: *(entering at a run)*
What the devil, Miss Lawson! have you not raised Zimmerman yet? All hell's breaking loose downstairs.

SCARTH: And what is the meaning of this, Dr. Holman?

HOLMAN: Wha' – ?

SCARTH: Get Zimmerman while I put some clothes on. *(exit)*

AGATHA: Miss Zimmerman is a very sound sleeper, Doctor; or could it be she's not in her room?

(tape: further knocking and echoes)

HOLMAN: *(knocking on door)*
But she must be. She knows she's on call. Hello, Renée. Wake up. It's Peter. Unlock the door.

AGATHA: Oh – it wasn't locked.

HOLMAN: It wasn't locked? Oh – ?

(She pushes open the door; up above, red-orange hair.)

AGATHA: Miss Zimmerman lay in the glow of the pink twilight of her bedside lamp – her pretty throat cut from ear to ear.

(We see the image of the dead nurse, a carefully prepared waxworks.)

AGATHA: At that moment Miss Scarth, the head nurse, appeared by my shoulder buttoning up her uniform. I always say there's something indelicate about nurses. Buttoning up her uniform in front of us all – ! Ugh!

HOLMAN: Thank God you're back, Miss Scarth. Look after Miss Lawson, will you? – while I run downstairs and find Dr. Lennox. There's a murderer loose among us! *(exit)*

PARSONS: *(entering)*
What's the matter, what's ever the matter, Agatha?

SCARTH: Stop making a fuss, my dear. Come now, come now...

PARSONS: I don't understand it... *(continues whimpering softly)*

FRY: *(we are back in the interview)*
What was your reaction to the sight of Miss Zimmerman's body?

AGATHA: *(pause)*
Nothing. At first, nothing. What bothered me far more was the sight of Miss Scarth hovering over me still buttoning up her uniform.

FRY: Did that bother – a little thing like that – more than a dead body, the corpse of a highly esteemed nurse?

AGATHA: Yes. Miss Zimmerman was highly esteemed in certain quarters.

FRY: Go on, Agatha.

AGATHA: 'A little thing like that' – ! Mister Fry, how would you feel in my position if a man, a male nurse, came hovering over you still buttoning himself up?

FRY: What – what certain quarters was Miss Zimmerman esteemed in?

(From behind a curtained alcove in the vestibule comes the sound of a tumbling jardinière, which comes rolling out across the floor.)

(tape: light crash; vessel teetering)

(A shoe protrudes, then disappears at the bottom of the curtain. Fry goes to curtain, yanks it aside to reveal Dr. Lennox looking rather abashed.)

LENNOX: Fry, I really felt that... felt that...

FRY: Doctor Lennox, I know Miss Lawson is your patient and you have only her good health in mind, but the rules are no supervision, please, of my interviews unless I ask.

LENNOX: You don't know what you're doing to me. I have no opportunity to defend myself against –

FRY: *(leading him out)*
You've been through a good deal – your boy, these other attacks. Go back to your study; I'll see you when I'm through with Agatha here.

(*Returns from escorting Lennox out; takes up notebook again. Scene resumes.*)

FRY: What certain quarters was Miss Zimmerman esteemed in?

Dr. Lennox

(*Parsons has been whimpering and moaning under the foregoing, and now screams like a dormant volcano that suddenly realizes what it must do. Scarth slaps Parsons' face.*)

AGATHA: I'll tell you something that's been hushed up. (*The screaming stops.*) Miss Zimmerman had been having an affair with our head – Dr. Lennox. At the autopsy, they found she was three months pregnant.

TIM: God almighty, she's going to scream too!

(*tape: amplifying screams and slaps*)

(*She screams and Scarth slaps her face repeatedly. Blackout with music. Frisson!*)

(*Musical interlude covers costume change: Performer playing Agatha is now Scarth, and manipulates Agatha as a doll-puppet; we appear to get outside of Agatha's mind if she appears as a puppet in this scene.*)

(*Similarly, the performer playing Fry is now Hogan, and (later) manipulates Fry as a doll-puppet. The inmates of Elmhurst have been called together for questioning. Miss Scarth brings forward Madame Dupont.*)

SCARTH: Lieutenant Hogan, Madame Dupont.

HOGAN: Mrs. Dupont...

DUPONT: Je suis Madame; je ne suis pas 'Mrs.' – je suis Madame!

HOGAN: God, Miss Scarth, is everyone here nuts?

SCARTH: Lieutenant, we don't say things like that in front of the patients.

HOGAN: Well, there's been a murder, and – nuts or not – I'm going to find out who did it. Now who've we got? Let's see your charts.

SCARTH: (*showing him the charts*)
Mrs. Johnston. Mrs. Parsons. Miss Lawson. (*She goes from chart to puppets.*) Each an heiress to a fortune in her own right.

HOGAN: Johnston?

SCARTH: Restless last night. Moaning a great deal. Has to have continuous baths. (*Mrs. Parsons is thin, Mrs. Johnston a flapper gone to seed and chunkiness.*)

HOGAN: Parsons?

SCARTH: Came out into the hall just at the moment of my finding the body. Hysterical – made dreadful accusations.

HOGAN: Lawson?

SCARTH: Has the freedom of the house. May go wherever she pleases. In fact I've told her she may use the staff sitting room. Dr. Lennox says she may as well take her final exam tomorrow. Such a great help to me last night. Miss Lawson, Lieutenant, I might as well tell you, Miss Lawson is a lamb. When Parsons lost control, I said, 'You'd better get some sleep, Miss Lawson. Go to your room and I'll get you a sedative.'

HOGAN: What time was that, Miss Lawson?

AGATHA: I've no idea, Lieutenant. My room was dark; no luminous dial on my watch.

HOGAN: What woke you?

AGATHA: Madame Dupont with her 'Nous partirons pour l'Europe.'

HOGAN: You may go, Miss Lawson. (*But Agatha lingers in the background.*)

SCARTH: The male patients: Mr. Small and – Dr. John Lang.

HOGAN: A doctor a patient? By Heaven, he's holding a doll in his hand.

SCARTH: Never without it. Former head of this institution. He suffers from Folie Circulaire.

HOGAN: Circular Folly?

SCARTH: He gets well and performs brain operations – a genius. Then he collapses and asks for his Norah Wellings gypsy

Fry/Hogan

doll. Then he gets well again and performs operations of genius.

HOGAN: Jeez – he has a record number of escape attempts too. (*consulting chart*)

(*tape: whirling carousel*)

(*The doll-puppets move in a circle: crazy carousel.*)

SCARTH: On staff: Nurse Currie to replace Nurse Jones. Poor Jones – she's still unconscious.

HOGAN: Miss Currie. From our department, isn't she?

SCARTH: And she looks it too. You know, the patients are clever, Lieutenant. They'll catch on she's a policewoman unless she learns to be more loving.

HOGAN: But she's a fast worker. She'll ferret out the killer within twenty-four hours.

SCARTH: Nurse Maclean – just a novice. Rather nervous about what happened to Zimmerman.

HOGAN: (*noting*)
A novice, rather nervous...

SCARTH: Male nurses: Tim O'Connor...

HOGAN: O'Connor: big shoulders, big hands... The doctors?

SCARTH: Dr. Lennox, Dr. Greer, Intern Holman...

(*a sudden scream*)

SCARTH: It's Mrs. Johnston. She's developed a mania about someone looking in her window.

AGATHA: (*aside to audience*)
Why any man would look in her window was quite beyond me.

(*tape: a clock strikes the half hour. Whirling carousel again; A whiff of twilight sound and fade*)

(*Performer playing Scarth is now dressed again as Agatha. A 'crowd'*) *gathers. Small has turned his back to Hogan and will not listen to him. Murmur...)*

HOGAN: *(addressing them all)*
Now look here, you people. I'm going to get to the bottom of this if it's the last thing I do.

(Murmur...)

AGATHA: As I sat there, I felt I didn't want to leave Elmhurst after all. I thought of offering my services to Dr. Lennox. I could solve the murder quicker than this Lieutenant Hogan. I could ferret things out better than Miss Currie.

HOGAN: Hey, somebody! *(to Currie)* You, angel of mercy, get the old guy to turn around. He's not listening to me.

CURRIE: Come now, Mr. Small, there's a gentleman to see you. Turn your chair around and answer his questions.

(Small refuses.)

AGATHA: Miss Currie, let me talk to him. I know him quite well. I'm sure I can get him to turn around.

CURRIE: What makes you so sure?

AGATHA: Mr. Small. *(She whispers to him.)*

SMALL: *(feebly turning around)*
Well, well well well well. Who is this gentleman?

AGATHA: Now then, Lieutenant.

HOGAN: Now look here, all of you. Whoever murdered

Zimmerman must have (*strepitoso*) got into her room with Nurse Jones's keys, left the door unlocked and got back – got them back to Jones's pocket. (*Murmur...*) But how did he – or she – get past Tim at his station by the stairs?

TIM: Lieutenant, I was I was... had to go to the bathroom. (*laughter*)

(*tape: amplifying laughter*)

AGATHA: (*to audience*)
And the rest of the day passed with circular follies of this sort.

(*The assembly dissolves, carousel is quiet.*)

AGATHA: But after supper...

(*Pianist and Percussionist hold up a window and Tim leers through it at Johnston who screams every time he appears. He ducks back, he comes forward... Maclean and Currie attend Johnston.*)

(*tape: moaning and faint echoes of screams*)

MACLEAN: Tell me, Mrs. Johnston, what frightens you?

JOHNSTON: Someone looked in my window.

AGATHA: (*appearing, aside to audience*)
Why any man should look in her window was quite beyond me.

MACLEAN: Miss Lawson, how ever did you get Mr. Small to turn around this morning? That was remarkable.

AGATHA: I said, 'We're having ice cream for dinner, Mr. Small' – always works.

(*light glows on Small puppet briefly*)

MACLEAN: Perhaps then you can persuade Mrs. Johnston to tell us what she saw at her window.

AGATHA: Amy Johnston, what frightened you?

(*No reaction. Enter Greer.*)

CURRIE: I'm afraid your magic doesn't always work. Now, Mrs. Johnston, here's Miss Lawson, who may be leaving us quite soon. Won't you tell her what it was that frightened you?

(Johnston screams and points to window.)

AGATHA: Amy Johnston, stop that. We've had enough disturbance around here this last while. Tell me what frightened you – or take your pills and go to sleep.

JOHNSTON: Oh, Aggie, I did see a man's face. A horrible face rather like Tim's – leering at me.

GREER: Golly, I wonder if there was someone outside. Miss Currie, you put Mrs. Johnston to bed, and –

(Exeunt Maclean, Currie and Johnston.)

AGATHA: Shall we go outside and have a look, Dr. Greer? There might be telltale tracksteps under her window. Shall I put on my outdoor walking boots and help you?

GREER: I couldn't think of allowing you to do such a thing.

AGATHA: I'd be honoured if you would trust me. I like to feel I'm of assistance.

GREER: Golly, it's true – we're rather shorthanded. Holman has Small troubling him and – I don't mind telling you in strictest confidence, Miss Lawson – we're having a terrible time with Dr. John Lang.

AGATHA: What sort of trouble?

GREER: He's out in the grounds somewhere and we can't find his gypsy doll. It controls him, you may have gathered.

AGATHA: Doctor, have you informed Lieutenant Hogan about the missing Dr. Lang and about Mrs. Johnston's obsession with her 'voyeur'?

GREER: You think you saw someone?

AGATHA: There's a large bed of delphiniums there outside her window. I myself detected movement there. If we went out with a flashlight we could – there might be footprints in the flower bed.

(*During this sequence, she sits and puts on her stout walking boots. Like the scene with the sadistic surgeon in* Kings Row, *she robes herself for action – rain poncho, rain hat.*)

GREER: (*excited*)

Wait a sec, Agatha. I'll get a *couple* of flashlights – from the office. (*Exits.*)

AGATHA: (*calls after him*)

Why not *three* flashlights – and bring along Tim for protection?

(*Scene changes. Darkness descends. We are outside Mrs. Johnston's window. We see three flashlights, then two, raking the ground about the mysterious delphiniums.*)

GREER: Keep right with me, Miss Lawson. Tim, take the other side of the flower bed and keep your eyes open for footprints. If you see any, give us a yell – but not too loud. Nurse Maclean is in there with Mrs. Johnston; she's not used to it all yet.

AGATHA: It all – meaning such difficult patients?

GREER: Sorry, Miss Lawson. I never think of you as being a patient, nor difficult.

TIM: Whaddya wunt to look for tracks for?

AGATHA: Dr. Greer and I are investigating.

TIM: Okay, tootsie. Keep you britches on. Or I suppose you're still wearing them old-fashioned *drawers*. (*laughs*)

(*The flashlights make searching patterns. The delphiniums occasionally show up. One flashlight goes out, goes on, goes out. The music and projection screen know what is going to happen.*)

GREER: There was someone here! Golly, there are footprints, Miss Lawson and big ones too. They've been here for some time, proving you see that – Jove, I must apologize to Mrs. Johnston.

AGATHA: Is there anything more satisfying than finding out

one's guesses have been correct?

GREER: Hogan will love this. So far he's had so little to go on. *(pause)* Tim? *(pause)* There's his flashlight on the ground. Tim – come inside with us now.

AGATHA: Tim is so refractory, Doctor. How do you put up with –

GREER: Oh, Tim's all right, just a bit –

(Lights go on. We see a delphinium bed blazing with cheap shock blue and buzzing with bees, alive with earwigs.)

(tape: whirring, buzzing)

AGATHA: In the delphinium bushes we saw a large foot encased in a thick black shoe.

(Delphinium bed is whisked up to reveal the full-size figure of Tim, its head gruesomely pulped. Uproar: puppets moving all over the place. Screen a blue rectangle, followed by an aching yellow afterimage.)

(tape: conversational excitement)

AGATHA: Tim's head had been bashed in by one of the half stones that bordered the flower bed. The jagged edge of the stone had done awful things to his skull. Hogan said it took great brute strength to bash in his head, it was so thick.

(tape: whispers, fading…)

(The uproar fades. Barely visible in the shadows, Agatha and Amy Johnston talk in the latter's room.)

JOHNSTON: Oh, Aggie Lawson. Imagine that man trying to scare me and then helping you people discover his own foot-tracks – and then?!

AGATHA: Calm now, Mrs. Johnston.

JOHNSTON: *(pause)*
Did you hear about Nurse Jones, Aggie?

AGATHA: Mrs. Johnston, don't –

JOHNSTON: They found out at the autopsy-turvy: Miss Jones was about to have a baby.

Amy Johnston

AGATHA: Amy, surely you're mistaken. Nurse Jones is not dead but in a coma. Perhaps you mean – Nurse Zimmerman?

JOHNSTON: She was found dead in bed and she was about to have a baby.

AGATHA: What fellow was responsible for that?

JOHNSTON: They say – oh, this will be the end of Elmhurst Asylum for millionairesses – they say it's Dr. Greer.

AGATHA: *(aside, to audience)*
But I can't be sure that was what she said because just as her words became so interesting, Miss Scarth came along and made me leave and go back to my room.

(Scarth appears and escorts Agatha away. Scene shifts to the staff sitting-room. Hogan plots strategy, addressing a group of staff He holds up a jagged stone.)

HOGAN: Hell, no! She wouldn't be strong enough. Miss Lawson? She's sixty-one years old. She's five feet one-and-a-half; weight, a hundred pounds. I still can't get it. Tim was six feet two; this stone is heavy. No, Lawson is not strong enough.

AGATHA: *(appearing suddenly)*
May I enter a protest, sir? I don't mind vile accusations as to my being a murderer. But I do resent being called a weak little old lady.

HOGAN: You're not supposed to be here, Miss Lawson.

AGATHA: I alone am allowed to use the staff sitting-room, sir.

HOGAN: And you don't like being left out of the picture. So – you think you're strong enough, eh?

AGATHA: 'But definitely.'

HOGAN: Well, maybe this will put you *in* the picture – a simple test.

(He goes flat on the floor and commences doing pushups.)

AGATHA: What test is that?

HOGAN: Lie down on the floor and try to push yourself up with your arms. *(She does so.)* Keep your body stiff. Use your arms. *(Agatha fails the test.)*

Your arms aren't worth a hoot.

AGATHA: Does that mean... *(out of breath)* I'm not the murderer?

HOGAN: Afraid so, Miss Lawson.

AGATHA: Who *is* it then? Who is left?

HOGAN: Oh, it's Dr. Greer. Or Dr. Lang. Or–

AGATHA: Oh. Or Dr. Lennox. Why not Lennox?

HOGAN: Dr. Greer. It's Greer.

AGATHA: Why?

HOGAN: That I cannot reveal in mixed company, Miss Lawson.

AGATHA: *(narrating)*

They had a terrible time arresting Dr. Greer. The poor man fought them like a tiger.

(We see in silhouette the struggle with the Greer doll-puppet. All others watching, off he goes in a paddy wagon.)

(tape: siren, fading)

AGATHA: We all watched it from the front porch and the odd thing is – we all seemed the better for it. I felt sorry for the poor fellow. But we were better, calm, even happy.

(tape: a phrase of whistling)

AGATHA: Some of the male patients even started to whistle tunes. Wasn't there a country once where all the doctors went on strike and the death rate went dramatically down?

(Change of scene; caterpillar images on screen.)

AGATHA: *(narrating)*
Nurse Currie – that fuzzy-haired spy – was putting Madame Dupont to bed and I knew she would next move in on me.

CURRIE: Just lie down, Mrs. Dupont.

DUPONT: Mon frère est en Amérique.

CURRIE: Izzatso? Let me pull the covers a little higher; these late summer nights are chill.

DUPONT: Mais, nous irons à la campagne, mon frère et moi.

CURRIE: I'm sure that will be very nice – but get going, you little old bag lady.

DUPONT: Pardon? Pardon?

CURRIE: Oh, never mind, Mrs. Dupont. Just go to sleep like a good girl. *(moving towards Agatha)* And are you all right, Mrs. Lawson?

AGATHA: La clef avec laquelle on ouvre la porte…

CURRIE: Oh, no! Miss Lawson, please. Haven't I had enough?

AGATHA: I'm sorry, Miss Currie. Madame certainly is a handful, isn't she?

CURRIE: This whole set-up's a handful. I replaced Miss Jones after she went down. Who will replace me when I –

AGATHA: But the murderer's been caught. Surely there's nothing to fear.

CURRIE: The murderer caught? Why, Dr. Greer is no more the murderer than you are.

AGATHA: Why did Lt. Hogan arrest him, then?

CURRIE: Because he's a fat-headed big ape! Why on earth would Dr. Greer murder Tim?

AGATHA: I know that Dr. Greer didn't murder Tim. He wasn't out of my sight for a moment among the delphiniums. I told Lt. Hogan that.

CURRIE: You see how much your judgement is regarded, don't you? I mean – you're not discharged yet.

AGATHA: This is news to me, Nurse Currie. I came up before the board on Friday, passed the test with flying colours.

CURRIE: But since then – you're too upset, you're still sick.

AGATHA: Am I not soon to leave, then?

CURRIE: Most unlikely. More treatment, Miss Lawson.

AGATHA: But I was told –

CURRIE: Good night, Miss Lawson. I'll be just down the hall if you need me. (*Moves towards hallway.*)

AGATHA: Good night, Miss Currie. (*She retires for the night.*)

(*Currie stops in hallway, removes her shoe and rubs her foot. Dupont strolls by.*)

DUPONT: Mlle. Currie tire son soulier, hein? Mademoiselle, vous avez du mal au pied, hein?

(*Currie limps to the nursing station and draws the curtain. Dupont stares after her.*)

DUPONT: Avec ce soulier-là je vois que vous êtes trompée, et puis – parce que vous m'avez appelé une clochardette – les mains seront une ficelle pour votre gorge, hein? Ah –

(*Exits to her room. Agatha now gets out of bed.*)

AGATHA: Why does Miss Currie not stop that Dupont woman blathering on in parle-toi zig-zag et passe-partout? (*She disappears.*)

DUPONT: (*offstage*)
Ah – une ficelle pour votre gorge –

AGATHA: (*re-entering and moving along hallway*) Miss Currie? Why, there are her keys in the doorway. How careless of her. Any of us could get out. Miss Currie?

(*She pulls back the curtain. A body doll of Currie, full size, is slouched back in the chair.*)

AGATHA: Oh dear, those dark marks on her throat. One of us has murdered her. Ring the bell, the alarm bell. (*Screams as she does so.*)

(*tape: amplifying bell, screams, crescendo of babble*)

(*The doll-puppets suddenly are all there with Hogan.*)

AGATHA: (*to herself*)
Parsons? Lang?
Small? Dupont?

PARSONS: What's ever the matter, Agatha? Agatha?

HOGAN: Miss Lawson? What in God's name – ?

DUPONT: Nous partirons pour l'Europe.

AGATHA: Johnston is too stupid to have.

PARSONS:
I don't understand it, Agatha. Agatha, Agatha...

HOGAN: (*after examining body*)
She's been dead for at least half an hour.

DUPONT: Décrasse-toi le crâne!

PARSONS: Miss Jones, now Miss Currie...

AGATHA: (*regaining composure*) The keys are in the door, Lieutenant.

DUPONT: Mon frère est en Amérique.

HOGAN: Get out of my sight, Agatha! Go in and see if Mrs. Johnston is all right. She's the only patient not here.

PARSONS: Agatha, Agatha...

DUPONT: Nous partirons pour l'Europe, aha, aha...

AGATHA: (*Goes to Johnston's door. Screams.*) Oh – ! Lt. Hogan, Mrs. Johnston's bed is empty!

HOGAN: Sgt. Coombe, get your men and search this damned place from cellar to garret. Do the servants' quarters. Tear the place apart, but find Mrs. Johnston! And you – ! (*to Agatha*) Get back to your room and stay there!

AGATHA: M-m-m –

HOGAN: Don't say anything. Just go to your room.

(*Agatha shuts herself in her room and goes to bed.*)

COOMBE: Lt. Hogan, sir, the Johnston woman is on the edge of the gravel pit. We can't get her to come down.

(*A shift of doll-puppets and lighting suggests a new locale.*)
(*Way high up on a stepladder we see Johnston.*)

COOMBE: Sir, we can't get her to – If we take a step towards her, she moves back. If we rush her, she'll go over.

HOGAN: Miss Maclean, help me get Mrs. Johnston off of that cliff.

(*tape: teeter-totter; background babble*)

MACLEAN: No sirree. I have Parsons and Dupont to deal with.

HOGAN: Where do you angels of mercy hide when you're needed? D'you suppose I could find another nurse around this dump?

MACLEAN: Not if you let us nurses get killed night after night. Ask Agatha Lawson. She knows Johnston well. She got Mr. Small to turn around. The other nurses need their sleep.

(*Crowd reacts as Mrs. Johnston almost topples.*)

(*tape: increased babble, fading*)

HOGAN: (*Knocks on Agatha's door.*)
Agatha, Agatha, I need you to help us out here. (*silence*) Look, I'm sorry if I offended, but things have changed. We can't get Mrs. Johnston to move away from the edge of the gravel pit. (*silence*)

MACLEAN: Dr. Holman. Promise her something. Get her to come out.

HOLMAN: Miss Lawson, you may leave tomorrow if you will help us with the suspect tonight.

(*Agatha emerges with raincoat and umbrella. She marches over the fields to the cliff.*)

AGATHA: Amy, can you see me down here – amid this sea of flashlights? Hello – well, hello.

JOHNSTON: Aggie? Aggie Lawson, is that you?

AGATHA: Fancy meeting you here, Mrs. Johnston.

JOHNSTON: Land's sake, Agatha! –

AGATHA: Brr! It's cold. Let's go back to the house. I'm nearly frozen.

JOHNSTON: So am I.

AGATHA: Then come on down and get warmed up.

(*Johnston comes down from the 'cliff.'*)

(*tape: crowd sighs.*)

HOGAN: Nice going, Miss Lawson.

AGATHA: So Dr. Greer's not the killer then?

HOGAN: Looks it's a patient.

AGATHA: I can hardly believe it of any of them. They all play a nice game of bridge. Except for Mrs. Johnston.

HOGAN: Don't say such things, Agatha. Go back to bed – and thanks.

(Agatha retires.)

JOHNSTON: But I didn't want to get out. It's too cold. 'Don't you push me out,' I said.

HOGAN: Mrs. Johnston, who was it? Who forced you to go outside?

JOHNSTON: Why should we all be cooped up here like a flock of hens?

HOGAN: (raising his fist)
You lunatic, I warn you – ! Try to recollect: who was it? Who shoved you outside to be their patsy?

(Johnston collapses, sobbing and is led away by Maclean. Hogan retreats, angry. Fry enters with a bouquet of flowers.)

FRY: Not that way, Hogan. Not that way.

(Light fades on the flowers.)

AGATHA: Dr. Holman heard my heart and gave me a sedative. I reckon I slept. But, despite the sedation, I awoke with the – strangest feeling of terror. Ah!

(tape: soft, restless commotion)

(In the dimly lit bedroom we see a figure searching in bureau drawers, then under bed (collision with chamberpot), padding of feet, a figure looming against the window.)

AGATHA: I longed to move, to turn over and face the thing – even if it meant facing a madman, a killer, the killer who'd been stalking the halls of Elmhurst, strangling and slashing – Ah! Unh! (gagging)

(Through music and projections we dimly perceive a struggle, preluded by mysterious movements around the bedroom by an unknown figure. It wraps hands around Agatha's throat.

PIANIST: *(falsetto)* Répondez à ma question!

(Descent into unconsciousness, then slow re-awakening. Maclean and Holman work at reviving Agatha.)

HOLMAN: Come on, Miss Lawson. Fight!

MACLEAN: Come on, Miss Lawson.

HOLMAN: You've been asleep all morning now. Time to wake up. Come on. Time to wake up.	MACLEAN: Come on. See the pretty flowers on your bureau? Who could've brought them, I wonder? Such pretty flowers.

(Agatha sighs. Enter Hogan.)

HOLMAN AND MACLEAN: Good girl. Keep on trying, keep on trying. She's coming round.

HOGAN: Someone damned clever is having a lot of fun, at my expense!

AGATHA: *(croakily)*
I'll help you find that person. They came and searched my room, tried to choke me.

HOGAN: Did they say anything?

AGATHA: 'Répondez à ma question.'

HOGAN: Miss Lawson, I owe you an apology. I've had doubts about you.

AGATHA: About me?

HOGAN: Somehow you've muscled in on all these murders: Zimmerman, O'Connor, Miss Jones (she's recovering, but she still can't remember how it happened) – and now Miss

Currie.

AGATHA: I was there each and every time, Lieutenant.

HOGAN: But you didn't do them?

AGATHA: No – and I didn't choke myself either.

HOGAN: In fact I know that. Someone wants to do you in, because you know too much. Someone has been just as close to each murder as you have and you've seen him – or her.

AGATHA: Why would they want to choke me? And why search my room?

HOGAN: Whether you know it or not, you know who the murderer is. Think, Miss Lawson. Think.

(Interlude covering costume change. A clock strikes eleven. We return to the first scene's setting.)

FRY: *(now live, not a puppet; looking up from his notes)* And what do you think, Agatha?

AGATHA: You know, Mr. Fry, I've helped you all I can. When I saw the bruises on Miss Currie, I thought: this looks like one of us – a patient. And – it's someone doing it who doesn't know they're doing it.

FRY: How could that be, Agatha?

AGATHA: La Sonnambula – ever hear of it? Somnambulism, or self-mesmerism? *(starts slow exit through audience)* But I'm no detective, Mr. Fry. I'm going to leave Elmhurst forever. I don't want to be like the others.

(She continues into the audience as if proceeding outside the rest home. She exults in the freedom, clouds (projection) racing above her through the sky, a line of poplars waving in an avenue before her that leads to the gatehouse with its last barrier to freedom. Fry disappears for a second, then returns with the flowers.)

FRY: Agatha, wait! You've forgotten the flowers I gave you.

(He tries to lure her back with flowers.)

AGATHA: (*turning back*)
>   You gave me those flowers? (*pause*) It's been a long time since anyone has given me them.

FRY: Don't you see? I do care about you.

AGATHA: (*unsure*)
>   Yes, I see. Well, then, Mr. Fry, what?

FRY: Stay one more night!

AGATHA: Stay one more night? All because of a bunch of flowers?

FRY: We'll find out who choked you.

AGATHA: No. Nosiree! It's what mother used to say: 'They're just after your money, Agatha.' I'm going to walk home.

FRY: Aren't you going to take a cab – or a train?

AGATHA: Nonsense. I'll be a gypsy! (*resumes slow exit*)

FRY: (*calls after her*)
>   All right, but we may not let you back in.

AGATHA: Down the avenue of trees,
>   Waving poplars in the breeze...

FRY: Safe home then – and farewell.

(*She is out of sight. Fry muses at her retreating figure, goes to a phone.*)

(*tape: phone line crackles*)

FRY: Hogan? Detective Fry. Hogan, she's just coming down the drive now. (*pause*) No, let her go. (*pause*) She's intent on walking to her sister's house – sixty miles. I know the weather's not good, but I say let her try. She'll come back. (*pause*) Because she loves me.

(*tape: louder phone static – Hogan's raucous reaction.*)

(*Fry hangs up, exits.*)

(*Lights blink on and off.*)

PIANIST, PERCUSSIONIST: (*as chorus*)

'A thunderstorm shook Elmhurst as if it were a rat.'

(*tape: wind, a few thunderclaps*)

FRY: (*appears in hospital corridor with Krug*)
Miss Krug? Remember: wait till Lawson's asleep before you disturb her.

(*The storm rages. Stage darkens.*)

FRY: (*to Percussionist*)
I want you to take this luminous paint and put the numbers on the patients' doors, so Mrs. Johnston will see them no matter how dark it is.

(*tape: storm gradually subsiding; a large door opening and closing; whimpering*)

(*The thunderstorm has settled into a steady downpour. We hear but do not see Agatha return exhausted and battered. She is crying. She is put to bed. Fleeting glimpses in dim light. Then the room numbers glow in the dark.*)

KRUG: Are you asleep, Miss Lawson?

AGATHA: (*groggy and flailing, as if coming out of a nightmare*) How could I be, with you in here!

KRUG: Quiet! Listen, I'm your new nurse, Miss Krug. We must be quiet now to see if we can catch –
(*a struggle*)

AGATHA: Who is it?

KRUG: Are you nuts? What's the big idea?

AGATHA: (*still flailing*) Who is it – ?

KRUG: (*rubbing her throat*)
You pack quite a wallop for a frail-looking old dame. Remember what happened last night? Well, they're liable to come back.

AGATHA: I thought Nurse Maclean confessed.

KRUG: Lying. She lied to us.

AGATHA: So it's not Maclean?

KRUG: Keep quiet! – and we'll see who it really is.

AGATHA: Thank you, I'm quite able to take care of myself.

KRUG: You're telling me.

AGATHA: Look, Miss Krug, I'm sorry if –

KRUG: Shuddup!

AGATHA: In the silence, I could smell her hair.

(*Johnston stands in the hallway beside Fry. She has numbered doors to patients' rooms to choose from.*)

FRY: Mrs. Johnston, I want you to go to the door of the patient, the fellow patient, who last night woke you up and pushed you onto the verandah and then locked the door behind you. (*She re-enters her own room.*) No, no, Mrs. Johnston. That's your room. You didn't push yourself out onto the verandah, did you?

JOHNSTON: Can I try again, sweetie? There's no one I know in that room.

(*tape: footsteps echoing*)

AGATHA: I heard them pause at Mme. Dupont's door. Then the steps approached – mine. The knob turned slowly and silently... Oh, that nurse, I could not escape her. The smell of her hair!

(*Krug puts a hand over Agatha's mouth to shut her up.*)

JOHNSTON: (*turning on pink bedroom light*)
Are you awake, Agatha? (*pause*) There's something I've been meaning to ask you all day, but I couldn't find you. pause Aggie, what had you in mind when you got me up last night and made me go out on the grounds? You said I'd find supper out there, but – was it a practical joke, dear?

(*Lights all up. Fry plus a great many doll-puppets look down at Agatha on her bed.*)

FRY: Agatha, it's all right. You've helped solve the case. We just wanted to hear what Mrs. Johnston had to say to you. It was

at this time last night that Nurse Currie was choked by –
someone who never knew she was doing such hideous and
unnatural deeds.

AGATHA: So – is this your experiment? May I now leave this
place as you promised me?

FRY: You will now leave this place, yes –

FRY, KRUG, PIANIST, PERCUSSIONIST: (*as chorus*) – for the Asylum
for the Criminally Insane.

AGATHA: Don't be ridiculous. You might tell me how that
wretched Johnston woman managed to murder three peo-
ple. Amy, I no more told you to find your supper in the grav-
el pit than a cat needs sand fleas.

FRY: Agatha, you've got what it takes.

HOGAN: (*as puppet; just putting two and two together*)
I wouldn't a believed it, Fry. I guess I've got to hand it to
you. It takes a nut to catch a nut.

FRY: You're a cool one, Agatha. We're fellow artists. We told you
you knew who the murderer was, didn't we?

AGATHA: (*roaring*)
Well, I may know, sir, but perhaps you'd spell it out for me.
Seems I'm condemned by the most unreliable bridge play-
er I ever knew. Amy, did I push you onto the verandah last
night?

JOHNSTON: (*terrified by Agatha's stare*)
No.

AGATHA: We're in a book, a detective story. It's a dream I've
often had. I'm trapped in a book I'm writing. I wander from
cover to cover, I try to crawl up the reader's arms, her eyes;
the covers close in on me. Here it is: you're all in this book.
(*Holds up a large book.*)

FRY: First time I've heard that one. Give me the book.

(*He shows it to the others. We see that it is a blank. Pause as Agatha exam-
ines the book.*)

Jean Stilwell (Agatha), centre, in the 1989 première at the Guelph Spring Festival. The doll puppets were by Anna Wagner-Ott.

AGATHA: You've washed away the print – it was there just a minute ago. Ah! the blood, the blood! Ah! horror, horror, horror!

(*She now realizes she is the killer and stumbles down howling, then suddenly recovering, sullen, sulking, then flashing from modality to modality as the visual symbols of her mental states come thunderously on.*)

AGATHA: It all started (*laughs*) with a boy and a garter snake.

(*Taking over the production, she shoves Pianist off bench and starts to accompany herself.*)

AGATHA: Let me play that piano. And you, detective, get on those drums. Fry does so. Ah, Dr. Lennox, at last you've come to tell us a thing or two.

(*Menacing sound; he will shortly be her last victim.*)

AGATHA: While I sat sewing in the garden, the Lennox boy dropped a little snake onto
the bench beside me...

Twas then and there Miss Lawson
Decided that young scamp

Did need a lesson taught to him
At the gravel pit's high ramp.
(She comes striding towards us, pushing Pianist back to the piano.)

I pushed him down, 'twas rather fun
His mistake to correct,
And then more situations noted
That needed some improvement!

Behaving very foolishly
With you, Dr. Lennox!
Nurse Zimmerman, ah! he so well
Remembers her red locks.

(Lennox runs out in anguish, followed by Fry but not until it is too late, so mesmerizing is Agatha – purposely so, her enemy doing what she wants him to.)

Miss Jones at the desk had the keys
Her pretty back was to me;
Choked her and got what I wanted –
To Zimmerman – entry!

Coming back from rectification
Of this young maid misled,
I put the keys back in the pocket
Of Miss Jones who's still not dead.

Tim's turn next for insulting me,
You delphinium skulker;
Turned off my flashlight, jagged stone –
I, of rudeness revenger.

Now everything should have been
Much better at Elmhurst
Save for police spy, Miss Currie,
Making it so much worse!

On the floor of this hall she knelt,
Her shoe off, rubbing a corn;
Hit her with the shoe, her own shoe!
Choked her till life was gone.

I needed a stooge – Amy Johnston,

> She maundered near the doorway;
> Amy, I said, let us go out,
> For dinner on the fairway.

(A musical interruption as Lennox dies. Fry runs off.)

> But now there's one thing more to do
> For Elmhurst's mental health,
> And that's to tumble from his throne
> Our head jailer himself.

> So much impressed has been Lennox
> Of late by his own incompetence
> That some seconds ago he left
> This room, he walked thence

> Through the lobby and up the stairs
> To his quiet study cell
> At whose desk he found the means
> To do one thing well.

(tape: scurrying running feet)

(Fry dashes upstairs to Lennox's study, opens door.)

AGATHA: Dr. Lennox, as you lie face down at that desk of yours heaped with our charts, about your recent ways what are you thinking now?

(Fry's footsteps coming downstairs more slowly and towards us.)

FRY: Agatha, you've achieved your masterpiece – death by word, so much more difficult than mere death by deed. Dr. Lennox has just taken his own life. I found this note on his desk; the ink is still wet…

LENNOX: *(voice pre-recorded?)*
> By my misconduct with Renée Zimmerman, I see now that like a domino I upset this patient so deeply that it needed only the further innocent mischief of my child to undo all the work my institution had accomplished with Agatha Lawson. Why should I, how can I, go on with you, every one of you, knowing what she told you, what I knew and should have known?

AGATHA: So – (*pause*) I guess I must have done all these things, but – it's strange – I still don't feel that I did.

FRY: (*off*)
Sunlight slides across the floor...

AGATHA: It's not like me, is it?

(*Light fades on her in tableau. Enter Fry. Exit Percussionist.*)

FRY: After it was all over and Agatha left Elmhurst for the Asylum for the Criminally Insane, I used to visit her there.

(*Lights up. We move to the Asylum. Agatha is typing.*)

FRY: Her research at Elmhurst was complete and she sat at the typewriter we gave her and wrote the story you have just heard.

(*tape: typing*)

(*He gives a bouquet to a red-haired Nurse who places it in a vase nearby. Exit Fry. Nurse walks out, but remains dimly seen in background, disturbing us with memories of – Nurse Zimmerman?*)

AGATHA: That nurse reminds me of – (*Exit Pianist.*) The only way you knew it was Easter Sunday at Elmhurst was that on that day they served roast lamb.

(*tape: typing continues in fade-out*)

The Sharon Temple in a nineteeth-century photo…

Serinette

… and in a colour photo taken in the fall of 2002.

Serinette

Opera in two acts

Libretto, James Reaney   Music, Harry Somers

First performance, Sharon Temple, Sharon, Ontario, 7 July 1990.

Singers:
Kristine Anderson, Lynn Blaser, Benjamin Butterfield, Jeffrey Carl, André Clouthier, Leslie Fagan, John Fanning, Carol Ann Feldstein, Dennis Giesbrecht, Aline Kutan, Brian McIntosh, Erik Oland, Jackalyn Pipher, Laura Pudwell

Victor Feldbrill *conductor*
Keith Turnbull *director*

Concert revival, St. James' Cathedral, Toronto, 31 May 2001.

Singers: Mehgan Atchison, John Avey, Michael Colvin, Alain Coulombe, Sally Dibblee, Doug MacNaughton, Allyson McHardy, Lambroula Maria Pappas, David Pomeroy, Marcia Swanson

Victor Feldbrill *conductor*

Main characters, in order of appearance:

Act One
Major-domo *baritone*
Colonel Molyneux *bass*
Samuel Jarvis Sr. *bass*
Padre *baritone*
Samuel Jarvis Jr. *tenor*
Colin Jarvis *tenor*
Lady One *soprano*
Ann Smith *soprano*
Mrs. Jarvis *mezzo-soprano*
Lady Two *mezzo-soprano*
Bird girl *soprano*
Three Quaker farmers
Three Maids
Choirmaster *baritone*
Ridout *baritone*

Act Two
David Willson *baritone*
Treasurer *baritone*
Mary Stogdill *mezzo-soprano*
Young girl *soprano*
Farmer *bass*
Farm wife *mezzo-soprano*
Reverend Trueblood *baritone*

Orchestra:
Flute, oboe, clarinet, bassoon, horn, trumpet, trombone, percussion, piano, violin, viola, cello

Act One
    Scene One, Bivouac – Scene Two, Dinner at Hazelburn, York, Upper Canada – Scene Three, The bird box – Scene Four, Parchment – Scene Five, On the piazza – Scene Six, Pagan darkness – Scene Seven, The brothers – Scene Eight, A musical evening.

Act Two
    Scene One, Almsgiving Day at Sharon – Scene Two, The penny – Scene Three, The widow's store – Scene Four, Monday night singing school, and variations – Scene Five, Barrel organ – In David Willson's study – Scene Six, Run-through – Scene Seven, Cabbages – Scene Eight, Interrupted ceremony – Scene Nine, Farewell to Sharon – naked and beautiful – Scene Ten, The serinette – Scene Eleven, 'My own song.'

SERINETTE
ACT ONE

SCENE ONE
BIVOUAC

(*Some distance from the Sharon Temple, the entire cast of performers, both musical and vocal, start marching towards the west door. They march to a spirited piece of Doric carnivore music in the spirit of the Redcoat suicide advances of the era. As the march ends, a Major-domo standing in front of the west door says:*)

MAJOR-DOMO: Regiment Nineteenth of the Centre – Halt! Attenshun! Colonel Molyneux will speak to you. Sir! (*Saluting as the colonel comes forward to mount a box provided for him by two privates.*)

COLONEL: At ease! Officers and Men of the brave nineteenth. Tomorrow, but thirty miles away from here, from this old barn, tomorrow we will disband on the common of York and say farewell to each other after two years of bloody combat defending our frontiers against the American foe. As I recall, it was at this very barn here, where we shall bivouac this evening, that we turned the Yankees back and chased them through the villages and towns they had destroyed until – why, glorious moment –

ALL: We invaded their territory and burnt down Buffalo.

COLONEL: So the war is over, but remember, men – keep those swords sharp. Do not let them rust in the scabbard. Three cheers for King and Country! Quartermaster – have the barn made ready.

(*As the quartermaster opens the doors of the Temple, the cast cheers.*)

ALL: Huzzah! For King and Country!
Huzzah! For King and Country!
Huzzah! For King and Country!

(*Then, as bugler blows reveille and drummer drums, the company files into the 'barn.' So does the audience. Inside, the musicians have already started playing a dinner-party divertimento to cover the audience hum and keep up the feeling of 'we're all in a play.'*)

SCENE TWO

DINNER AT HAZELBURN, YORK, UPPER CANADA

(Two evenings later at the Jarvises' house, Hazelburn, on Queen Street, York. Mr. and Mrs. Jarvis are honouring their two sons' return from the wars with a dinner for their friends. Represent table with, simply, a held cloth, ladies already withdrawn. Among the men present: Samuel Jarvis Sr., Samuel Jarvis Jr., Colin Jarvis, other gentlemen. The two sons face their father and the others across the cloth with their backs to us. In the other playing area, the ladies are gathered around Mrs. Jarvis and a birdcage swathed in a white cloth, all dimly lit so as not to distract from the after-dinner scene.)

JARVIS SR.: Since, gentlemen, I became Provincial Secretary, many years ago, I have not experienced a happier day perhaps than yesterday when my son, Samuel Jarvis Junior, returned triumphant from our frontiers. Padre, put that into your Latin for a toast to the lad.

PADRE: *(clearing throat)* Samuel Jarvis Junior – Omnipotens, Victor Redens!

ALL: *(raising their glasses)* Samuel Jarvis Junior – Samuel Jarvis Junior – Omnipotens, Victor Redens!

(They strike the table for a speech.)

SAM JR.: My dear pater, dear friends, my brother Colin – here beside me. Well, as I guess you know, I am far better at battle than prattle. Always – so I can but suggest another toast – to my young brother here beside me – Colin Jarvis. A returned warrior of sorts as well.

JARVIS SR.: Warrior? Nay, Samuel, Colin was but the drummer boy in your regiment. Doubt very much whether he's blooded yet.

(Colin dives under the table in embarrassment and has to be fished up by his brother.)

SAM JR.: Out of that, you cub. Up here and tell us about yourself. Worth a try; come on, Colin!

COLIN: I drummed for them marching
I drummed for them fighting
And bugled there too
Helped the regimental cook

ALL: (*laughing*) 'Helped the regimental cook'

COLIN: Helped find the wounded
Helped the surgeon deal with them
Helped make bandages and nurse
Helped bury the fallen
Helped wash their corpses
Helped clean out latrines.

(*He hangs his head.*)

REACTION: (*laughter, applause, bravos*)

JARVIS SR.: And all that, although you did not fight, lad, surely deserves a toast of sorts. Padre!

PADRE: (*clearing his throat*) Colin Jarvis Junissimus –
succurens coquere
succurens pulsare tympanum
succurens vivos et mortuos
purgator latrinorum
Ave! Salve! Puer!

ALL: Colin Jarvis Junissimus
Ave! Salve! Puer!

SAM JR.: Here, you aren't going to crawl under the table again. Stay here and reply to – a longer toast than I got!

COLIN: No, no. I can't.

JARVIS SR.: Leave him be, Sam. He'll play for the dancing instead.

SAM JR.: Very well, Colin. We'll let you off, but we'll make a killer of you yet come the next war, brother.

COLIN: Never.

JARVIS SR.: First of all we shall make him, starting tomorrow, a junior clerk in my office. But to more interesting matters. Gentlemen, shall we join the ladies?

SCENE THREE

THE BIRD BOX

LADY ONE: A serinette, Mrs. Jarvis?

MRS. JARVIS: A serinette, Mrs. Robinson. Five years ago, I ordered it from Paris. Yesterday it arrived here and I find that you turn this handle and out comes the tune of an aria.

(*After a pause, a series of miniature tootles skims through the fretwork: glissades of a faraway aria.*)

(*The ladies react, the gentlemen enter.*)

JARVIS SR.: Mrs. Jarvis, ladies. Is it to be a musical evening? Colin, off to the instrument. Take Miss Smith with you. It seems to me that in antebellum days I recall you played duets with her.

(*Colin and Ann Smith actually get a good start at a minuet before … *)

JARVIS SR.: What's this? Can't make out the tune.

MRS. JARVIS: Now, Mr. Jarvis.

JARVIS SR.: New fangled stuff.

MRS. JARVIS: Oh, S.J.

MRS. JARVIS: Mr. Jarvis, don't let them start dancing. Quiet! I was about to show the ladies how this small barrel organ – the serinette you gave me, remember? – has taught our wild finch over there in that cage to sing Rossini. Sam Junior – take that sheet off that cage. Shhh!

(*With great authority, Sam Jr. starts pulling the cover off the cage. The serinette begins to play, but its music goes wild as Sam inadvertently opens the door of the cage and the Bird Girl escapes. From being a bunch of voyeurs around a bird prison, the cast fan out to catch that bird! Improvise*) *or compose chase music here. Colin and Ann do not take part in the chase. Eventually, Sam Jr. catches the bird and she is brutally shoved back into her prison and her cage is covered. As before, Sam Jr. ceremoniously pulls off the cover and as he does so, a singer in yellow dances in and repeats vocally the Rossini aria. Applause. Cover restored. Dancer off.)*

LADY TWO: What else can it sing, Mrs. Jarvis?

MRS. JARVIS: A month ago, that bird could not sing a thing worth listening to.

LADY ONE: Oh, play another one, Mrs. Jarvis. Pray do. How many do you have on each barrel? Of this bird box?

MRS. JARVIS: Two per barrel and we got twelve barrels! This is 'O cessate di piagarmi, toglietemi la vita ancor.' Hush!

(As the Lilliputian music sounds, the men retreat a bit.)

JARVIS SR.: Well, padre, it gives my old woman something to do.

PADRE: And when the bird hears this pretty tune?

COLIN: It will sing exactly what it has heard, sir.

SAM JR.: Opera. Pater, ain't that why our ancestors left them old countries in Europe?

(Serinette music, possibly bird's reply, under. Time passes – rusty bells of a colonial town, street traffic until) ...

SCENE FOUR
PARCHMENT

(Three Quaker Farmers and Jarvis Sr. in his office.)

JARVIS SR.: Gentlemen, can I be of any assistance to you?

FARMER ONE: Mr. Secretary Jarvis – we have come again about the deeds to our land. We want the deeds to our land.

JARVIS SR.: Names?

FARMER ONE: Hezekiah Titus.

FARMER TWO: Ezra Flummerfilt.

FARMER THREE: Methusaleh Chapman.

JARVIS SR.: Ah yes, good Quaker yeomen. Messrs. Titus, Flummerfilt and Master Chapman – I regret to say that the situation remains as before two years ago. Here in Upper Canada we have run out of supplies of parchment. Until some more arrives from Great Britain, we cannot here make out your deeds. Good morning, gentlemen.

(Just as they reluctantly leave, Colin emerges from the back of his father's office with an armful of parchment.)

COLIN: Father, isn't this parchment?

JARVIS SR.: *(pause)* Yes, Colin. But it is not the sort of parchment out of which we make deeds for Quaker yeomen who won't fight for their country.

COLIN: *(pause)* And when, father, does that sort of parchment arrive?

JARVIS SR.: Parchment for Quakers shall come in – *(yawn)* another two years. Colin, our policy is to make them wait for it.

(The lights fade slowly on Colin's face and his armful of parchment.)

SCENE FIVE
ON THE PIAZZA

(We hear the sounds of the serinette, then the maidservants at Hazelburn reporting to Mrs. Jarvis on their morning activities.)

MAID ONE: Mistress Jarvis, I have made both the young gentlemen's beds. Mr. Jarvis Junior's was not slept in, but I made it up anyhow and found under his pillow the following book.

MRS. JARVIS: *(setting down the serinette)* Give it here, Kitty. Ah – *The Complete Handbook to Duelling with Sabre, Pistol, Club Etc.* And what, Brown, have you found?

MAID TWO: Under his mattress, Master Colin has concealed this pamphlet, Mistress Jarvis.

MRS. JARVIS: *The Rights of Christ, according to the principles and doctrines of the Children of Peace.* (*pause*) Could be a very dangerous little document. (*pocketing it*) Hill – ?

MAID THREE: Oh, madam, there's a dead drunk man lying face down on the piazza – I couldn't finish sweeping up because of him.

(*In the other playing area* (*lately the Provincial Secretary's office*) *we see Sam Jr. lying on the floor, one arm bandaged. Raising himself.*)

SAM JR.: Not dead drunk, you fool. Do you not recognize the heir to your master's house – that stately mansion of Hazelburn – from the back? If I fall down on my parents' own piazza from loss of blood, do I have to fall face up before any of you jades will attend to me?

MRS. JARVIS: Loss of blood!

(*The women scurry down to the piazza.*)

MRS. JARVIS: What's this pickle you've got yourself and us into now, Sam?

(*The maids help him to a chaise longue.*)

SAM JR.: Brandy! Why, don't you know? Everyone in town must but my own mother and father. I was challenged to a duel at six o'clock this morning and I've been winged in the arm by my opponent. At last!

(*As a maid brings him brandy.*)

MRS. JARVIS: Get upstairs. I want to take a look at that arm. How'd you like to lose it?

SAM JR.: Mother, I can't understand how I missed him.

MRS. JARVIS: Surely, the whole point of a duel is to hit them before they hit you.

SAM JR.: Mother, it all started late last night at Roche's Hotel...

(*As the ladies help him off, we switch focus to a choir rehearsal at St. James' Cathedral which Colin attends.*)

SCENE SIX
PAGAN DARKNESS

CHOIRMASTER: Have you all your parts? Latecomers shall be
fined and –

(*Choir sight-reading under difficulties – the windows in the church are
very narrow though numerous. There is barely enough light.*)

CHOIR: O'er the realms of Pagan darkness
Let the eye of pity gaze.
See the kindreds of the people
Lost in sin's bewildering maze,
Darkness brooding
On the face of all the earth.

CHOIRMASTER: Why are some of you lighting those ridiculous
candles?

COLIN: Sir, there isn't enough light in this church to read our
parts by.

CHOIRMASTER: But the sun is still high in the sky on a bright
midsummer evening.

RIDOUT: I know, sir, but the windows are so narrow.

CHOIRMASTER: Have you not heard of a dim, religious light?
Put those candles out and squint your eyes.
We will have no candles in St. James'.

CHOIR: Light of them that sit in darkness,
Rise and shine, Thy blessings bring;
Light to lighten all the gentiles,
Rise with healing in Thy wing;
To Thy brightness
Let all kings and nations come.

May the heathen, now adoring
Idol-gods of wood and stone,
Come and worshipping before Him
Serve the living God alone:
Let Thy glory
Fill the earth as floods the sea.

CHOIRMASTER: Matins at seven this Sunday. No loitering in the chancel, please. I wish to lock everything up and be out of here before curfew bell.

ALL: Curfew bell. Let us go home and cover our fires!

RIDOUT: When do we come to your house on Saturday night?

COLIN: As early as seven – in the cellar so as not to disturb my parents. Bring all your musical instruments. I have new music just arrived from Montreal, Vienna, Paris. I extracted a seed cake, the promise of one from our cook with mother's permission and my father says we can have a certain amount of small beer with ginger beer for the ladies.

(*A cheer*)

CHOIR SINGER 1: Who's chaperoning the ladies?

COLIN: One of their governesses.

CHOIR SINGER 2: Which one of their governesses?

COLIN: Mademoiselle Bobinette.

(*Groans*)

CHOIR SINGER 2: Anybody else?

COLIN: Miss Slinger.

(*To which there are cheers, groans, cheers, fading away in the distance as the names are repeated.*)

SCENE SEVEN
THE BROTHERS

(*At the door of Hazelburn, Mr. and Mrs. Jarvis prepare for an outing. Their eldest son is lounging on the piazza, reading a Family Bible.*)

MRS. JARVIS: Remember, Samuel. While Mr. Jarvis and I are away this afternoon at the Fort for the Lieutenant Governor's reception, you may allow Colin as far as the piazza steps, but no farther.

JARVIS SR.: Your younger brother, Sam, is impounded till such time as it is safe to let him loose, but I suppose he won't want to leave this evening – his musical friends, at that time, God help us, are descending on us.

MRS. JARVIS: By that time, they will have left town.

SAM JR.: Who will have left town, mother?

MRS. JARVIS: Why, the Children of Peace. Don't you know, their Mohammed and his harem along with an orchestra, a band and a choir are coming to town this afternoon to preach in the Market Square. I don't want my younger son to have anything more to do with those people.

SAM JR.: They sound rather interesting. The Children of Peace – where and what are they?

JARVIS SR.: They live up in the bush thirty miles north of here and keep their property and women in common. Fine singers and musicians, though.

MRS. JARVIS: Fine singers and musicians? Music of the devil. That's what attracts converts – fine singing and music, especially aimed at my youngest impressionable.

SAM JR.: Sharing the women in common! (*whistles*)

JARVIS SR.: None of that, now. Wait till I inspect the horses, Mrs. Jarvis – then I'll hand you up.

(*As the coach drives away crunching the gravel, Colin comes out of the piazza, hands in pockets, dejected. He has brought out with him the music for the evening musicale.*)

SAM JR.: Well, aren't you going to ask me why I'm reading the Family Bible?

COLIN: Sam, I want to go downtown and hear the Children of Peace.

SAM JR.: Did you know that we were both christened on the same day at St. Matthew's in Newark, Upper Canada?

COLIN: But, Sam, we were born in Newark, New Jersey. I do so want to go hear their music, Sam.

SAM JR.: Why aren't our birth dates in this Bible?

COLIN: Mother and father didn't use this Bible down in the
States. They'll be just starting to play in the Market Square.

SAM JR.: Colin. If you get me the other Bible, maybe I'll let you
go and listen to these wild people in the Market Square.

COLIN: It's up in the attic.

(*Climbing up the Jacob's ladder, he soon returns with an older Bible.
Meanwhile, we hear in the distance the Sharon Band and choir.*)

COLIN: The only trouble is, Sam, this Bible won't open.

SAM JR.: Why would a Bible be locked?

COLIN: There might be things in there Mother and Father
don't want us to know.

SAM JR.: Such as?

COLIN: Why do you want to know when you were born?

SAM JR.: Because I've fallen in love with a girl who works at
Roche's Hotel and I figure they won't let me marry her. But
if I'm twenty-one, I can and light out for the bush some-
wheres.

COLIN: That's why the Bible is locked, then.

SAM JR.: Where's the key?

COLIN: Father has a little key on his watch chain.

SAM JR.: If you get me that key, I'll let you go hear the Children
of Peace.

(*Colin makes a run for freedom. We hear the Sharon Band. But Sam Jr.
trips him up with his invalid cane, places a foot on his chest, holds him
down.*)

SAM JR.: Is young Ridout coming to your musical soiree
tonight?

COLIN: Sam, leave Ridout alone.

SAM JR.: I hear he's spreading slander about me and I want to clear my honour with him. Doesn't he sing in the choir with you?

COLIN: You can hear the trombone and the bass viol so much better when you're close to the ground like this. Thank you, Sam.

(Sam Jr. raises his cane and foot to administer a beating; nimbly Colin rolls over and skids away to the market square. The Sharon music grows louder. The musicians are outside the building at this point. Unsuccessful at opening the locked bible, on the crest of the peaceful music, Sam Jr. sings.)

SAM JR.: No, not a child of peace am I
But Mars' own boy until I die.
I love the art of spilling life
More than I would to take a wife
And find within me Death's delight
In duelling with his neophyte.
His son am I, I turn and fire
Conceived once more by his desire!

I'll teach you to be so happy, drummer boy. All this music –

(He picks up a pile of music which Colin was sorting for this evening and exits with the same.)

SCENE EIGHT
A MUSICAL EVENING

(The Jarvises have returned from the reception at the fort and are retiring early.)

JARVIS SR.: I have stood all that I can stand
At the governor's reception.

MRS. JARVIS: That was the trouble – nowhere to sit
Everywhere to stand.

JARVIS SR.: Not a chance to rest one's buttocks
From two in the afternoon till eight o'clock tonight.

(His wife looks under the bed.)

MRS. JARVIS: Are all our dogs to lie under the bed tonight?

JARVIS: Better with us than biting and barking the ankles of the young musicians. Wife, if they wake me up once – out they go.

MRS. JARVIS: Mezzo piano in the basement I commanded.

JARVIS SR.: Damn the British connection. We Loyalists from the old colonies of New York, New Jersey and Pennsylvania received twice as less cake than Johnny come lately from Scotland.

MRS. JARVIS: I wish they'd send us a tall lieutenant-governor. The last two have been runts.

JARVIS SR.: I have stood all I can stand. (*snore*)

MRS. JARVIS: That was the trouble. (*snore*)

JARVIS SR.: To rest one's buttocks.

MRS. JARVIS: Everywhere to stand.

(*A bell rings an evening hour – rustily – but in the basement the rest of the cast have arrived with their instruments.*)

COLIN: Never mind being late, Ridout. We have no music to play. It has all disappeared.

RIDOUT: Colin, on the way here, I met your brother. He had a message for me and one for you. Here is yours.

COLIN: 'Dear brother, I have hidden all your new music under the bed of our mother and father. Good luck.' Ladies and gentlemen, until I find our new music, you shall have to improvise your own.

GIRLS: (*pensively*) Make our own music?

MEN: Impossible. What is there to sing about? To play about? In this town!

COLIN: While I creep into my parents' bedroom and rummage beneath it for my new music from Europe, why – Ann, show them how my mother's serinette works.

MAN ONE: Ridout, what was the brother's message to you?

RIDOUT: From Colin's brother, that son of Mars? *(pause)* He is challenging me to a duel. Tell neither Colin nor any of the women.

MAN TWO: Pay no heed to his bullying.

RIDOUT: And be placarded as a coward all over town? *(pause)* Which one of you will act as my second? *(pause)*

MAN THREE: *(raising his hand)* Ridout, I shall.

(The serinette sounds. In the bedroom, a routine develops. Every time Colin makes some progress with almost touching the pile of new music, a dog growls or a parent stops snoring. He does pick something from his father's night table, but returns, eventually, to the basement and spreads his hands as a sign of failure.)

ANN: But we have thought up a story about the serinette. *(reaction)* I will direct the fable. Mr. Jarvis shall lead you musically.

ALL: *(murmur)*

MAN ONE: Miss Smith, what is this fantasia's title?

ANN: 'Serinette.' *(At the pianoforte she plays various motifs.)* The story concerns a wild bird girl. *(Out dances the girl dressed in yellow.)* She lives in the forest happily singing – my own song. *(Motif)* *(Ann points at the instrumentalist involved here.)* A servant is sent to snare her and bring her to a fine house in York in a cage.

(She plays and assigns the cage motif.)

ANN: There her native song is ridiculed. *(Motif)* With the aid of a bird box *(Motif)* she is forced to learn very sophisticated metropolitan arias. *(Motif)* But one of the family's boys falls in love with the wild bird and takes pity on her. *(Motif)* He schemes how to free her and find the key to her cage. Which is what motif? *(This is played.)* Meanwhile his bad brother plots how to get the poor bird into trouble with his parents. *(Motif)* by rearranging the pins on the bird box so they will play an ugly tune. *(Motif)*

(Pause)

COLIN: Then what happened?

ANN: Let's sing that when we come to it. The muse will take care of us and you are the father, you are the mother, you, of course, are the bird, you all over there are the good brother, you are the bad brother and you all are the ser-inette and

COLIN: Play the motifs in order and we have the overture?

THE OVERTURE

(Bird Girl sings her wild song.)

BIRD THIEF: Such a silly little song you sing.
I shall catch you in this cage.
Soon you'll learn to sing a better something
More fitting to this polished age.

(He catches her and sells her to the parodies of Colin's parents.)

PARENTS: Children, take the bird away. Here's the serinette.
By the end of this summer day, have her learn this aria cor-rect!

(The brothers take turns at cranking the serinette (mime) whose ornate mechanics are illustrated by all the instruments very floridly. The parents sit down formally, a clock strikes seven, the boys enter with the bird.)

BIRD GIRL: Please, may I sing my own song?

PARENTS: Sing it then, if not too long.

(Her native air is ridiculed. With a cue from the serinette, she launches into the aria.)

PARENTS: *(applaud)* We'll be the envy of our neighbours
With our bird so operatic.

Train her in some other arias –
Now we're truly aristocratic.

GOOD BROTHER: My dear, your only hope is to pretend to be dead.

(The Bird Girl keels over.)

PARENTS: Throw her out, then and we'll find another.

BAD BROTHER: Nonsense, she's not dead but shamming, Mother, Father. Let me have the serinette training of her.

ANN: *(as narrator)* Now the cunning brother on the serinette the tune changes
Until chaotic discords are all that emerge.
(The Bird Girl holds her ears, but Bad Brother motions Good Brother to wind the serinette or else. Then he forces her to listen.)

PARENTS: *(to guests)* Tonight, friends, you will hear the new aria our bird has learned to sing.

(Bird Girl sings discordantly. Holding their ears, the guests leave.)

PARENTS: Take her away to the bush
There may she be forever be lost
For she has deeply disgraced us.

ANN: And there she lives unto this day
Free from singing mechanically.

BIRD GIRL: All the day long
Happily free
Singing my own song
Merrily.

(The postlude rises to great heights and suddenly diminuendos as Colin realizes that his parents have stopped snoring. With great suspense everyone waits – at last they resume.)

(Colin, to Ridout and Sutherland who are preparing to leave)

COLIN: Are you not going to sing till dawn with the rest of us?

RIDOUT: Like nightingales? Colin, we are promised elsewhere.

(*He embraces Colin; Man Three shakes his hand. Colin looks after them. Then the company improvises a final summing up which gets louder and louder until a dog barks. Silence. The snoring wavers, then resumes on a certain uncertain level. The guests take leave of Colin. A clock strikes a very early hour.*)

COLIN: Ah, my friends of the basement musicals – must you leave? Even that did not quite wake my papa or my mama.

VARIOUS VOICES: It is morning. Our chaperones say our parents will be worried. Goodnight, Colin. Thank you for the new music. Thank you, Ann. Good night. Good morning! (*Laughter fades away*)

COLIN: Ann Smith – Miss Smith, must you leave?

ANN: So says my chaperone.

COLIN: Ann, this may be the last time you see me. I am thinking of running away to Sharon to be with the Children of Peace and learn their music. They told me this afternoon that they needed a new singing master for their singing school.

ANN: How I would love to hear their music!

COLIN: Come with me then. (*Kisses her. She slaps him.*)

ANN: Chaperone!

(*Then leaving, laughs, waves back at him, Colin recovers sufficiently to wave back. Quiet reflection on evening, dawn, then his brother enters.*)

SAM JR.: Brother, bring me a towel and a basin of water.

COLIN: Sam, have you got hurt again?

SAM JR.: Where – where were you this afternoon when I needed you? You ran off and left me to my own devices.

(*Colin comes back with basin and towel.*)

COLIN: Sam, why did you hide all my music?

SAM JR.: Perhaps it was a call for help.

COLIN: (*pause*) You aren't hurt.

SAM JR.: Nah. I've hurt him. I've shot your pal, Colin. Ridout. Affair of honour. Shot him.

(*Colin holds his ears. Some hint of serinette theme. In the other playing area, Ridout on bed surrounded by cast (perhaps as mourning relatives, not all though): we're having a reprise of Act One with all hands on deck. Colin kneels by bed to pray for Ridout's soul. Back in the other area, Sam Jr. washes his hands and dries them. Colin stands and addresses us directly.*)

COLIN: LEAVE! Leave! As I looked down at my fellow musician dead – his voice I kept hearing saying

RIDOUT'S VOICE: Colin, leave this town too. Run away.

ALL: … invaded their territory… burnt down Buffalo…

COLIN: My friend's voice further said: Run away – in what you wear. Those shoes. That shirt. Dangerous to wait.

ALL: Colin Jarvis Junissimus – succurens vivos et mortuos

SAM JR.: – But we'll make a killer of you yet come next war, brother.

COLIN: Never!

(*Serinette music, then Bird Girl singing torturedly.*)

COLIN: It will sing exactly what it has heard, sir.

SAM JR.: Opera, Pater, ain't that why our ancestors left them old countries in Europe?

(*Serinette fortissimo*)

JARVIS SR.: Because, Colin… 'Deed not issued because of lack of parchment.'

MRS. JARVIS: *The Rights of Christ, according to the principles and doctrines of the Children of Peace* (*pause*)… could be a very dangerous little document.

ALL: May the heathen, now adoring
Idol-gods of wood and stone…

CHOIRMASTER: No loitering in the chancel, please.

MRS. JARVIS: … along with an orchestra, a band and a choir… music of the devil.

(Serinette music)

SAM JR.: Ridout. Isn't he in your choir? Doesn't he spread stories about me?

COLIN: Never… to return, I hope, for henceforth I shall be –

SAM JR.: And find within me Death's delight.

COLIN: – Numbered not with the Children of War
Whose music is the martial clarion.

MAJOR-DOMO: Regiment Nineteenth of the Centre… Halt!

ALL: *(quietly)* Huzzah! For King and Country!

COLIN: Hurrah! For Christ my King
And his own Children of Peace who sing
Of music sweeter far to me
Than this town's martial clarion,
Trained bands of killing men,
Henceforth, I'll live, not here at York
But oh forever there at Sharon!

Harry Somers cavorting on the lawns of the Temple, during one of the première performances, July 1990.

ACT TWO

(The members of the company, led by David Willson, women bearing banners, dressed in white, as many as possible playing musical instruments, march from a place they have foregathered – either on the banks of the Holland River or the site of the old meeting house – to the Temple for the monthly almsgiving ceremony. The marching music the band plays should sound like 'Jack o' Hazeldean, The Prussian March, the New Rigged Ship, the Recorder,' mentioned as procession music of theirs by Mackenzie in his Advocate, Feb. 27, 1834. *At the east door of the temple, the company forms about Willson, who says, or sings, as they file in:)*

SCENE ONE

ALMSGIVING DAY AT SHARON

WILLSON: Come in before the Lord in the following manner with clean garments and with clean feet. Prepare with fasting from one meal in the day on this, the last seventh day of each month in the year.

Abstain from your twelve o'clock meal for half of Israel's sabbath is restored unto us on this day.

I shall see his name but the glory of this house I shall not see with mine eyes and I may not partake of it because it is forbidden of the Lord for causes not lawful for me to reveal. *(He does not enter with the others.)*

Our meeting of worship is open at all times for all people that may respectfully attend. All the branches of the Church of Christ are equal without distinction. We have no written Creed. We have monthly sacrifice in the Temple of the Lord, a sacrifice for the poor and afflicted, twelve sacrifices a year.

(As we, the audience, now enter the Temple following the singers and players, we should see him over our shoulders walking across to the study singing to himself:)

WILLSON: 'A person is but a waymark of the soul.'
     'While lines are so distinctly drawn
     A Saviour's absent and he's gone.'

(The musicians ascend to the gallery, blow trumpets three times, then come

down, put instruments in centre of a table dressed in green. The congrega-
tion all seated and silent. Elders arise, walk around altar eastward fol-
lowed by four lines of men, women from the congregation. They place
their sacrifices on four small tables – women's tables separate from men's.
A counter comes to count the men's, a small scrap of paper with name of
contributor. Colin, disguised as 'Tobias Brown,' is the last to contribute.
Given the small numbers of cast, repeat the circlings. Willson made the
'collection' plate an eye-dizzying ritual. Before the treasurer stands up to
receive the sacrifices from the counters, the cast should start singing or
chanting the following which can go under, come up, should weave a net-
work of names around the counter's and treasurer's statements.)

SCENE TWO
THE PENNY

ALL: John Doan Senior, ten shillings. Esther Lundy, two
shillings, six pence.

COUNTER: I give thee in trust this day the Lord's money for
which thou shalt be accountable to God and the congrega-
tion. Pounds, shillings and pence received. Do thou give me
a signed receipt and read aloud the Sum annexed.

(In the ritual, after the last sacrifice has been made, the four tables become
two, then are counted and a male counter and a female counter bring the
sacrifices together; another counter takes these to the treasurer.)

TREASURER: Israel Willson, two shillings, six pence. Mary
Willson, two shillings, six pence. Amos Hughes, five
shillings. Rachel Hughes, two shillings, six pence. Phoebe
Dunham, one shilling, three pence. George Hollingshead,
two shillings, six pence. Mary Stogdill, one shilling, three
pence. Peter Leppard, two shillings, six pence. Ira Doan, one
shilling, ten pence and a half pence. Tobias Brown, one
penny.

(The Treasurer holds up the penny (there are several ways of timing this
scene and arranging it) but does not immediately drop it back into the
golden bowl (silver) – this gleaming ritual vessel should blind the eyes of
the audience when it is raised. From the congregation come scattered voic-

es in argument about the acceptance of this penny. The effect should be the remembering of phrases and sentences they have learned here, in the meeting house and at school and from being in the Children of Peace a long time.)

VOICE ONE: This is the new young singing master for the children.

TREASURER: Strangers and sojourners shall be excluded from acting in matters of the church, as a decision can be of no heartfelt interest to them.

VOICE TWO: Who is not for us is against us.

COLIN (TOBIAS): But I am no stranger. I am most for you. Please accept my sacrifice.

VOICE THREE: But if a stranger be poor, settle him at a distance by consent of the assembly and let him be tried for seven years to see if he shall be for or against the house of the Lord.

VOICE FOUR: Dispose not of God's ground to strangers.

VOICE FIVE: While lines of division are so distinctly drawn
A Saviour's absent and he's gone.

VOICE ONE: *(slowly joined by other)* All strangers may sacrifice that will and inherit *(pause)* the outside seats of the assembly.

TREASURER: *(accepts penny)* I have received in trust of the Lord's people the sum of four pounds, eight shillings, one penny and – a half penny – sacrificed to his most holy name, at the hands of the counter and receipted the same in trust accountable when called for in the congregation.

(The tables and vessel of collection are removed, a person in black at the west side of the altar faces east and gives out the lines for the following hymn, everyone still seated.)

PERSON IN BLACK CHORUS: I'll haste away to Jordan's stream
Where wisdom doth chastise,
I'll bow my neck and wash me clean
And watch with wakeful eyes.

I'll offer God my hands and feet,
I'll make my offerings clean,
And when the lamb of God I meet
My sin shall not be seen.

ALL: We're counting thy favours,
    Because they are known,
    Thou gav'st us a Saviour,
    A Son of thine own;
    Our praise is to bless him,
    The pearl of our joy,
    May nations embrace him,
    Nor kingdoms destroy.

    His name is salvation,
    And glory and peace,
    The light of the nation,
    That never will cease;
    He gave us this building,
    His name to adore,
    The serpent he's stilling,
    The lions that roar!

(*The trumpeters sound again. Dividing into four groups, the congregation leaves by four doors.*)

SCENE THREE
THE WIDOW'S STORE

(*The widow, Mrs. Mary Stogdill, has lately taken in to help her a young man named 'Raphael Smith.' In reality this is Ann Smith disguised as a boy. Mary Stodgill returns to her store to find Raphael repricing all the goods with a piece of chalk.*)

RAPHAEL: While you were away, Mrs. Stogdill, business was very poor. Not a soul came in the door. Were the whole village at the meeting of the Children of Peace?

MRS. STOGDILL: No, Raphael. That just shows you how little time you've spent in this village. Everyone knows that for the Children of Peace, the afternoon of the last Saturday in every month is to be kept until midnight as a Sabbath.

RAPHAEL: So your store will not be open?

MRS. STOGDILL: I, myself, will not serve a customer.

RAPHAEL: And then at midnight, the other Sunday begins?

MRS. STOGDILL: The other Sunday begins. (*pause*) Have you reduced all my prices by thirty percent, Raphael?

RAPHAEL: In as much as I could figure it out, Mrs. Stogdill. Seems to me where I come from they always raised prices unless bankruptcy occurred.

MRS. STOGDILL: Raphael, you saw me adding up my books when you first came?

RAPHAEL: And saw you running a profitable store.

MRS. STOGDILL: I was making too much money. My dead husband warned me: If you, Mary, make too much money, there will be poor again in Sharon.

RAPHAEL: And so – next accounting you aim at a loss.

MRS. STOGDILL: Aiming at being more of a Child of Peace than just a merchant.

RAPHAEL: What shall I do now, Mrs. Stogdill?

MRS. STOGDILL: I'd like nothing better, child, than for you to read this story from the newspapers.

RAPHAEL: (*pause*) Why, here's a story about a duel – fought last month between Mr. Samuel Jarvis Junior and young Ridout. Perhaps you remember, but the last named young man was killed.

MRS. STOGDILL: Murdered. And they have tried his murderer?

(*The shop doorbell rings. Colin enters.*)

MRS. STOGDILL: Oh, it's the singing master, Mr. Brown. Mr. Brown, you'll have to go to another store. It's our almsgiving day, remember?

COLIN: I wanted to invite Raphael, your apprentice, to my singing class Monday evening, Mrs. Stogdill. Wasn't it wonderful, Mrs. Stogdill, Raphael? At the meeting, they accepted my sacrifice.

RAPHAEL: And what did you sacrifice, Mr. Brown?

COLIN: A penny.

(*Amused reaction*)

It was all I had.

MRS. STOGDILL: Continue reading about the trial of the murderer, Jarvis Jr.

RAPHAEL: Mrs. Stogdill, I would rather not.

MRS. STOGDILL: Perhaps Mr. Brown would like to?

COLIN: Mrs. Stogdill, I do not need to, for the accused is my brother. It mentions that his younger brother has run away from the family. From the Children of War I have come to the Children of Peace.

MRS. STOGDILL: Then you are a runaway. Will your parents not send the constables after you?

COLIN: Not if both of you keep my secret from them and for me.

MRS. STOGDILL: That, in this peaceful, simple place, will be the first secret I have ever had. Good afternoon, Mr. Brown.

COLIN: Thank you, Mrs. Stogdill. Raphael, remember Monday night singing class. (*exits*)

MRS. STOGDILL: And now I have a second secret to keep.

RAPHAEL: A second secret, Mrs. Stogdill?

MRS. STOGDILL: Yes, you have been acquainted with that young man somewhere else before – although he seems not to know you.

RAPHAEL: The secret's even bigger than that, Mrs. Stogdill.

MRS. STOGDILL: Whom am I entertaining unawares?

RAPHAEL: This will make things more exciting. *(She starts to remove apparel, takes off cap to reveal long hair.)*

MRS. STOGDILL: Raphael Smith! If you intend removing your pantaloons, remember that I have been fasting all day and this is likely to bring on a fainting attack. *(But Raphael reveals a skirt under the pantaloons.) (Pause)* So, I am to keep as my larger secret – that you are a young woman. *(groans)*

RAPHAEL: Madly in love with that young man, followed him here to Sharon, don't know how to reveal myself to him just yet because at our last meeting in York I slapped his face.

MRS. STOGDILL: Why on earth did you do that?

RAPHAEL: Did you never slap a boy's face because you loved him so?

MRS. STOGDILL: Not since I've become a Child of Peace. Maybe when I was a young Methodist.

RAPHAEL: He had the nerve to ask me to come up here with him.

MRS. STOGDILL: I've got to have something to eat. I'm starving. But you have come up here to be near him –

RAPHAEL: The dishonour of it! *(rapidly slicing a loaf of bread)* Are you going to tell on me?

MRS. STOGDILL: Almsgiving Day! Weak from fasting. Please – *(reaching up to the slice of bread)*

RAPHAEL: *(pause)* Promise?

SCENE FOUR
MONDAY NIGHT SINGING SCHOOL AND VARIATIONS

(The young people are sight singing certain intervals from a blackboard Colin has inscribed with musical notes.)

COLIN: Now – if you know those intervals, you should be able to sing the following. From sight, please.

(He gives them the key note on a set of small bells. Raphael enters and takes a place.)

CHORUS: Tell me little housewife,
    Toiling in the sun
    How many minutes till the pie is done?
    John builds the oven,
    Katie rolls the crust,
    Daisy finds the flour,
    all of golden dust.
    Turn it so and roll it so!
    What a dainty size!
    All the plums are pebbles,
    Hot mud pies!

COLIN: Not bad. Now, if the men – if the men sing the list of intervals I gave you earlier and the girls sing the tune we've just sung, we'll have two-part harmony. (*This gets a laugh. Pause.*) Wait a minute. I'd like to test the male voices for range. What I've written may be too high for some of you. From the tonic sing in thirds. Ascending – upwards and…

(*As the men sing higher and higher, most of them drop away, but Raphael sings on, higher and higher until everyone's mouths fall open.*)

RAPHAEL: (*clearing throat apologetically*)
    My voice hasn't changed yet.

COLIN: (*pause*) Well – are you sure? Try the second verse in three parts. I anticipate no range problems and –

(*Chorus in two parts with embellishments by Raphael.*)

CHORUS: Hands that never weary toiling in the deep
    Shut the oven door now,
    Soon we'll take a peep.
    Wish we had a shower,
    think we need it so,
    For it would make the road sides –
    such a heap of dough.
    Turn them in, turn them out,
    how the morning flies,
    Ring the bell for dinner –
    Hot mud pies.

RAPHAEL: (*as the scene fades, spreading hands*) Some days it's changed, some days I can't get above Middle C – if you shot me.

SCENE FIVE
BARREL ORGAN – IN DAVID WILLSON'S STUDY

(*Sitting at his writing desk, Willson composes a hymn while a young woman dressed in white turns a hymn tune on the smaller barrel organ.*)

WILLSON: My dear sister, the Spirit is not supplying me with words for that tune. Go on to the next one.

YOUNG GIRL: Oh, Mr. Willson, here comes the Singing Master to relieve me – it's my turn at school at the loom. Mr. Jackson's going to show me how to make the patterns.

(*She races off; Colin takes up the apparatus.*)

WILLSON: You seem to have caught on to the proper turning of that barrel organ rather quickly, Mr. Brown.

COLIN: I have had deep experience of barrel organs, Mr. Willson. We had one at home to train a bird to sing with.

WILLSON: A serinette. And did your brother the duellist enjoy listening to its pretty tunes?

COLIN: Ah, sir, I see my secret is out. (*pause*) No, my brother did not enjoy music.

WILLSON: Yet he is closer to Christ than you are at present.

COLIN: Well, the jury acquitted him.

SAM JR.'S VOICE: Perhaps it was a call for help.

WILLSON: You are not seeing what I mean.

COLIN: Am I farther away from Christ than he is?

SAM JR.: Where – where were you this afternoon when I needed you?

WILLSON: Your brother has dared to descend into the flames

where it is most flaming. If he repents now – God destroyeth his first mind in the flame and will give him a new mind.

SAM JR.: You ran off and left me to my own devices.

COLIN: Should I become a duellist then?

WILLSON: No, no, Tobias Brown. You will find your own version of the dark fire through which all of us must pass before we come to the light. (*pause*) You do not like playing the barrel organ?

COLIN: I like it when it is used to help you write new songs.

WILLSON: No one up here offers me new tunes.

COLIN: Well, there is a ghost of a new tune, Mr. Willson, in between the old tunes.

WILLSON: Ah yes, Mr. Coates, when he was making this instrument, he put in some transition chords of his own.

COLIN: In between 'China' and 'Wilmot' there is – this.

(*Through manipulation he plays the in-between chords over and over and over again, then starts to improvise vocally against the chords. David Willson smiles and begins to write rapidly. A text for the memorial verses set by Colin:*)

Gather up the fragments that nothing be lost;
I think your spirit calls on me
To mark the things mine eyes do see,
Nor lose them in the dust.

SCENE SIX
RUN-THROUGH

(*At her store, the Widow Stogdill with flageolet, a Farmer of her acquaintance and Raphael are sight-reading Colin's setting of Willson's 'Memorial Hymn for Leppard' from some expedition abroad. Colin enters the store, overhears their practising and only reveals himself after they have finished a run-through.*)

COLIN: Thank you for going ahead, Mrs. Stogdill, I didn't know you could play flageolet.

(*Reaction at his having heard them.*)

MRS. STOGDILL: Of course, everyone in Sharon can play anything on something. What does it sound like?

COLIN: May I make some changes?

(*He calls in the parts and begins to, with pen and ink, adjust notes here and there. Then he hands them back.*)

You know such is the vanity of artists – but I feel less sorrow for the man these verses mourn (after all, I never met Mr. Leppard) and more joy at being asked to use my faculty for original composition. In my excitement, I have arranged for an invitation to be sent to a musical friend of mine in York to come up here the day of the funeral.

RAPHAEL: What musical friend down in York could this be, Mr. Brown?

COLIN: Ah, it is the young lady who brought me to my senses with a sound slap the night I left.

MRS. STOGDILL: How are you sending the note – in a glove?

COLIN: No, Mrs. Stogdill. I have an arrangement with her maid-servant by which when our people here at Sharon go down to market at York tomorrow morning, a certain cabbage they have for sale is to be examined carefully for hollowness. Now –

(*He conducts another sing-through, while on the other side of the stage, a Farmer and his Wife are counting cabbages before packing them into bushel baskets. We hear the singing rehearsal of the new elegy, but watch the farm couple. A clock strikes, Raphael appears and –*)

SCENE SEVEN
CABBAGES

RAPHAEL: You good people need some help counting your cabbages?

Poster design based on Harold Town's painting *Stages #14*, for the first production, Sharon, Ontario, July 1990, by Music at Sharon and Cultural Support Services.

FARMER: Fifty-two?

FARMWIFE: Fifty-two – why this sudden desire of a passerby to help us count our cabbages? You never offered to help us before.

RAPHAEL: I hear that there's one light cabbage.

FARMER: Well, yes – I won't lie, I cannot, never did. There is a light cabbage we're taking down especially.

RAPHAEL: The note in it is really for me – and I want to read it here and now.

FARMWIFE: How can it be, Raphael Smith? It's a love note to a young woman down in York whose servant is to pick up this cabbage at the St. Lawrence Market tomorrow.

RAPHAEL: Let me explain...

SCENE EIGHT
INTERRUPTED CEREMONY

(At the cemetery, Colin's parents and brother await the arrival of the cortege for the recently deceased Child of Peace. This now arrives, the choir bearing black banners centred with gold stars, the band playing a slow march.)

MRS. JARVIS: Colin – we've come up to bring you back, you naughty boy.

(But the service moves forward immediately into the memorial song. Underneath it we can just perceive the Parents trying to drag Colin away with angry words, his brother drawing a sword or a pistol, until at last he breaks away and they disappear after him. But this never disturbs the ceremonious singing – now under as ...)

SCENE NINE
FAREWELL TO SHARON – NAKED AND BEAUTIFUL

(In a forest glade Colin kneels staring up into the light. Raphael enters.)

COLIN: How close are they, Raphael?

RAPHAEL: They're just entering the forest.

COLIN: I'm saying farewell to Sharon. I don't want my presence to be a nuisance to the Children of Peace. If only I could have the visions here he must have had – must have, he tells us. Raphael – kneel down with me, let me put my hands on your shoulders – this is the vision David Willson had as he told me:

(*Other playing area – a younger David Willson sings; band and singers back him. Black banners change to vision ones.*)

WILLSON: I was called to retire into secret from all men. Accordingly I obeyed the call and came forth by myself into the forest. It was expressly spoken to me that if I would go I should see the angel of God. Half believing that such a thing should be and still fearing the event of not going, I obeyed the command.

According to divine promise, I saw a beautiful young man clothed in a scarlet robe.

This robe was the blood of Christ Jesus and a mission for me.

He stood at my left hand, I could have touched him and he signified by motion this covering was for me.

He gently stripped the garment from his own shoulders and laid it on mine and told me that through the sorrows of his sin I must minister to the Christian Church – this redeeming blood was laid upon me, which I must be baptized in.

He disappeared from me naked and beautiful and I saw him no more.

(*Raphael takes off his cap, Ann's hair falls down about her face.*)

COLIN: So you did come with me to Sharon, Ann, and have been at my side all these months.

ANN: Colin, I am a free woman now – my parents cannot haul

me back as yours can. Hide from them – let me hide you in the wilderness and I shall feed you.

(*Enter Colin's relatives.*)

SAM JR.: You'll do no such silly thing, my girl. Colin – take my hand – Father and Mother are waiting up there with the carriage.

(*He drags Colin off; Ann gestures towards the light. The memorial and vision music finishes.*)

SCENE TEN
THE SERINETTE

(*We hear the serinette music, then see the figure of Colin back at Hazelburn siting very neatly in a chair, as if tied to it, while a Young Anglican Clergyman in full regalia, with cane, finishes up an examination of Colin's faith. A blackboard has on it: 'Thirty-nine articles, questions from catechism, the problem of non-juring bishops.'*)

CLERIC: (*not sung*) Very well, Master Colin Jarvis, now that you have recited the thirty-nine articles of your faith, answered correctly all the questions a somewhat older than usual catechumen should know and shown at least some understanding of the history of the state church, as one final demonstration of renewed faith in the faith of your fathers (*lighting cigarette*) I want you, if you please, to do two things: first, denounce David Willson for the fornicating pig that he is and, second, recite, nay chant, the Nicene Creed.

COLIN: Oh Reverend Trueblood, yes! I denounce David Willson as being the only true Christian in our province and I will not chant any barren and Grecian creed, but instead –

Hurrah! for Christ is my King
And His Children of Peace who sing
Of music sweeter far to me...

SAM JR.: Enough! (*Reverend Trueblood is beating Colin with his cane to shut him up*) Trueblood Padre! You hit him one more time and I'll wipe this floor with you. You have not got a notion of how to effectively torture a nonconforming prisoner of war. We're the sons of a father who had all his toenails pulled out of him up in the Mohawk Valley in 1778 and he didn't bat an eyelid. And Colin's got the same guts to my everlasting admiration (*pause*) and my pity because I do know how to torture him into submission.

TRUEBLOOD: Tell me how, then.

SAM JR.: Why, he can't stand to hear music played out of tune. And don't tell mater, but I tampered with one of the rolls in that damned serinette and I've spent hours secretly training this bird to sing 'Aria baloney spumoza di sorbetto' as if she had a varicose larynx and a burr on her tonsils.

(*Maids bring Bird Girl out of cage and hold her as Sam Jr. plays the serinette music we heard in Act One in the opera within an opera.*)

SAM JR.: (*tossing aside the serinette*) Sing, you wretched finch of the grove! Sing that!

(*Bird Girl does the out-of-tune she did in Act One.*)

(*Colin holds his ears, but Trueblood and Sam Jr. bend his arms down. He eventually screams.*)

COLIN: Sam, get me out of here. I am going insane!

SAM JR.: (*motions Trueblood away*) Denounce David Willson then.

COLIN: (*shakes his head*) No!

SAM JR.: What about reciting the Creed for our friend here?

COLIN: (*shakes his head*)

SAM JR.: Colin, you can surely do a thing like that and in private not mean what you say. All my life, I've been doing all sorts of stupid things just to make life a bit easier for us all.

COLIN: Like killing Ridout!

SAM JR.: Colin, they trained me to kill and not stop killing. (*pause*) Please do the Creed and we'll get out of here and head for the bush.

(Colin rises from the floor and is stuffed into the cage with the Bird Girl. The Reverend Trueblood advances with a cane just as the two prisoners break out of the cage and repeat the escape sequence of Act One. When Bird is back in the cage, Colin back in the chair, Trueblood continues:)

TRUEBLOOD: Remember the lessons in chanting I have given you. Breath should not be taken at a comma, an unfortunate habit you seem to have fallen into up there in Sharon among those strange sectarians without a written creed. Chant!

COLIN: *(chanting mechanically but efficiently)* I believe in one God the Father Almighty, Maker of heaven and earth and of all things visible and invisible. And in one Lord Jesus Christ, the only begotten Son of God, begotten of his Father before all worlds, God of God, Light of Light, Very God of very God, Begotten, not made, Being of one substance with the Father...

(Our attention swings to the next room where Colin's parents sit listening, birdcage close by.)

JARVIS SR.: Egad, old woman, the Reverend Mr. Trueblood has brought our son around to right reason at last.

MRS. JARVIS: Sam, I mistrust such sudden giving in after such months of rebellious fire. Being away so long up there may have taught him to act with guile.

JARVIS SR.: Like a woman, I'm half ashamed a son of mine should give in so to that super-refined honeymouth. The Reverend Trueblood has drunk our cellars literally dry until I had to beg him to visit a tavern and give our barrels a rest.

MRS. JARVIS: Well, the task of rooting out our younger son's new beliefs is not a pleasant one. And, Samuel, they do say that the Fortieth Article, never published, is 'Thou Shalt Drink.'

COLIN: And I believe in the Holy Ghost, the Lord and Giver of life, who proceedeth from the Father and the Son, Who with the Father and the Son together is worshipped and glorified.

SAM JR.: (*entering*) Get him into some secret confinement, will you, pater and mater?

MRS. JARVIS: Don't you dare disturb them, Sammy. His soul lies in the balance. Don't you realize that this is the first time he has obeyed his religious instructor? Wait – now, why?

SAM JR.: They've come to town to sell and perform in the market place with their whole band. They're asking after him – and they say they'll pass through every one of our streets until they've found where we've hidden him.

(*We hear in the distance the sound of Sharon Band and Sharon singing.*)

COLIN: And I look for the Resurrection of the dead,
And the life of the world to come, Amen.

MRS. JARVIS: All right. Now's a good time. He's finished the Creed. Lock him away till they've gone by our house.

(*Reverend Mr. Trueblood wearily slumps in a chair. Colin's father and brother lead Colin upstairs, then rejoin the Cleric and Mrs. Jarvis in the parlour with the birdcage in evidence. As if to fight the approaching tide of Sharon music, they unhood the bird, play the serinette. From up above we hear a trumpet being blown. Dashing out, Sam Jr. returns to say:*)

SAM JR.: Couldn't you think of any other place to put him but upstairs – he's climbed out somehow and is up on the roof playing a trumpet to them.

COLIN (*descending laughing*) And now – entering his parents' drawing room with this in his hands.

MRS. JARVIS: What do you want to bring down that silly old book for? We have a nice new one not all coming to pieces like that silly old thing.

COLIN: Mother, an old copy of a Family Bible up in the attic is not to be called silly. (*pause*)

JARVIS SR.: How the devil did you get that book open? Why, you've stolen the key to it off my watch chain.

COLIN: The night of the musicale, Father. When you were

asleep and I couldn't get my music out from under your bed.

(*Looks of amazement cross parental faces.*)

SAM JR.: (*laughs*) Which I had hidden there.

JARVIS SR.: Sam and Colin, there were good reasons for keeping that Bible locked up.

COLIN: Yes, you and Mother were once Baptists in New Jersey.

MRS. JARVIS: Certainly not. I was a Congregationalist. It was your father who was the Baptist.

JARVIS SR.: Well, they'd never have made a Baptist Provincial Secretary. You had to change to the official religion.

COLIN: To get all this.

MRS. JARVIS: And raise you and Sam Jr. as gentlemen.

SAM JR.: Wish you hadn't, mater. Then I could have married my sweetheart. (*pause*) Though the duelling's been fun.

MRS. JARVIS: The upstairs chambermaid at Roche's Hotel.

COLIN: Mother and Father. I have recently obeyed you and honoured you. In return, I want your permission to travel up to Sharon for a few days and see the harvest festival. (*pause*)

JARVIS SR.: Why do you ask for permission, son? If you know I'm a renegade Baptist, you also know that we hid your true age from you.

COLIN: I know. Sam over there is twenty-two and by some miracle, today happens to be my twenty-first birthday. But I want us to be friends.

MRS. JARVIS: If deception was practised, son, what you want to do now proves we were right.

SAM JR.: What about me, mater?

MRS. JARVIS: Marry her. She's already provided us with a grandchild, I hear.

SAM JR.: No, she hasn't quite yet. Another month, I think.

COLIN: I'll only be away for a couple of days. (*He salutes his parents and his brother.*) So don't send after me. (*At the door he turns around. Combine outside music and Bird Girl here to go along with the next crucial moments.*) You do know where I'm going, don't you? With my new friends to the village whose first name was Hope and now is called Sharon. Why don't you come with me? They'll illuminate the Temple tonight.

(*Rigidly the parents sit, but Sam Jr. stirs and slowly comes over and takes Colin's hand. They leave together. Our last image of the parents as we leave is them rigidly sitting, their bird singing counterpoint to the music outside. By direction in the program, the audience will know that the end of the play does not occur until they now move outside, where they will find the Temple illuminated and hear the cast sing the following hymn written long ago by David Willson for that event:*)

SCENE ELEVEN
MY OWN SONG

ALL: Bless'd is the garden of the Lord
     Where ev'ry plant do grow,
     The vine the joyful fruit doth bear,
     Nor moth, nor thief can steal.
     Messiah is our shepherd there,
     And doth his heart reveal.

     'Tis there the flocks of Jacob feed,
     And distant tribes are one:
     There grow the pasture that we need,
     And crystal streams do run.

     The walls around are strong and high,
     No partialist can rise
     Our love and kindness to deny,
     Our love to all, despise.

     Our gates are as the open door,
     And ev'ry kind comes in;

The wise, the great, the rich, the poor,
And all the souls that sin.

The Lord hath made our off'rings free,
And unrestricted love,
We own, O Lord, hath come from thee,
As dew from heav'n above.

As rain that waters distant hills,
By thee our plants do grow;
Thy love to all, the bosom fills,
To all, our cup doth flow.

Taptoo!

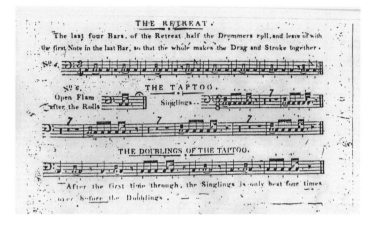

Fife and drum elements from the traditional 'taptoo' ceremony, from various late eighteenth and early nineteenth-century sources.

Taptoo!
Opera in two acts

Libretto, James Reaney   Music, John Beckwith

First performance (piano and drums), McGill Opera
Department, Crane School of Music, Potsdam, New York, 13
March 1999.
Singers: Kevin Arnstrong, Jonathan Carle, Rena Detlefsen,
Stephan Fehr, Jake Feldman, Kelly Hodson, Luc Lalonde, Felicia
Locas, John Loyer, Chris MacRae, Chantal Richard, Sally Rogers,
Zoe Tarshis
James Higgins *music director,* Brenda Anderson *director*

First performance with orchestra, MacMillan Theatre,
University of Toronto, 7 March 2003.
Singers (two casts): Michael Adair, Laura Albino, Allison Bent,
Philip Carmichael, Saemi Chang, Trevor Eliot Bowes, Hélène
Couture, Jon-Paul Décosse, David Dellaire, Melinda Delorme,
Stephen Erickson, Tyrsa Gawrachynsky, Leah Gordon, Wayne
Gwillim, Virginia Hatfield, Joni Henson, Chloé Hunter, Kathryn
Knapp, Megan Latham, Matthew Leigh, Michael McBride,
Peter McGillivray, Eve McLeod, Jason Paul Nedecky, Julien
Patenaude, Calvin Powell, Eric Shaw, Stephen Sherwood, Giles
Tomkins, Katherine Whyte, Jillian Yemen
Sandra Horst *conductor*, Michael Patrick Albano *director*,
Fred Perruzza *designer,* Alison Grant, *choreographer*

Main characters, in order of appearance:

Act One
Seth as a boy *treble*
Jesse Harple *bass*
Mrs Harple *mezzo-soprano*
Ebenezer as a boy *treble*
Colonel (later General),
    'Mad Anthony' Wayne *baritone*
Drum Major *baritone*
An Adjutant *tenor*
Major (later Lieutenant-General),
    John Graves Simcoe *baritone*

A Sentinel *tenor* or *soprano*
Jarvis *baritone*
A Sergeant *bass*
Mrs. Felswad *mezzo-soprano*
Mr Felswad *baritone*
Williams *treble*
Lakeman *soprano*
Hartley *soprano*
MacKay *tenor*
A Soldier *baritone*

Act Two
Seth as a man *tenor*
Atahentsic *soprano*
Ebenezer as a man *tenor*
Elizabeth Posthuma Simcoe *mezzo-soprano*
Speaker of the Legislature *baritone*
Parson *baritone*
Mrs. Jarvis *soprano*
Attorney-General *baritone or mezzo-soprano*

Orchestra:
flute/fife 1, oboe/fife 2, clarinet/bass clarinet, bassoon, horn, trumpet 1, trumpet 2/Fluegelhorn, trombone/euphonium, tuba, 2 percussion, accordion, non-pedal harp, string quartet, contrabass/mandolin

NOTE: The opera is based on events surrounding the establishment of the town of York, Upper Canada (now Toronto). Scenes cover a period roughly from 1780 to 1810. Some characters are historical, others imaginary. The performance requires a minimum of fifteen singers – three trebles, three sopranos, two mezzo-sopranos, three tenors, three baritones, one bass – each of whom participates in tuttis when needed and each of whom assumes several solo roles, involving in some cases crossing of genders. The music incorporates many period quotations, identified in the libretto as they occur.

Act One
Overture – Scene One, Vulgus mobile strepitoso! – Scene Two, On the road to Philadelphia – Scene Three, How to play the drum – Scene Four, The chicken thief – Scene Five, 'Draw your swords, Rangers, the rebels are coming' – Scene Six, 'Why, soldiers, why?'

Act Two
Prelude – Scene One, Under two flags – Scene Two, In the Ohio wilderness – Scene Three, An old friend at Fort Defiance – Scene Four, Loyal she began... – Scene Five, Parliament Oak – Scene Six, The ball – Scene Seven, Toronto becomes York – Scene Eight, Finale

TAPTOO!
ACT ONE

OVERTURE

(Two drummers walk slowly to their places, entering from opposite sides and performing short signals to each other. These sounds cut across the conversation of the spectators and the growing murmur of the cast assembling outside the performance tent. Then, to the tune of 'Yankee Doodle,' we hear a band of eighteenth-century revolutionaries serenading an effigy of King George III they have tarred and feathered. Scornful, scoffing, some are banging on pots and pans in shivaree fashion. 'Serenade for Pig Gelder' music.)

MOB: We've tarred and feathered
    Old King George the Third,
    We've tarred and feathered
    Mad King George the Third,
    That old tyrannical
    Antiquated turd!
    From now on our king's the more agreeable
    Our king'sssss uusss! *(pause)* We, the people!

(Seth heads into the performance tent with a pail of water he has just pumped at the fort's well. An official tries to stop him but he dodges past him. The mob, now closer, carries banners with revolutionary symbols: a rattlesnake, a snake divided into thirteen pieces, a triangle centred with a huge eye. All bear violent mottoes: 'Don't step on me!' 'Join us or die!' and 'E pluribus unum!')

SCENE ONE: VULGUS MOBILE STREPITOSO!

REBEL SONG
(BASED ON 'WASHINGTON'S MARCH,' ANON, 1794–5)

MOB: What's this? You call us rebels?
    You drink the English tea?
    The American eagle's after you.
    Don't step on us! Join us or die!
    Tear off the tyrant's crown,
        Throw it down!

Join us or die!
And wear the cap of liberty!

1 VOICE: Where's that boy going with the water?

SETH: You'll see.

2 VOICES: Where're you taking it now?

SETH: Find out.

(*He enters the tent again. The mob disappears into same also, carrying effigy and banners.*)

MOB: What's in this tent? What's... in this ... ?

(*We now enter the tent and can see the front stoop of a colonial house bearing a sign: 'Jesse Harple – Scrivener & Conveyancer.' In front, Seth plays at a naval battle between a British and Yankee pair of ships, using bellows to propel the toy boats around the tub and a squirt gun to sink them.*)

SETH: Lookout reporting
            Privateer to larboard
                  Under false colours!

MOB: (*sotto voce, offstage*)
      False colours!

SETH: All men on deck!
            Yankee rebel, I suspect!

MOB: Did he say 'rebel'?

(*Enter Jesse Harple, Seth's father, with a cup of tea. He is hatted in the Quaker style.*)

JESSE: Seth, I wish
        Thee would desist
        From such
        A warlike
        Game.

SETH: Be thou patient,
        Father, with me,
        My man o' war must sink
        This privateer into the sea.

(He keeps missing the target boat with the squirt gun and a toy cannon.)

MOB: What's this he's up to? This is no game.

(Enter Mrs. Harple, with teapot. She pours long tea, short tea.)

MRS. HARPLE: Jesse, thou knowest
  Since in Boston they threw tea
  Into the sea
  I am nervous of thee
  Drinking it so – publicly.

JESSE: *(calming her)* But – drinking it so – harmlessly.

(They drink. Ebenezer darts in and out and returns, leading the rebel mob.)

EBENEZER: This way, citizens, for treachery,
  Traitors – young, old, come and see!

MOB: Traitors! Traitors!

MRS. HARPLE: Jesse!

(She confiscates cup, heads into house, turns back.)

MRS. HARPLE: Tell Seth to hide.
  Hurry! Hurry! Take off
  Those little flags.
  Dear Lord deliver us! *(Exit)*

MOB: *(assembling)*   Who dares to fly the British flag
  In this town?

SETH: My sailors on this boat do –
  'Give her a broadside, my hearties!'

MOB: Are you going to let them sink our ship?

SETH: Yes! Down the Yankee privateer,
  Down she goes to Davy Jones's locker!

1 VOICE: *(to Jesse)*
  You Quaker pacifist!
  Make your tyke desist
  From desecrating our flag!

MOB: Our flag, our flag!

JESSE: Friends! This is a tempest in a tub!

EBENEZER: He was drinking British tea!

JESSE: … a tempest in a teapot!

1 VOICE: *(spoken)*
     Take off your hat, 'Friend.'

MOB: Take off your hat
     To the emblem of our state,
     Our state, our state!

2 VOICES: *(shouting)* … The rattlesnake!

JESSE: *(firm but quiet)* Friends, I will
     Take off my hat
     To neither king nor republic
     Nor a flag, nor a…

MOB: You don't want freedom?

JESSE: *(more defiant)* Yes. Freedom from all oppressors
     Kings or – mobs like yourselves!

MOB: *(shouting in unison)*
     Take off your hat!

(Jesse does not move. Pause, then sudden quick action as they seize him.)

MOB: Tar and feather him!
          Seize that tub,
                    Burn that little flag there!

MRS. HARPLE: Put my husband down,
                              Give me back my tub

SETH: Father, father!

JESSE: Courage, my son, courage!

MOB: Take off his hat!
     Catch that imp!
          Set their house afire!
               Haul him off to the market square!

Humil-i-ate him
There!

(One last glimpse of utter chaos – fire, Mrs. Harple at window, Jesse being led off on a rail, Seth dodging eager hands. Then: blackout (gong boom mysterious) – dawn, at a crossroads in a dense primeval forest – green, green, green.)

SCENE TWO: ON THE ROAD TO PHILADELPHIA

ARIA

SETH: Waiting for my mother and father
When she finds where they've left him
Waiting for my parents to join me
Long shadows shorten as the sun
Separates them, separates the shadows
Searching out, the sunlight shows me
Nameless forms, secret fearings.
(Full sun now. He looks about warily.)
What is heard and what is seen?
Boy with red hair hidden watching me
Woodpecker   Mourning dove
(War and peace)
Sometimes... men in shades of green
Moving about the trees are heard, are seen,
Disappearing, reappearing.
No shadows now, no shadows
Noon
Hungry

(To the tune of Albert G. Emerick's song 'Mad Anthony Wayne,' some American soldiers enter led by Colonel 'Mad Anthony' Wayne, dressed in splendour. He superintends the posting of a recruiting poster on a tree.)

WAYNE: *(reading poster)* All Intrepid Able-Bodied Heroes!
Join the American Light Corps
(Formerly Wayne's Irish Pennsylvanians)
Help
The Whelps

> Defeat the British Lion (mangy old beast
> Eager to despotize our liberty!)
> Five dollars & equipment!
> At the end of the War
> 50 acres of land
> Where every gallant Hero may retire,
> To enjoy his bottle and his lass!

SOLDIERS: Where every gallant Hero may retire,
To enjoy his bottle and his lass!

WAYNE: Well – ?

SETH: I'll join. (*laughter*)

WAYNE: Don't laugh, men – there's always the drum corps
But... (*to Seth*) Wherefore do you wish to join us?

SETH: Hunger. (*more laughter*)

WAYNE: Hmm. Not wishing to be accused of plagiarism,
Where are your parents?

SETH: Waited two days for them –
Supposed to meet them here.

WAYNE: (*to Seth*) Stay put there, juvenile
For a while.
(*to soldiers*) Is he too young to be a spy, men?
A Loyalist spy? – or is he just old and quick enough?

(*The red-haired boy, Ebenezer Hatchway, appears up in a tree.*)

EBENEZER: Just three miles from here, Colonel Wayne.
That Tory imp raised the British colours
And – to our flag his father would not
Take off his hat!

WAYNE: That little gaffer a Tory and he so young?

EBENEZER: It's not fair...

WAYNE: Well, redhead, didn't you apply to be a drummer
And we turned you down?

EBENEZER: Never! And it's not fair to...

SOLDIERS: What's not fair?
A turncoat's as good as you!
After him, after him!

(*Ebenezer jumps down from tree; some of them chase him off, others exit in a more leisurely way to the 'Wayne' tune. Seth, alone again, hears the woodpecker and mourning dove – then, in the distance, Simcoe's rangers singing. Tune, 'Over the Hills and Far Away.'*)

RANGERS: Hark now, the drums beat up again
For all true soldier gentlemen;
Then let us list and march, I say,
Over the hills and far away.
O'er the hills and o'er the main
To Flanders, Portugal and Spain.
Queen Anne commands and we'll obey:
Over the hills and far away.

(*As with Wayne, Simcoe and his men sing their recruiting poster as they nail it up on another tree.*)

MAJOR: All Aspiring Heroes
Can now distinguish themselves by joining...

ALL: The Queen's Ranger Huzzars!

MAJOR: Commanded by...

MAJOR, ADJUTANT: (*together*) Major John Graves Simcoe!

MAJOR: Fresh from victory at Brandywine!

MAJOR, ADJUTANT: Vivant Rex et Regina!

ALL: Vivant Rex et Regina!

(*Seth has put a stick over his shoulder and marches back and forth, strutting.*)

MAJOR: (*spoken*) Look here.

SETH: I'll join. (*laughter*)

SIMCOE: Well, my small rustic, what's your pleasure?

SETH: Soldiering, your honour. (*roars of laughter*)

SIMCOE: Lad, if I were to let you join my Rangers
I should prefer some talk with your parents.

SETH: My parents have deserted me.

ADJUTANT: Sir! There was a couple, rather beggarly and tramp-
ish,
The woman wheeling the man in a wheelbarrow.
We passed them a mile back.

SETH: My parents have a horse and cart –
They wouldn't ride in a wheelbarrow.

MAJOR: We need another drummer boy, Major Simcoe.

SIMCOE: *(pondering)* He may miss his parents, though.
(decides to accept Seth) Where were they rendezvousing for,
lad?

SETH: Philadelphia.

ADJUTANT: *(with a forward sign to the company)* Let's get moving
again.

(They begin tramping again, joined by Seth.)

SIMCOE: Major Armstrong, leave a note for the parents,
with our address, just in case.

*(Major salutes and lingers to carry out the order, then follows the others
off.)*

RANGERS: The 'prentice Tom, he may refuse
To wipe his angry master's shoes,
For then he's free to sing and play –
Over the hills and far away.
O'er the hills and far away...
Flanders, Portugal and Spain...
Queen Anne commands and we obey...

*(As this fades in the distance, the parents enter, he in wheelbarrow, she
pushing. Seeing the note, she drops the barrow and studies same.)*

JESSE: Oh, good wife!
Let the barrow down next time more gently,

For it hurts so.

MRS. HARPLE: Oh, Jesse, Seth's gone.

JESSE: Gone?

MRS. HARPLE: Gone with the Queen's Rangers.

JESSE: If only I could walk, we might have saved him.

MRS. HARPLE: Surely, we'll catch up with him.

JESSE, MRS. HARPLE: (*together*) We'll catch up with him in Philadelphia.

(*They resume their travels, singing a hymn by George Fox, to the tune of William Billings's 'Canon 4 in 1.'*)

HYMN

JESSE, MRS. HARPLE: (*together*) Walk cheerfully over the world
Answering that of God in every man,
For He lies like a dull stone of flint
In even the hardest-hearted wicked man

Friends! Strike that stone with patient peace,
Bring light and love to souls so dark.
As he did, love your enemies,
And Lo! Your love may strike a spark. (*Exeunt*)

SCENE THREE: HOW TO PLAY THE DRUM

(*Drum major and a model drummer prepare to teach a lesson.*)

MAJOR: The first thing
previous to a Boy
Practicing on the Drum
is to place him perfectly upright!

(*Seth appears. They show him the proper position.*)

MAJOR: Left heel in the hollow of the Right Foot.

(*Pause to adjust.*)

MAJOR: Then put the Drum Sticks into his hands
Secondly, let the Boys Drum be slung on the Neck

The Drum bearing on the left thigh so that...

(*Adjusting again.*)

MAJOR: Thirdly, previous to commencing to learn the Long Roll...

(*Model illustrates by placing his arms up with his elbows nearly level with his ears. Seth copies. Then the model plays the long roll, throwing his arms up between each phrase, lowering them according to the closing of the roll. Seth imitates.*)

MAJOR: Don't hit your knees, Master Harple.
Try to hit the centre of the drum!

(*Eventually, Seth plays a perfect long roll.*)

MAJOR: Well, now then, today, now that we've learnt the
Roll! The Open Flam! The Ten-Stroke Roll! The Close
Flam from Hand to Hand! The Drag! The Drag and Stroke!
Let's try the Eleven-Stroke Roll!

(*Seth repeats this figure after the model a couple of times.*)

SETH: Learning to play the drum, why you may hear
My drumming, drumming!
As if I had been given a five-mile-long
Woodpecker's beak thrumming, thrumming!

MAJOR: (*shouting, an order*) Plain beating of a march!

(*Troops enter and march to the drum.*)

SOLDIERS: How many miles do we go
Before – bang! bang! – we meet the foe?

(*Two fife players march, with model drummer leading. Tune is 'The General.' Major introduces Seth to the marching drill.*)

MAJOR: Carrying the Drum
When marching and Beating
At the same time!

(*Seth begins to move while drumming, falters and then – breakthrough!*)

SETH: After many months of practice
when I finally, finally,

could play for real soldiers
marching, marching,
I felt so close to our Commander.
There were no written orders.
We drummers and buglers were
extensions of his mind.
We were his voice, his thunderous voice,
commanding, commanding.

(Stage fills up as soldiers, women and children enact patterns of camp life.)

MAJOR: *(shouting)* Break camp!

SOLDIERS: Our secret camp in the wilderness.

WOMEN: Good spring water to wash their bloodied shirts in.

(Seth looks up at Simcoe, appearing in a spotlight.)

SIMCOE: For the Queen's Rangers,
No, there are to be no slow
Marches. Fast marches only.
From nowhere we strike – and vanish!

(Spotlight fades. Seth goes on drumming.)

SOLDIERS: Charge them, surprise them – and kill them!

TUTTI: Charge them – and die!

(They march while singing 'The girl I left behind me.')

SOLDIERS: In hurried words her name I blest,
I breathed the vows that bind me,
And to my heart in anguish pressed
The girl I left behind me.

(Each one of the following sets of drum/bugle signals suggests a different drill pattern involving the whole company and also suggests what a drummer's day is like. Ending in the taptoo and the snores of the barracks.)

MAJOR: Reveille! *(Bugles and drums give signal.)*

SOLDIERS: You damn rebels! You got us into this!

MAJOR: Sighting the Enemy! (*Do.*)

WOMEN, CHILDREN: 'The shot heard round the world.'

MAJOR: Prepare to commence Firing! (*Do.*)

A SOLDIER: My tinderbox... dammit... won't light!

MAJOR: Cease firing! (*Do.*)

A SOLDIER: (*spoken*) Good idea, that.

TUTTI: Aye, angry hordes about to come after us! A-a-a!

MAJOR: Retreat! (*Do.*)

A SOLDIER: (*spoken, brightly*)... to where there is a *tavern*?

TUTTI: A tavern!

MAJOR: Dinner Call! (*Do.; voices join in*)

SOLDIERS: When mighty roast beef was the Englishman's food,
    It ennobled our hearts and enrichèd our blood.

A BOY: The best cows George Washington ever raised.

A WOMAN: Six more bloody shirts to wash!

SOLDIERS: Oh, the roast beef of Old England and
    Oh for Old England's roast beef!

(*A bell sounds. The drummers, Seth among them, initiate the taptoo ceremony. Twilight. Major sings against the first taptoo, 'St. Patrick's Day in the Morning.'*)

MAJOR: Time to go about the town
    And too the taps,
    Roust them out of their taverns and canteens
    Gather up the stragglers and wanderers...

(*Crowd cheers, claps in time to the music.*)

TUTTI: Taptoo! Taptoo!

(*With the second taptoo tune, 'Go to the Devil and Shake Yourself,' the tavern singing and dancing become more animated, rowdier.*)

TUTTI: 'Molly, dear Molly, come dance with me.'

Hickory-dock, a-diddle-de-die-do,
'Go to the devil and shake yourself!'
Riddle me, rattle me, fiddle-de-dee!
'Stir yourself, shake yourself, dance with me.'
Hippety-hop, a diddle-de-die-do,
'Go to the devil and shake yourself!'
Riddle me, rattle me, fiddle-de-dee!

(*Jollity subsides as soldiers bid goodnight and head back to camp. Stage empties and darkens.*)

TWO SOLDIERS (*one reads, one sings, lines from Gray's 'Elegy.'*):
'Now fades the glimmering landscape on the sight
And all the air a solemn stillness holds.'

TWO BOYS: Taptoo! (*last signal to stragglers*) Taptoo!

(*Ad-lib humming, snatches of songs, distant laughter, snorings in sleepy barracks, drummer boys asleep, taking off their drums, some still playing drums in their dreams.*)

SCENE FOUR: THE CHICKEN THIEF

(*The last watch of the night at Wayne's encampment.*)

ARIETTA

SENTINEL: Stretch myself. Yawn.
Got to keep... awake
Or...Wayne will have...
Me sho(t) – (*turns into yawn*)
(*spoken*) Oh! The soles of my boots are just sieves
for these little stones.
(*cock crows in the distance*)
(*glancing towards camp*) At last it's time for...
Me to sleep...
And you to wake.
(*spoken*) My sore-toe bandage has slipped off! Ouch!!
(*suddenly, as Wayne approaches*) Halt! Who's there?
Stand and declare yourself in the name of the Republic!

WAYNE: A friend, you idiot.

(*Holding closed lantern, Sentinel examines Colonel's face and uniform.*)

SENTINEL: Give the password, then.

WAYNE: I'm your colonel, you nutmeg-head.

SENTINEL: What would *he* be doing out here so late?

WAYNE: There's one of our drummer boys missing.

SENTINEL: (*sceptical*) Sure. Give the password.

WAYNE: Um... Er... (*Mutters as his memory fails.*)

SENTINEL: You could be that Simcoe fellow, stole your crazy uniform off a clothesline. The password?

WAYNE: Eh... Er...

SENTINEL: You're the one thought it up. Or so you believe.

WAYNE: Um... (*finally*) 'It is me, I, Charles.'

SENTINEL: That's better. No drummer boy's got past me, sir, your honour. Not past me, he hasn't.

WAYNE: But past you (Corcoran, isn't it?) – no drummer boy it was stealthed by you.

(*Starts to stretch a rope across the path.*)

SENTINEL: Then what did, sir?

WAYNE: A goddamn little two-faced about-to-desert weasel!

SENTINEL: Throw me the end of the rope, sir.

WAYNE: That's more like it, Private Corcoran. We'll trip him up.

WAYNE, SENTINEL: (*together*) We'll trip him up, this young pup, Tie him up and trip him up!

WAYNE: Hsst! There's someone loping up the path.

(*They crouch on either side of the path, holding ends of the cord. We hear Ebenezer stamping along, cackles from burlap bag he has stuffed some chickens into. Offstage voices supply the cackles. He trips, Wayne grabs him, Sentinel holds the bag.*)

WAYNE: You chicken-purloiner! (*sarcastic*) Next time leave us a note where you're going. I was sick of worry for you.

EBENEZER: Yah! You never give us enough to eat!

SENTINEL: I can second that remark, Colonel.

EBERNEZER, SENTINEL: Hoo! Join up with Wayne, farewell to food!

SENTINEL: Yes and farewell to *shoes*!

WAYNE: (*trying to keep calm*) One thing at a time. (*to Ebenezer*) Where did you steal these? (*No response. Then, suddenly threatening.*) Hatchway, do you want a whipping?

EBENEZER: (*cheeky*) Yes, I do.

WAYNE: You can't play the drum worth a damn, but you can spread discontent like you were the spirit of sour apples.

EBENEZER: Why don't you drum me out of the regiment, Colonel?

SENTINEL: Yes, why not drum him out, drum him out?

WAYNE: You aren't worth that. Get up!

EBENEZER: (*arms about Wayne's knees*) Don't shoot me, sir!

WAYNE: (*hoisting him up and kicking him*) Bah! No wonder the local farmers hate us – with your like thieving them blind. Back to camp!

(*Ebenezer runs off laughing. As if mourning their departing master, the bag of chickens set up a big cackle. Light fades on the Sentinel proffering the sack to his colonel with*)

SENTINEL: Your honour?

SCENE FIVE: 'DRAW YOUR SWORDS, RANGERS, THE REBELS ARE COMING!'

(*Rangers line up against a green sheet, backs to audience.*)

SIMCOE: Draw your swords, Rangers, the rebels are coming.

RANGERS: Draw your swords, Rangers, the rebels are coming.

(*Sheet is withdrawn, Rangers face a line of various Yankee rebel corps. During Simcoe's discourse, the two groups mime a confrontation.*)

DISCOURSE

SIMCOE: The enemy will wonder, after they have fired their
        one rifle shot,
Why you, running at them, bayonets at the ready, did not
Fire your one musket shot: but
The soldier in the Queen's Rangers
        on the victim's
Eye
With leonine ferocity fixes
His eye,
And without looking at the point of it
        (By which I mean his bayonet!),
Consigns, certain of conquest, his enemy,
Screaming to – eternity!

(*By now the rebels are swept offstage. Rangers line up again in front of green sheet.*)

RANGERS 1, 2: (*to audience*) The surprise of the rebels at Hancock's Public House.

(*Sheet is withdrawn: a cut-out tavern with many unshuttered windows. A blue sheet represents Aloes Creek.*)

SIMCOE: (*to audience*) There was a bridge across Aloes Creek.

RANGERS 1, 2: (*to audience*) In the swamp their army did not see us.

SIMCOE: (*entering scene*) Jarvis, you and your men
Go into that public house and hide.
The rest of the Rangers will retreat
        Past the tavern.

(*Women in house resist the soldiers of Jarvis.*)

WOMEN: (*brandishing brooms*) Here, get out of here, you damn Tories!

(Brooms at windows suddenly disappear as soldiers grab women and stuff them down the cellar. Windows are shut.)

JARVIS: Sorry, ma'am, but we need your tavern for an ambush.

WOMEN: Ambush our brave Yankees, is it? Ha!

WOMAN 1: Scream, everybody! *(They scream.)*

JARVIS: Stop that!

MEN: Stop that!

WOMEN: We won't stop that!

MEN: Down into the cellars with you.

WOMEN: We shall not be put down into the cellars of our own house.

JARVIS: Ladies, this is not your house now, it is the King's house.

(More loud vocal reactions.)

WOMAN 2: What?

WOMEN: Gagged with our own kerchiefs, is it? Our house the King's house?

MEN: Yes, ladies.

WOMEN: Our republican cellar a dungeon?

MEN: No, ladies.

WOMAN 3: Take that and that! Take that and that!

JARVIS: Tie them to those barrels.

WOMEN: Our own barrels? We *(smothered)* shall *(smothered)* not...

MEN: Quiet, quiet!

(Screams subside.)

RANGER 1: At last.

SIMCOE: *(to audience)* The rest of the Rangers retreated up the road

In full view of the enemy.

(*Backing up, the demi corps lures the enemy corps to pass the house.*)

REBEL OFFICER: After those Rangers, men.

(*As they cross the bridge, the shutters fly open and muskets fire out. As they tumble down into the 'creek,' the blue sheet billows up to reveal rebels struggling, floats down as they drown.*)

VARIOUS VOICES: It's an ambush / Retreat, you bloody
fools! / Get out of range – forward! / I can't
swim! Help, help! / Let go of me, let go of…
(*gurgle*) / Where's the… (*gurgle*)

SIMCOE: (*to audience*) The greater part of the rebel division…

SIMCOE, RANGERS 1, 2: (*to audience*)… were drowned in Aloes
Creek.

RANGERS 1, 2: (*to audience*) And then, some weeks later…

(*Twilight. Simcoe is talking to some rebel soldiers.*)

SIMCOE: Good evening, men and where are you off to?

REBEL 1: Your honour, fat cattle from New England
That General Washington's desirous of having.

SIMCOE: Where?

REBELS 1, 2: Sleepy-hoe Ferry.

REBEL 2: Your honour, any news of that
British general (what's his name, Pat?) –

REBEL 1: General Clinton.

REBELS 1, 2: General Clinton?

SIMCOE: (*motioning for assistance*) You shall ask him yourselves
for, you see,
We are British.

(*Rangers appear and arrest them.*)

REBELS 1, 2: (*as they are borne off*) British?
But you're supposed to be redcoats!

SIMCOE: *(to them)* Best colour for light troops is green.

MEN: Best colour for light troops is green.

SIMCOE: *(to audience, resuming narrating/lecturing mode)*
Green: Put it on in the spring, the men can scarcely be seen.
Barely discernible at a distance,
As on the enemy we secretly advance.
Draw your swords, Rangers, the rebels are coming...

MEN: The rebels are coming.

(Stage is empty as Rangers prepare another ambuscade. Far-off sounds of horses' harnesses jangling, marching feet, drums, approaching disaster. As tension dissolves, we hear rain beating on the roof of the Rangers' winter quarters.)

SIMCOE: Mr. Quartermaster, scour the country for cabbages.
We've a duty to keep the men from scurvy this winter.
(to audience) In messing, I prescribe cleanliness and
regularity,
In caps, in clothing, absolute uniformity.
Yes, Sergeant?

SERGEANT: *(saluting)* Colonel Simcoe. A farmer and his wife,
Mr. and Mrs. Felswad. They have a complaint.

SIMCOE: Good day, sir and madam. *(pushing ahead)* You do have
some cabbages?

MRS. FELSWAD: Yes, Colonel, cabbages we do have, but –

SIMCOE: But – ?

MR. & MRS. FELSWAD: *(together)* Colonel Simcoe, we're not
selling you
Any cabbages unless, unless, unless
You can stop your soldiers from pilfering
Our apples.

SIMCOE: Your apples?

MRS. FELSWAD: Not an apple left by the public highway.

MR. & MRS. FELSWAD: *(together)* All gone, all gone.

SIMCOE: All gone?

MR. FELSWAD: All gone, Simcoe.

MR & MRS. FELSWAD: No cabbages, no apples.

SIMCOE: No cabbages?

MR. FELSWAD: No apples.

MR & MRS. FELSWAD: *(starting to leave)* No cabbages, no apples.

SIMCOE: No apples?

MRS. FELSWAD: No cabbages.

SIMCOE, MR. & MRS. FELSWAD: *(together, as Simcoe follows them out)*
No cabbages, no apples; no cabbages, no apples …

SIMCOE: No apples …

SCENE SIX: 'WHY, SOLDIERS, WHY?'

(Drummer boys are making an effigy of a Queen's Ranger sentinel. Ebenezer Hatchway, deserted to them, is not helping but juggling some apples.)

WILLIAMS: Hey! It's the turncoat, Hatchway.

LAKEMAN: Turncoat! Steals apples but still can't drum.

WILLIAMS: Hatchway, put the apples away and give us a hand.

EBENEZER: Simcoe's making us do this. What for?

WILLIAMS: Your former associates have been shooting our sentries, so – we're going to give them *this* to shoot at.

SETH: Make them feel ashamed. Shooting sentries.

EBENEZER: I remember now and Simcoe said: *(mimicking)* 'They're not supposed to do that. But then, they're rebels: no true grasp of milit'ry discipline.' *(laughs)*

LAKEMAN: You're still a rebel, Hatchway. What're you rebelling against?

EBENEZER: What h'ya got?

LAKEMAN: Aw, go back to Wayne's bunch if you don't –

EBENEZER: For two cents I would.

BOYS: For two cents? For two cents? Here!

(*A shower of pennies is thrown at him.*)

EBENEZER: Hurray! Williams, Lakeman, Hartley... I thought
you'd never buy my apples – you're so honest.
So, take delivery – two a penny.

(*He throws apples at each boy. They won't touch the apples. Drum major
enters, they line up and all salute.*)

DRUM MAJOR: At ease. Lakeman, assist the drum corps in draw-
ing lots.

(*Calls the roll. Each boy replies with 'here' and takes a straw from
Lakeman as his name is called.*)

MAJOR: Williams, Hartley, Dudgeon, Corolinia, MacKay, Harple.

EBENEZER: Sir! And Ebenezer Hatchway.

MAJOR: Eh?

EBENEZER: Sir, don't I get a chance to draw?

MAJOR: (*shaking head*) Hatchway, it's to draw for the pleasure
Of kicking you in the butt as we drum you out
Of the regiment for thieving.
Well, Lakeman?

LAKEMAN: It's Seth Harple, sir.

(*They form two parallel lines for gauntlet ritual. Ebenezer makes a break
for it, but is caught and held by the drum major. They force Ebenezer
through the scrum, hitting, jeering, tearing his uniform. Those in front
run around to end of the line for a second turn. Seth stands apart rather
awkwardly. Fifes, bugle and drum accompany the action with 'The
Rogue's March.' As excitement mounts, Simcoe enters and observes from
sidelines. It is Seth's turn to administer the final kick. He runs down the
gamut to do this, but at the last moment pauses.*)

SIMCOE: What's the matter with the lad?

MAJOR: Harple, you were allotted to kick this young rogue.
Kick him and he's out of the regiment.

BOYS: Kick him, kick him.

SETH: It's cruel. I can't do it.

SIMCOE, MAJOR: *(together)* *What?!*

EBENEZER: *(laughing)* Yah! Afraid to kick me? You'd better. This is all your fault, Harple.

SIMCOE: It's MacKay then. And I want to see Harple after mess.

(Exit)

(The interrupted ceremony proceeds. At the top of the march, Mackay kicks Ebenezer. The boys chase Ebenezer off, Scarecrow Sentinel is carried off as well and Seth is left alone. Simcoe walks slowly up towards Seth from a great distance, i.e, from the back of the performance space.)

SIMCOE: Master Harple, it's supposed to be cruel.

SETH: I know, sir.

SIMCOE: You were raised among the Society of Friends.

SETH: Yes, sir.

(Far away we hear the dull thuds of bullets hitting the effigy.)

SIMCOE: Not everything in the army is based on cruelty.
    For example, listen.

(He points off; they both hearken.)

SETH: It's the rebels trying to kill the soldier we made out of straw.

ARIA

SIMCOE: And they will keep on until
    It dawns on the thick colonial skull
    That we mock their barbarity.
    One day, Seth, for probably the same reason, man
    Will stop butchering his brothers
    But until that day men like me
    Must go on fighting – fighting so well that we
    Get all that over and done,

The fighting over and done and then
Peace, peace.

SETH: What's going to happen to me, sir?

SIMCOE: Oh! (*ironic*) I'm going to punish you very severely.
Your parents have been writing to me.
I think you should go back to Philadelphia.

(*They salute. A parting handshake and Simcoe goes off. Seth stands facing audience.*)

GLEE

(*Based on 'How Stands the Glass Around?' (Anon)*)

A SOLDIER: (*offstage*) Why, soldiers, why
Should we be melancholy, boys?
Why, soldiers, why?
Whose business 'tis to die.

SETH: (*to audience*) There was a song the soldiers sang as I left that night.

(*Carousing troops assemble on stage. Seth exits slowly.*)

SOLDIERS: Why, soldiers, why
Should we be melancholy, boys?
Why, soldiers, why?
Whose business 'tis to die.

A SOLDIER: (*now on stage*) What, sighing? Fie!
Damn fear, drink on, be jolly, boys!
'Tis he, you or I.
Hot, cold, wet or dry,
We're always bound to follow, boys,
And scorn to fly.

SETH: (*re-emerging with a pack-bag*) It broke my heart to leave that man. But –
I went back to my mother and father and they
Finished bringing me up.

(*He shoulders the bag and slowly exits.*)

SOLDIERS: What, sighing? Fie!
  Damn fear, drink on, be jolly, boys!
  'Tis he, you or I
  Hot, cold, wet or dry,
  We're always bound to follow, boys,
  And scorn to fly.

(*During this reprise they start to disperse. Solo voice is now heard offstage.*)

A SOLDIER: … always bound to follow, boys…
  … and scorn… to fly.

(*All are now off. Faint cheers, a distant guttural laugh or two, as song fades.*)

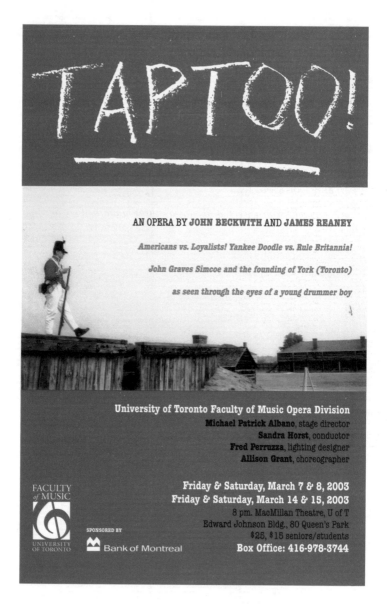

Poster design for the 2003 produtions by the Opera division, faculty
of music, University of Toronto.

Curtain call, Toronto opening night. The motif for the poster and the backdrop
is from a colour snap taken at Fort Henry, Niagara-on-the-Lake, Ontario, during
a historical re-enactment of a military excercise.

ACT TWO

PRELUDE

(We open outisde the theatre tent. In the distance, a band of immigrant loyalists starts walking towards us, the men holding ox-goads. The tune is 'Windham,' Daniel Read, 1785.)

ALL: Exiles are we
           Who in 1783
      Walked up from the Mohawk Valley
      To the border river of Niagara.
      Crossing Jordan into promised lands,
      We came in our thousands.
           Ten-mile Creek;
           Ten-mile, Twenty-mile Creek;
           Ten-mile, Twenty-mile, Forty-mile Creek.

      Before we left for these wilderness roads,
      We cut ourselves some ox-goads,

SOLO: From the Balm of Gilead tree by the house where I was bred,

ALL: And you'll never see it again, we said.
           Ten-mile Creek, etc. ...

      Those sticks we drove our oxen with:
      We planted them up here in our youth,
      And watered them with our exile's tears.
      Have they withered with the passing years?
           Ten-mile Creek, etc. ...

      No, just as we have, they've taken root,
      Oh so slowly new leaves show,
      And with any luck perhaps we'll grow
      And flourish and bear fruit.
           Ten-mile Creek, etc. ...

(They disappear into the tent.)

SCENE ONE: UNDER TWO FLAGS

(At first we think we're back in the New Jersey town where we started. But although the house with its 'Scrivener & Notary' sign is the same, we are really in York, Upper Canada, not long before the War of 1812. As long ago, a boy (Seth Junior) pulls (a bit different from the other time) a low trolley with a tub upon it and places it downstage left.)

JESSE: What's that, little Seth?

JESSE, MRS. HARPLE: What's that, my boy?

SETH JUNIOR: It's Lake Ontario, Commodore!

(He goes back and forth filling tub from a pail.)

SETH SENIOR: *(entering)* You've seen the house before too, Mother, Father.

MRS. HARPLE: Why, it's so like the house we used to have in New Jersey.
Didst thou move it up here, Seth?

JESSE: Oh, Mrs. Harple, that house was burnt down by the mob.

SETH SENIOR: Well, I built it up again – from memory.

(Tune: 'Celestial Waterings,' 1805)

MRS. HARPLE: Yes, my son, thee were always for trying something different.

SETH SENIOR: When I finished school in Philadelphia, I was saved by the Methodists.

JESSE: Such noisy people.

SETH JUNIOR, MRS. HARPLE: 'Praise the Lord!'

SETH JUNIOR, MRS. HARPLE, SETH SENIOR: 'Brother Jones has seen the Light!'

JESSE: Noisy people.

SETH JUNIOR, MRS. HARPLE: 'Hallelujah!'

MRS. HARPLE: And we trained thee up in such a quiet profession.

SETH SENIOR: I know: scrivening and accountancy.

JESSE: And took you every First Day to such a quiet meeting house.

SETH SENIOR: I know. But mild maketh wild, they say.
Always the same makes for – change.

SETH JUNIOR, MRS. HARPLE: 'Hallelujah!'

(*Exit Seth Junior. He re-enters with a second tub, this time on a slightly higher trolley and places it downstage right.*)

SETH SENIOR: What's that one, little Seth?

SETH SENIOR, JESSE, MRS. HARPLE: What's that one, my boy?

SETH JUNIOR: It's Lake Erie, Commodore!

SETH SENIOR: Leave it there for a while, lad. Mother, Father:
when you lit out for Canada, you may remember,
I didn't.

JESSE: Thou used to write us, about teaching –

JESSE, MRS. HARPLE: – at the Methodist seminary in Pennsyl-
vania.

SETH SENIOR: That's where I met Atahentsic.

(*The door of the house opens. An Indian woman, Atahentsic, holds two model boats in her hands.*)

ATAHENTSIC: Sethy, here are your toy ships. All sails and flags
mended now.

SETH JUNIOR: (*coming to her*) Thank thee, Mamma.

(*He takes them over to the Lake Erie tub.*)

SETH SENIOR: (*resuming*) When school broke up –

ATAHENTSIC: I went back to my father's house, across the
Ohio River. My father told me he would not fight
the Americans this time. There was no stopping them.

SETH SENIOR: I received a letter from General Wayne.

WAYNE: (*appearing in a spot stage right*) Harple, how
would you like to be drum major in my army of the Ohio?

(Spot out.)

SETH SENIOR: And I also had news about my friend, Major Simcoe.

GEORGE III: *(appearing – the effigy from overture to Act One – in spot stage left)*
Divide the colony in two and let that Simcoe chap be lieutenant-governor of Upper Canada.

(Spot out.)

QUINTET

JESSE, MRS. HARPLE: Yes, we remember.

ATAHENTSIC: My father's house stood in Ohio.

JESSE, MRS. HARPLE: We remember wondering which he would choose.

SETH JUNIOR: My father was in love –

SETH SENIOR: – Not with General Wayne so much as you! *(gesture to Atahentsic)*

JESSE, MRS. HARPLE: Which would he choose: Simcoe in Upper Canada or Wayne in Ohio?

SETH JUNIOR: It was love that led my father to decide for Wayne then.

SETH SENIOR: It was love that led me to decide for Wayne then.

ATAHENTSIC: His love for me, my love for him.

ALL: Love – love led him (me) to Ohio.
Love led him (me) to Ohio.

SCENE TWO: IN THE OHIO WILDERNESS

(Light fades. As in Act One, Scene Two, a transition to a wilderness setting: Wayne's camp, with a stars-and-stripes flying. Drums, overlapping the end of the previous scene, foretell the situation. A small party of soldiers prepares to set up the general's tent. Seth is signalling them to place it far away from a tall buttonwood tree but Hatchway, with his drum, signals

them to put it right under the tree. So the tent (represented by a small pup tent) moves back and forth. To fragments of the patriotic song 'Hail! Columbia,' two soldiers attempt to follow the conflicting directions.)

1ST SOLDIER: Oh, oh! Move it near this big tree.

2ND SOLDIER: Oh, no! Move it farther away.

1ST & 2ND SOLDIERS: It's a battle of the drummers
　　With their contradictory drums
　　And we're underneath their thumbs!

(Whole group now sings the song while Seth and Ebenezer interject orders.)

SOLDIERS: Hail! Columbia, happy land!
　　Hail! Ye heroes, heav'n-born band…

SETH: I'm in charge of pitching General Wayne's tent.

EBENEZER: *I'm* in charge of pitching General Wayne's tent.

SOLDIERS: Who fought and bled in freedom's cause,
　　Who fought and bled in freedom's cause.

(Tree gives a sudden lurch.)

SETH: Not beneath that tree.

EBENEZER: *Right* beneath that tree!

SETH: Isn't it leaning rather?

EBENEZER: All the more shade for the general!

SOLDIERS: Let Independence be our boast…

SETH: This way, men. Paramount is General Wayne's safety!

SOLDIERS: …Ever mindful what it cost.

EBENEZER: *This* way, men. Paramount is General Wayne's *comfort*!

SETH, SOLDIERS: Firm, united, let us be…

EBENEZER, SOLDIERS: … Rallying round our liberty,

TUTTI: … As a band of brothers…

(All freeze as Wayne enters.)

WAYNE: What the Sam Hill's going on here?

SETH: Sir! Ensign Hatchway keeps countermanding me.
  I want your tent as far from that tree – *(tree sways again)*
  not a safe tree – fall over –

WAYNE: It's warm, Drum Major Harple. Take a chance. I
  need the shade.

(Seth gives in. Tent is now right under the tree. Soldiers disperse informally. Wayne is about to go inside the tent.)

EBENEZER: Sir, before you retire: a grave matter.

WAYNE: Yes, Hatchway. Grave matter of what?

EBENEZER: Sir, Drum Major Harple is a traitor.

WAYNE: Eh! How so?

EBENEZER: He's just married to an Indian woman.

WAYNE: *(pause)* Not necessarily treason, but –

DUO

WAYNE: Seth Harple, where was it you first met her?

SETH: Sir, she was a pupil of mine, at the school I taught at in
  Pennsylvania.

WAYNE: Her tribe and parentage – ?

SETH: She's a Maumee and the daughter of Chief Turtle.

WAYNE: Chief Turtle?! Do you not know, Seth Harple, what her
  father once expostulated?

SETH: No, I do not know what he 'expostulated.'

WAYNE: – After he demolished General St. Clair seven years
  back?

SETH: No, No, what *did* he *(pause)* 'say'?

WAYNE: – As he bade his men stuff our dead boys' mouths with
  earth?

SETH: *(exasperated)* No, General. What did Chief Turtle say?

WAYNE: 'You wanted our land,' said your wife's father.
'Here! Eat it!'

SETH: Well, it is their land!

(A tense silence. A group of soldiers surrounds them.)

WAYNE: *(furious)* Either leave her or leave me.
I could have you shot! Why'd you marry her? – You could
have slaked your appetite for copper no doubt without that!

(Seth raises his fist to strike the general but is restrained.)

WAYNE: Drum him out of the regiment, before I *do* shoot him!

*(Soldiers tie a halter round Seth's neck and form lines with drummer,
preparing a gauntlet similar to Act One, Scene Six. Tune is a different ver-
sion of the 'Rogues March.')*

SOLDIERS: Indian-lover! Loving the enemy! Indian-lover!
Two little, three little, four little...
Five little, six little, seven little...

EBENEZER: It's not cruel enough: do it again!

WAYNE: Hatchway!

SOLDIERS: *Eight* little... *(shouts, kicks...)*

EBENEZER: ... not cruel enough... !

WAYNE: Hatchway! Hatchway!

SOLDIERS: *Nine* little... *(final kicks...)*

WAYNE: That's enough! So he fell into passion: enough!

SOLDIERS: Indian-lover! Loving the enemy! Indian-lover!

WAYNE: Enough!

*(He persuades them to break up the lines. Exeunt, leaving Seth, ragged and
bruised, alone – as lights fade.)*

SCENE THREE: AN OLD FRIEND AT FORT DEFIANCE

(*Picking some herbs, Atahentsic applies them to Seth's many cuts and bruises. Also, if possible, she helps him get his torn clothing to look less so.*)

DUO

ATAHENTSIC: Oh, my husband,
       How they have torn you and
              Treated you cruelly
       Because you love me.

SETH: Oh, my dear wife,
       Because I love you more than life
              Your love for me is as a spell.
       I feel no pain though I am caught in fiercest Hell!

ATAHENTSIC, SETH: Where shall we go now?
              Not South where our enemies are. (*pause*)
       Wilderness, birds in flight,
       Shadows, light, earth, air
              Tell us, where? (*pause*)
       To the North! the North!

(*The pauses are filled with suggestive wilderness sounds (wind, etc.) including a hint of some distant pursuit. Their rapid progress through the forest brings them to the mysterious and silent gates of Fort Defiance – a fort in Ohio still under the British flag, like one of those mysterious castles that suddenly loom up in Arthurian romances.*)

SETH: (*out of breath*) Oh, are we saved at last? A new British fort.

(*A sign reading 'Fort Defiance' is poked up from within.*)

ATAHENTSIC: Fort – Fort De – Fort Defiance!
       Ah! How fortunate I learned to read!

(*She hammers at the gate. At first there is an ominous silence as a cannon is raised and pointed towards us. A hand reaches up with a torch and makes the cannon fire. Seth and Atahentsic hug each other in terror. Gates open; they pass in; gates shut again.*)

SIMCOE: (*from inside the fort*) Upon my word, it's Master Harple, grown up.

SETH: *(do.)* Colonel Simcoe! I didn't know you British still had a fort in Ohio.

SIMCOE: Why yes. We're holding on to nine forts. Fort Schlosser, Fort Niagara, Fort Oswego, Fort Détroit *(French pronunciation)* – five more with similar horrid names – till you Yankees pay our Loyalists for their confiscated property.

ATAHENTSIC: And until my people are guaranteed their land?

SIMCOE: Oh yes, our Indian allies will be protected too. Your wife, I presume?

SETH: Yes, sir.

SIMCOE: Properly married?

ATAHENTSIC: Two ceremonies.

SETH: Just in case, two wedding ceremonies.

ATAHENTSIC: Once by the rites of my father's tribe.

SETH:... and once by the rites of a Methodist parson.

ATAHENTSIC, SETH: Two times have we been married.

SIMCOE: *(pause)* I've had the most difficult time up in Upper Canada, persuading the settlers to get married properly.

(Drums beat as Wayne and rebel contingent, including Ebenezer, approach.)

WAYNE: What's that blasted abomination flag doing here?

SETH JUNIOR: *(as narrator)* There was no answer.

WAYNE: Son of a...

SETH JUNIOR: General Wayne swore at Fort Defiance.

WAYNE: ... You bastards... !

SETH JUNIOR: He swore, they said, for five hours.

WAYNE: By Christ, I'll bastinado you!

SETH JUNIOR: He wanted to storm Fort Defiance...

WAYNE: ... turkey you!...

SETH JUNIOR: ... and recapture my mother and father.

WAYNE: ... damn British bulldog!

SETH JUNIOR: But finally –

(*Simcoe pops up on the parapet.*)

WAYNE: Simcoe! You rapscallion marauder!

SIMCOE: Mr. Wayne, you sordid foul-mouthed rebel:
Go away, or I shall fire this cannon at you!

(*A soldier appears holding a torch.*)

WAYNE: What are you doing here, you – lootenant-governor of
Upper Canaday?

SIMCOE: Obeying orders from His Majesty's government.
One, two, three... By the way, it's pronounced 'Leftenant.'
Four, five... (*counting continues under*)

EBENEZER: General, we ain't got no cannon. Better retreat!

REBEL SOLDIERS: General! Anthony! Tony! Better retreat!

(*Seth and Atahentsic laugh, their heads bobbing up over parapet.*)

SETH AND ATAHENTSIC: Democracy rules, General Wayne.
Heed the voice of the people!

WAYNE: Hatchway, get on a fast horse and ride
Hell for leather down to Pittsburgh.
Tell them cannon personnel
To get off their posterior declivities
And get up here with them culverins and mortars!

(*Exit Ebenezer.*)

REBEL SOLDIERS: Help! Help! Culverins and mortars! Help!

(*Cannon explodes, dispersing them. Wayne exits last, gesturing angrily.
Fort disappears and we see Seth Junior blowing a toy ship across the Lake
Erie tub.*)

SETH JUNIOR: Those were very happy days for my mother and
father. Colonel Simcoe came back to Upper Canada and
they came too. First they helped with – naming places.

SCENE FOUR: LOYAL SHE BEGAN

(*On the floor a map of southern Ontario is projected.*)

SIMCOE: And what is this part of the 'bush' called?

ATAHENTSIC: Colonel Simcoe, it is called Wawanosh.

SIMCOE: Let's call it Kent County. And this?

SETH SENIOR: Sir, the Canadians call it Côte de Misère.

SIMCOE: Ah yes, well, we will call it – Essex County. This river?

ATAHENTSIC: Askunessippi.

SETH SENIOR: The French called it La Tranche.

SIMCOE: We shall call it – the Thames. And at the forks here we shall build our capital – New London.

MRS. SIMCOE: (*offstage, lapdogs barking*) Call it Georgina, Mr. Simcoe. That would be a compliment to his majesty, King George.

SIMCOE: A *capital* idea, my dear. And what the devil do we call these two townships here?

(*Atahentsic and Seth have run out of names.*)

MRS. SIMCOE: (*entering, two lapdogs in her arms*) Why not call them after these pretty lapdogs you gave me? (*pause*) Flossy? (*pause*) Tiny?

SIMCOE, SETH: Flossy? Tiny?

MRS. SIMCOE, ATAHENTSIC, SIMCOE, SETH: Flossy! (*short laugh*) Tiny! (*more extended laugh*)

(*She hands the yapping dogs to him. Exeunt Simcoe and Seth Senior. Map projection fades. We hear the increasingly loud roar of the falls at Niagara which earmarks our presence in Newark, first capital of Upper Canada – today's Niagara-on-the-Lake. Mrs. Simcoe sits and invites Atahentsic to sit beside her.*)

DUO

MRS. SIMCOE: Look, Atahentsic, look at my arms. Swollen up

like posts with mosquito bites.

ATAHENTSIC: Mrs. Simcoe, here is the cure. *(proffers herb)* Touch-me-not.

MRS. SIMCOE: Why is it called Touch-me-not?

ATAHENTSIC: Try and touch its seed pod.

MRS. SIMCOE: Are you supposed to?

ATAHENTSIC: Yes.

(She laughs as pod delicately explodes. Atahentsic rubs the lady's swollen arms with crushed stems of the herb.)

MRS. SIMCOE: Why, Atahentsic, my arms feel better right away!

(Gets up and invites Atahentsic to join her in a stroll.)

ATAHENTSIC: Smell this, Mrs. Simcoe. It is sweet grass.

MRS. SIMCOE: Ah! It smells just like a Tonkin bean.
What is that sound, Atahentsic?

ATAHENTSIC: That is the roaring of Niagara.
We are walking by Ontario, the beautiful lake.

(Niagara roar grows fainter.)

MRS. SIMCOE: Ah! Quite like the sea sometimes off Devon in England, only –

ATAHENTSIC: Only what, Mrs. Simcoe?

MRS. SIMCOE: Only it lacks the marine smell.
Atahentsic, will there be rattlesnakes this way?

ATAHENTSIC: No. More likely up on Table Rock. *(pause)* Some dried hurtle berries?

(Takes them out of her bag. Mrs. Simcoe samples them reflectively.)

ATAHENTSIC: Made by relatives of mine.

MRS. SIMCOE: Ah, hmmh – they taste just like – just like Irwin's patent currant lozenges back home, only –

ATAHENTSIC: Only, Mrs. Simcoe?

MRS. SIMCOE: Only they taste of smoke.

ATAHENTSIC: But they are not English currant lozenges
Just as I am not an English lady.
They are hurtle berries,
Dried over my people's fires –
And I have been cradled by those fires.

(*Niagara gradually louder. Atahentsic knocks some pebbles together to attract a rattlesnake.*)

ATAHENTSIC: This ball you will give, you and the governor. (*pause*) Are we invited?

MRS. SIMCOE: My dear woman, only if you are properly married.

ATAHENTSIC: But we have been properly married
By the earth and the sky,
By the sacred tortoise of my father's tribe,
By the cross of my husband's faith.
But most of all by our love for each other.

MRS. SIMCOE: But by an Anglican parson?

ATAHENTSIC: An Anglican parson?

MRS. SIMCOE: An Anglican parson.
Our King and Queen are Anglicans, you know.

ATAHENTSIC: My king and queen are Earth and Sky!

MRS. SIMCOE: Anglican, Anglican!

ATAHENTSIC: Earth and Sky!

MRS. SIMCOE: (*pause, with a gracious smile*) Ah! Table Rock!
The more dangerous a landscape is, the more picturesque!
Atahentsic, my dear, do you really think you should pick up that dangerous rattlesnake?

(*Rattling sound as Atahentsic lifts up a rattlesnake above her head.*)

ATAHENTSIC: Yes, Mrs. Simcoe, you have never seen a live one before, have you?

MRS. SIMCOE: No. (*rapidly taking out sketchbook*)

ATAHENTSIC: Look, Mrs. Simcoe, look!

MRS. SIMCOE: Now that! That is the most picturesque thing I've ever seen in British North America!

(*She sketches as she walks backward in front of the majestic advancing Atahentsic and rattling snake.*)

SCENE FIVE: PARLIAMENT OAK

(*Enter legislative members in two groups.*)

GROUP 1: We belong to the Upper House,
    Which is to say
    We have servants and more than one table.
    We never, never dine with our servants.

GROUP 2: We belong to the Lower House,
    Which is to say
    We have no servants, or, if we do,
    We eat at the same table with them.

(*A fanfare as Simcoe enters.*)

SIMCOE: I have summoned the Legislature of Upper Canada under the authority of an Act of Parliament, which has established the British Constitution.

ALL: 'We assert our determination to strengthen our union with the present Kingdom and add our mite (*pause*) to its splendour and glory!'

(*All sit. Behind Simcoe is the Parliament Oak. From time to time we hear the dull roar of the falls. Each member rises and says his name and place of birth as the governor names his riding.*)

SIMCOE: Glengarry.

SPEAKER: John Macdonell, Mohawk Valley.

SIMCOE: Stormont.

1ST MEMBER: Jeremiah French, North Carolina.

SIMCOE: Dundas.

2ND MEMBER: Alexander Campbell, Long Island.

SIMCOE: Grenville.

3RD MEMBER: Ephraim Jones, Philadelphia.

SIMCOE: (*perceiving an irregularity*) Why has the member for Adolphustown and Prince Edward County not taken the oath of allegiance? (*peers at the name*) Mr. Jesse Harple?

JESSE: Sir, I cannot conscientiously take the oath of allegiance.

SIMCOE: Hmn... and where are you from, Friend Harple?

JESSE: New Jersey.

(*Sergeant-at-arms motions Jesse to sit aside. Simcoe resumes roll call.*)

SIMCOE: Leeds and Frontenac.

4TH MEMBER: Richard Cartwright, Connecticut.

SIMCOE: York and Lincoln.

5TH MEMBER: Nathaniel Petit, Vermont.

SIMCOE: Norfolk.

6TH MEMBER: Parshall Terry, Philadelphia.

SIMCOE: Kent.

7TH MEMBER: Francis Baby. I was born in *Canada*. (*laughter*)

SIMCOE: Middlesex.

EBENEZER: Ebenezer Hatchway. I'm from New Jersey too.

SIMCOE: (*loudly, after reading a note passed to him*) Mr. Speaker?

(*He hands note to the speaker, who scans it briefly.*)

SPEAKER: Sergeant-at-arms, I order you to expel Ebenezer Hatchway from this House and a new writ for his Riding to be issued forthwith.

EBENEZER: What's the matter with me? Expel me from this

House? I don't see no house 'cept that hovel over there you call Navy Hall.

SPEAKER: You are not loyal to His Majesty the King.

EBENEZER: I am a subject of old mad King George, have been ever since I was born in New Jersey. (*chuckle*) I'm a late Loyalist.

SPEAKER: Mr. Harple, could you identify this interloper? Alas, the constitution forbids you to take your seat – you've been too honest – but, you know this fellow?

JESSE: I certainly do. He had me tarred and feathered years ago in New Jersey, had our house burnt down.

EBENEZER: You quaking, old fool, that was the iniquity of my youth. (*chuckle*) You're not doing so well…

SIMCOE: Enough! Mr. Speaker! Sergeant-at-arms!

EBENEZER: Call this a democracy? Call this liberty and the pursuit of (*pause*) happiness?

TIRADE

EBENEZER: I come from a nation you should imitate,
And not of kings and order always prate.
Your flag is like a bloody butcher's apron;
Our flag is much prettier to look upon:
It reminds me of the sta-a-a-rs so bright
    On a summer night!

For your emblematic beast
    You take that rodent one, the beaver,
Always shadowed by a lion ever eager
    To make of your beaver a big feast!

Well, let us Yankees show you our great eagle
Filled with virtues ethical, commercial, legal!
Eager is this eagle to free you from the ways,
    The e-e-e-evil and wicked ways,
Of tyrants, affear'd of nothing and resplendent

> This American Eagle is president
> Of aw-aw-aw-awl he surveys!!!

MEMBERS: President of all? Bah!

SIMCOE: Is not the feeling of this assembly that Mr. Hatchway might continue his surveying somewhere else?

MEMBERS: Yes! Throw him in the drink, the river, the Falls!

JESSE: No, my friends. (*pause*) Let him go in peace.

EBENEZER: And I'll return in war!

SPEAKER: Sergeant-at-arms, eject this man!

A MEMBER: President of all the drink!

MEMBERS: Throw him in the drink, the river, the Falls!

(*Sergeant is helped by some MPs to drive Ebenezer off. Roar of falls followed by a large splash.*)

SPEAKER: Recess, gentlemen. When we return, we have two bills to attend to: the abolition of slavery, and the regularization of marriages.

SCENE SIX: THE BALL

(*Atahentsic and Seth in front of parson's cottage.*)

TRIO

SETH: We're in luck, Atahentsic.

ATAHENTSIC: Yes, there's the only parson for miles and miles, hoeing his cabbages.

(*Tune, 'Wells,' 1753.*)

SETH, ATAHENTSIC: Reverend sir.

PARSON: (*cheerily, looking up*) Oh, we are being formal today!

SETH, ATAHENTSIC: We want to see about getting married.

PARSON: Don't be silly, you're married already.
  If you aren't, you should be in jail for fornication.

(*He turns away. Atahentsic laughs nervously. Seth tries again.*)

SETH: Reverend sir, we've been married twice as a matter of fact.

PARSON: The more often the better, they say. Why?

ATAHENTSIC: Once by the Methodists –

SETH: – And once by her people's rules.

PARSON: And you want to obey the new law, the law that says you must be married by a priest of the state church. Is that it?

SETH, ATAHENTSIC: (*awkwardly*) Not really.

PARSON: Aha!

ATAHENTSIC: (*summoning courage*) Reverend sir, we cannot go to the Governor's Ball unless we are married – your way.

PARSON: At last, some honest candour. And here is your reward. (*He gives them a card.*)

ATAHENTSIC: Seth! It's an invitation to the ball!

SETH: What do we do now, sir?

PARSON: Go to the ball, that's all, go to the ball.

SETH, ATAHENTSIC: We'll go to the ball, the Governor's Ball!

PARSON: You're the only ones to honestly say
  Why you wanted to marry.
  Married or no, off you go! Married or no, go to the ball!

SETH, ATAHENTSIC: Off we go to the ball, the Governor's Ball!

PARSON: Off you go! There has to be more than one table for whist!

(*He shoos them off and skips along after them. Cottage scene dissolves. Bright lights up. At the ball a small orchestra accompanies a set of dancers. The first dance, the reel, 'The Deil amang the Taylors,' is just concluding as*

Mrs. Jarvis enters, followed by her husband, a former member of the Queen's Rangers. She takes off her coat, surveys the scene disapprovingly and strides rapidly to face the Simcoes. Music ends; dancers bow and curtsy to one another, applaud the musicians.)

MRS JARVIS: Your Excellency, surely you have not begun the ball with a country dance.

MRS. SIMCOE: What should it begin with then, Mrs. Jarvis?

MRS. JARVIS: A proper ball always starts with a minuet – where I come from.

(Simcoe whispers to orchestra leader. Pause, as musicians change gears, with Mrs. Jarvis glaring at them.)

ORCHESTRA LEADER: *(announcing)* Ladies and gentlemen: General Burgoyne's Minuet!

(Under and over the music ('Gen. Burgoyne's Minuet,' Lord Kelly, 1774), we hear the following.)

MRS. SIMCOE: Mr. Simcoe, where does that Jarvis woman come from?

SIMCOE: New Jersey.

MRS. JARVIS: Look at the Simcoes, Samuel. He plays second fiddle to her even at a dance.

JARVIS: Yes, my dear.

MRS. SIMCOE: And of what religious persuasion is she?

SIMCOE: Episcopalian.

MRS. SIMCOE: Ah, but what of her husband?

SIMCOE: Oh, Samuel is a Baptist originally.

MRS. SIMCOE: And remains one?

SIMCOE: Not anymore.

MRS. SIMCOE: I should hope not. His issue would be bar sinistered. *(annoyed)* Still, a typical Dissenter's Trick – dissent, even at a dance!

SETH: Atahentsic, what think you of the dance?

ATAHENTSIC: It's like Heaven must be. Bless the parson. Look at him dancing with his wife.

SETH: I feel guilty.

ATAHENTSIC: Why?

SETH: The Society of Friends frowns on dancing.

ATAHENTSIC: King David danced before the Ark, didn't he?

(*Music slows and ends, dancers bow and curtsy.*)

SETH: I know, but a minuet? I always pictured him as stepdancing!

(*He executes a few steps nimbly. Others clap and laugh. Music (reel, 'The White Cockade') is interrupted by a group of marchers who make ready for the traditional dancing game, 'Marching Down to Old Quebec.' Here the dancers march in pairs, clapping and singing as they circle the room. Each verse becomes faster and at the refrain a new couple is chosen from onlookers to join the march.*)

DANCERS: We're marching down to old Quebec,
   Where the drums are loudly beating.
   And we shall meet with no attack
   For the Yankees are retreating.
      So we'll turn and come again
      To the place where we first started.
      We'll open the ring and take a couple in
      Since they proved they are true-hearted.

We're marching down to old Quebec,
The fifes and the drums are beating
For the British boys have gained the day
And the Yankees are retreating.
   So we'll turn and come again
   To the place where we first started.
   We'll open the ring and take a couple in
   Since they proved they are true-hearted.

We're marching down to Old Quebec,

Where the drums are loudly beating,
Yes, the British boys have gained the day
And the Yankees are retreating
    The war's all over, so we'll turn back,
    And nevermore be parted;
    So open the ring and choose a couple in…

(Dance game develops into frenzy. Simcoe is called away during the last verse and returns waving a dispatch. Dancers abruptly stop.)

SIMCOE: Ladies and gentlemen, I must interrupt the dance
With some rather important news.

VOICES: News? Good or bad? Cheerful or not?

SIMCOE: First, cheerful. A large tree recently fell over on a tent
occupied by our old friend, General 'Mad Anthony' Wayne.
(applause)

VOICES: Hurrah! Good, loyal tree!

SIMCOE: But, not so cheerful –

VOICES: Not – so – cheerful?

VOICE 1: You mean the tree didn't kill him?

SIMCOE: Less cheerful, but a shade more charitable: he was not
injured badly enough to remove him from the scene.
(groans) And, not cheerful at all: before this 'accident,' Mr.
Wayne had completely vanquished our Indian allies in Ohio

(Silence. Atahentsic buries her head in Seth's shoulder.)

In a week's time our soldiers must leave the protective line
of forts we have held on to in Ohio and New York states. Old
Fort Niagara, just across the river, has fallen into the hands
of the Americans. *(anxious murmur; a gasp or two)* This makes
our capital, here at Newark, untenable. *(silence)* Cheerful
news: we can move the capital to the Carrying Place of
Toronto.

VOICES: Move the capital, *again*?

VOICE 2: First I built a house in Kingston. Then he moved it to here where I built another house and now –

VOICES: He calls this cheerful news?

(*Ball scene has dissolved. Upturned chairs. Carts being loaded with domestic interiors. Disarray and disgruntlement.*)

MRS. JARVIS: I'm not moving! Start a ball without a minuet, start a province with a new capital every time you turn around – there is nothing at Toronto.

JARVIS: No, nothing at Toronto –

JARVIS, MRS. JARVIS: – nothing.

(*Ships and wagons filled with complainers.*)

VOICES: Move the capital, *again*?

ATTORNEY GENERAL: Attorney General I may be, but, but: Send the papers from Toronto Carrying Place to me at Newark – here!

SCENE SEVEN: TORONTO BECOMES YORK

(*Dissolve to green forest, blue waves, gulls screaming not far from the foot of Bathurst Street. Soldiers, townspeople assemble. Amid bugle tuckets and fragments of Arne's 'Rule Britannia,' Simcoe steps forward.*)

ALL: (*spoken*) August 24th, 1793!

SIMCOE: I order that on the raising of the Union Flag at noon today, there shall be a Royal salute fired to be answered by the shipping in the Harbour in respect to his royal Highness, the Duke of York, in commemoration of naming this Harbour with the title 'York.'

ALL: Grow, Toronto! Toronto, rule the –

SIMCOE: (*spoken*) Er, I've just changed the name to *York.*

ALL: Grow, great York, with temperance and work! Ye shall never, never shirk to grow, great York!

(*Cannon boom nearby, with echoes fading.*)

SETH JUNIOR: *(narrating)* For the five years this man was our Governor; he called up five Parliaments –

(Another cannon replies from a distance, also echoing.)

SETH JUNIOR: – the first five.

SIMCOE: *(becoming less formal)* Of course, this may be only a temporary ('temp'ry') capital *(groans from crowd)* – but a permanent arsenal. Someday, New London.

VOICE 1: Governor, how will we get to London? By balloon?

SIMCOE: In answer to that rather impertinent query –

(Music up, light fades, spot up on Seth Junior as narrator.)

QUARTET

SETH JUNIOR: That summer, he set the Queen's Rangers building Dundas Street to the west.

(A roll of burlap unfurls across stage; workers mime actions with pickaxes, clop-clop sounds as highway emerges.)

ATAHENTSIC: To the west, to the west.

SETH SENIOR: Each week on Wednesday the courier comes Running from Detroit –

ATAHENTSIC: – Fort Detroit.

SETH SENIOR: Forty miles on by the Thames River.

ATAHENTSIC: Brant's Settlement at the Grand River.

SIMCOE: A long road from Fort Detroit to York to Kingston –

ATAHENTSIC, SETH SENIOR, SIMCOE: – to Quebec by the St. Lawrence River.

SETH JUNIOR, ATAHENTSIC, SETH SENIOR, SIMCOE: Dundas Street: A giant long road, Dundas Street.

SETH JUNIOR: The next summer, he built a road north from York and called it Yonge Street.

SETH SENIOR: North, north... *(another burlap extravaganza)*

ATAHENTSIC: Past Holland Landing.

SETH SENIOR: As far as Penetanguishene.

ATAHENTSIC: Past a lake the French had called –

ATAHENTSIC, SETH SENIOR: – Lac des Rosiers.

SIMCOE: *(locating it on map)* Haven't named a thing after my late father yet. *(tries out the sound)* Lake Simcoe! Change the French name, Mr. Harple. Make a memorandum: not Lac des Rosiers but Lac de Simcoe!

ATAHENTSIC, SIMCOE: *(laughing)* Lac de Simcoe!

SETH SENIOR: Lake Simcoe it is, sir.

SETH JUNIOR, ATAHENTSIC, SETH SENIOR, SIMCOE: Yonge Street: Another long road, Yonge Street.

(Lighting change. Summer sunset on the beach. The Simcoes chance upon Seth and Atahentsic, looking south across the lake.)

SIMCOE: Looking south, Harple?

SETH SENIOR: Yes, sir, Atahentsic was born over there. So was I.

ATAHENTSIC: I still dream there, Colonel Simcoe. *(pause)* Mrs. Simcoe.

SIMCOE: *(pause)* I wouldn't mind going back – with a proper army – to see if they'd be loyal to the King again.

MRS. SIMCOE: Since coming to York, I haven't lost a rubber. It must be the air.

(In the background, increasing sounds of the taptoo (as in Act One, Scene Three) – as soldiers are drummed out of taverns into Fort York. This swells up briefly, then subsides, continuing under.)

MRS. SIMCOE: What are they drumming for now, Mr. Simcoe?

SIMCOE: Why not ask an authority such as Mr. Harple here? He was once my drummer boy.

SETH SENIOR: Mrs. Simcoe, it's 'taptoo': time for all taverners to shut their taps and for the soldiers to drink up and go back to their barracks for a good night's rest. *(music swells up again and subsides)*

SIMCOE: Speaking of 'rest,' something both Mrs. Simcoe and myself are in need of: this is entre nous, but in a week's time we're leaving for England.

(Atahentsic and Seth mime farewell to the Simcoes – salutes, handshakes, embraces – as chorus offstage repeats the Rangers' motto.)

CHORUS: 'Draw your swords, Rangers, the rebels are coming. Draw your swords, Rangers, the rebels are coming.`

SETH JUNIOR: My father says those are the words of Mr. Simcoe he will always remember. *(pause)* And so my mother and father said farewell to the Simcoes and were never to see them again.

SCENE EIGHT: FINALE

(Same as Act Two, Scene One: York, circa 1810. Seth Junior has advanced to the stage where his ships are in battle, American vs. British/Canadian – but the two flags are still the same as at the beginning of Act One, Scene One.)

SETH JUNIOR: *(assuming the role of Yankee gunboat cap'n)* Schooner to larboard, under British colours! *(assuming role of schooner cap'n)* All men on deck! Yankee gunboat starboard!

JESSE: Sethy, I wish thee would desist from such a warlike game. Didn't we send you a Bible picture book for your birthday?

SETH JUNIOR: Be thou patient with me, Grampa. I'll show you I can read that book as soon as this Yankee gunboat sinks this Canadian schooner. Keeps missing 'er!

ATAHENTSIC: More tea, Mr. and Mrs. Harple?

MRS. HARPLE: Ah, Seth, I keep fearing that red-haired boy will appear from nowhere.

(Passersby are stopping to watch the naval flight.)

SETH SENIOR: You mean Ebenezer? Mother, I received a letter from him yesterday. *(hauling it out of his pocket.)* This is what

Senator Hatchway of Kentucky has to say:

(The senator appears in a spotlight stage right.)

EBENEZER: Seth, my darling. My friends have been keeping track of you up there in Canaday. Soon as my friends can swing it with the next President – not the chicken-livered British parasite now incumbent – we're comin' up, to give you some liberty. And we'll take you and your Indian friend back with us to where you belong. Fair warning! Sethy!

PASSERBY 1: Is that the stars and stripes on that little boat, sonny? Why, look, Eliza, I haven't seen that flag for twenty-five years.

SETH JUNIOR: Aye, aye, commodore. Give it to the schooner full broadside! *(using toy cannon squirt gun)* Hurrah! The Yankee skipper downs the Britisher.

(He goes to the other tub and puts four toy boats in it.)

PASSERBY 2: *(to the crowd)* It's true what the child is saying. We haven't got a Provincial Marine. The old fort's falling down.

SETH JUNIOR: *(a toy-soldier authority on military strategy for a colony in dire danger)* This tub is Lake Ontario, ladies and gentlemen. This one is Lake Erie. If we had a navy on Lake Ontario, could it sail to Lake Erie?

CROWD: No, no...

SETH JUNIOR: It could not.

CROWD: So – ?

SETH JUNIOR: So: we have to build a separate navy for Lake Erie.

CROWD: Yes, but...

PASSERBY 2: Look at all those American gunboats chasing that big Britisher.

CROWD: ... But we don't have any sailors in Upper Canada.

SETH JUNIOR: Bring them in from Halifax. And hurry! President Madison said yesterday the U.S. of A. should take us over. Soon.

SETH SENIOR: But, Little Seth, how are we to do all this?

CROWD: How, how... ?

SETH SENIOR: Where's the money? Where's the –

CROWD: Expensive. Is it worth it? What should we do? What can we do?

(They close in on Seth Junior and tubs. Suddenly he shouts and, taking a big dipper, splashes them with a huge thwawp! They scatter, spluttering and exclaiming. Silence after this reaction as light fades. Last image is the boy's defiant face, a toy ship in either hand, young scion of an endangered baby colony.)

Still photos from the 1999 stage premiere at the Black Box Theatre, McGill University, Montreal: ball scene, Chantal Richard and Stephan Fehr (the Simcoes); final tableau, Rena Detlefsen (Seth Junior)

Notes

The Great Lakes Suite
First published in *The Red Heart and Other Poems*, McClelland and Stewart, Toronto, 1949.

Night-blooming Cereus
First published in *The Killdeer and Other Plays*, Macmillan, Toronto, 1962. Inspired by a newspaper item about a cereus plant which bloomed in Shakespeare, Ontario, near Stratford. The actual cereus blooms at night, once a year (not once a century, as suggested by poetic licence in the opera).

Twelve Letters to a Small Town
Cycle of 'performance poems' about Reaney's home town, Stratford, Ontario. First published by Ryerson Press, Toronto, 1962. Facsimile reprint, Guelph Spring Festival, 2002, with 'Afterword' by James Reaney. Incorporates previous poems by Reaney.

Canada Dash, Canada Dot
Previously unpublished. Incorporates previous poems by Reaney. The Sharon sequence of Part 2 anticipates *Serinette*.

All the Bees and All the Keys
First published by Press Porcépic, Erin, 1976. The final scene relates to the poem 'The Royal Visit' in *The Red Heart and Other Poems*. The narrator's part has sometimes been divided between two voices, female and male.

The Shivaree
Published by the authors, 1982. The Prologue was added for the production at the Banff Centre in December 1982. The wedding tradition of the shivaree (a North American corruption of 'charivari'), a mock serenade on homemade instruments played under the bridal chamber, prevailed in rural Ontario up to at least the 1920s. The custom called for the groom to pay a cash forfeit, with which the serenaders would buy drink.

Crazy to Kill

Published by Guelph Spring Festival, Guelph, 1989. The original mystery novel by the Stratford author Ann Cardwell (pseud. Jean Makins Pawley) was reprinted with an introduction by Reaney (Southwood Editions, London, Ontario, 1989).

Serinette

Published by Cultural Support Services, Toronto, 1990. A two-CD recording of the 2001 concert revival is available: Centrediscs CMCCD-76-7701. *Serinette* was designed for performance outside and inside the Temple of the Children of Peace at Sharon, Ontario.

Taptoo!

Published by the authors, 1999. 'Taptoo' is the old Dutch version of 'tattoo,' meaning a) the final military signal of the day, announcing the shutting off of taps in the taverns and the return of troops to their quarters and also b) the elaboration of this into a parting song-and-dance entertainment.

About the Author

The poet and playwright James Reaney was born near Stratford, Ontario, in 1926. He received Governor General's Literary Awards in 1949, 1959 and 1962. The best known of his more than two dozen major dramatic works are the two plays produced by the Stratford Festival (*Colours in the Dark,* 1967 and his adaptation of Carroll's *Alice Through the Looking Glass,* 1994 and 1995) and the trilogy *The Donnellys* (*Sticks and Stones,* 1973, *The St. Nicholas Hotel,* 1974, and *Handcuffs,* 1975), whose cross-country tour by the NDWT theatre company in 1976 was the subject of his travel diary, *Fourteen Barrels From Sea to Sea.* Recent premieres include *Zamorna,* Toronto, 1999 and *Gentle Rain Food Co-op,* London, Ontario, 2002.

Reaney has repeatedly taken up local themes in his dramatic writings — an 1890s student revolt at the University of Toronto in *The Dismissal,* a 1920s Stratford strike in *King Whistle,* the founding of a Kitchener music-publishing firm in *I, the Parade* and late-nineteenth-century barn burnings and vigilante murders in Biddulph in *The Donnellys.* Early Ontario history inspired his children's novel *The Boy with the "R" in his Hand,* as well as the operas *Serinette* and *Taptoo!*

There have been over forty productions of *Colours in the Dark* in schools and colleges of the U.S. and Canada and numerous productions of *Names and Nicknames* by children's theatres and schools. International productions include *The Killdeer,* Scotland, 1965; *Names and Nicknames,* Switzerland, 1980; *Sticks and Stones,* U.S. (New York University), 1985 and England, 1995; *Wacousta,* India, 1997; and *Colours in the Dark,* Japan, 1997.

Reaney was editor and publisher of the literary quarterly *Alphabet,* 1960-71 and has also been active as a theatre director and as a visual artist — there have been several exhibits of his paintings and he has created illustrations for some of his published works.

He lives with his wife, the poet Colleen Thibaudeau, in London, Ontario, where he was associated 1960-90 with the

English department of the University of Western Ontario. James Reaney is an officer of the Order of Canada.

About the Editor

John Beckwith is the composer of over 130 musical works, including operas, orchestral, choral and chamber pieces, piano works and songs. Besides his association with James Reaney going back more than fifty years, he has worked closely with other writers such as Jay Macpherson, Margaret Atwood, Dennis Lee and bpNichol. A collection of his writings has appeared under the title *Music Papers: Articles and Talks by a Canadian Composer, 1961-1994* (Ottawa 1997).